UNDERWATER

OPTIONS WHEN YOUR MORTGAGE IS UPSIDE DOWN

Chris Lauer

apress®

Underwater: Options When Your Mortgage Is Upside Down

Copyright © 2013 by Chris Lauer

ISBN-13 (pbk): 978-1-4302-4470-7
ISBN-13 (electronic): 978-1-4302-4471-4

Trademarked names may appear in this book. Rather than use a trademark symbol with every occurrence of a trademarked name, we use the names only in an editorial fashion and to the benefit of the trademark owner, with no intention of infringement of the trademark.

President and Publisher: Paul Manning

Acquisitions Editor: Jeff Olson

Editorial Board: Steve Anglin, Mark Beckner, Ewan Buckingham, Gary Cornell, Louise Corrigan, Morgan Ertel, Jonathan Gennick, Jonathan Hassell, Robert Hutchinson, Michelle Lowman, James Markham, Matthew Moodie, Jeff Olson, Jeffrey Pepper, Douglas Pundick, Ben Renow-Clarke, Dominic Shakeshaft, Gwenan Spearing, Matt Wade, Tom Welsh

Coordinating Editor: Rita Fernando

Copy Editors: Catherine Ohala and Deanna Hegle

Compositor: Bytheway Publishing Services

Indexer: SPi Global

Cover Designer: Anna Ishchenko

Distributed to the book trade worldwide by Springer-Verlag New York, Inc., 233 Spring Street, 6th Floor, New York, NY 10013. Phone 1-800-SPRINGER, fax 201-348-4505, e-mail orders-ny@springer-sbm.com, or visit www.springeronline.com.

For information on translations, please contact us by e-mail at info@apress.com, or visit www.apress.com.

Apress and friends of ED books may be purchased in bulk for academic, corporate, or promotional use. eBook versions and licenses are also available for most titles. For more information, reference our Special Bulk Sales–eBook Licensing web page at www.apress.com/bulk-sales. To place an order, email your request to support@apress.com

To Tracy Lee

Contents

About the Author

 **Chris Lauer** is the author of *Breaking Free: How to Quit Your Job and Start Your Own Business* (Praeger, 2009), *Southwest Airlines (Corporations That Changed the World Series;* Greenwood, 2010), and *The Management Gurus: Lessons from the Best Management Books of All Time* (Portfolio, 2008). He is also the owner and editor-in-chief of Lauer Editorial Services (www.laueredit.com), where he writes for businesses and publishers. As a journalist and editor with more than 20 years of experience, Lauer works in a variety of fields, including business, news, music, and art. After graduating with an English Journalism degree from the University of Delaware, where he was a Features editor at *The Review*, he worked as a writer and editor for the *SF Weekly* in San Francisco. Next, he owned and published *Edge City* and *Anthem Monthly*, two arts and entertainment magazines in northern California. After that, Lauer worked for the NBC affiliate in Eureka, California, KIEM-TV, as a news reporter, chief videographer, and assignment editor. In 2006, he founded Lauer Editorial Services. Today, he writes and teaches in Wilmington, Delaware.

Acknowledgments

Although only one name appears on the cover of this book, many other people deserve credit and recognition. First and foremost, a special thank you goes to my team at Apress. Executive editor extraordinaire Jeff Olson made this book possible. Rita Fernando kept it on track. Paul Manning, Anna Ishchenko, Catherine Ohala, Deanna Hegle, and all the other publishing professionals at Apress also get a big thank you, too.

The many generous people who gave me their valuable time and expertise also deserve acknowledgment and my appreciation, including Daniel Fink, Nancy Ringer, Dave Watlington, John Paunan, Michael Milligan, John Mulville, Brett Stimpson, Brendon DeSimone, Rob Wassmer, and Mark Fleming. A special thank you also goes to Les Kramsky, Esq., for his help and enthusiasm.

Additional credit goes out to all the other experts and homeowners who shared their stories with me. Each story helped make this book happen.

But the people who deserve the most thanks are Tracy, Toby, Hailey, and Emma. They provided the vital patience and encouragement that made this book possible. Pauline and Ken Lauer also get a warm thank you for their love and support.

Preface

This is a book of knowledge and hope for people who owe more for their homes than their homes are worth. It's a tough spot to be in, but there is a glow on the horizon. Things are starting to look up even during this sluggish time of recovery. Every homeowner watches for signs of good news as the real estate market begins to see the light of a new day.

Unfortunately, that light is difficult to see when you're under water. That's why underwater homeowners need the guidance of experts to help them choose the right path to a brighter future. There is no need to go it alone. Those who suffer from negative equity need help from people who have worked inside the real estate market long enough to understand its ebb and flow. This book is filled with the advice of experts who know about underwater mortgages from the inside out.

The stories, tips, and advice in this book come from those who have seen enough real estate transactions to know the score. These professionals were there on the frontlines when the real estate bubble burst 6 years ago, and they are ready to share their experience and knowledge vital to helping homeowners with underwater mortgages who are ready for relief.

Hope on the Way

Hope is on the way. The advice of the real estate professionals collected here offer you a better understanding of the real estate market and your place in it. This book distills their experiences, numbers, and expertise into a guidebook you can use to help you navigate the topsy-turvy world of owning a home in the United States today.

To help you get a handle on the underlying history that has shaped the current housing landscape, Part I is all about the real estate market and the underwater mortgage. Part I starts with Chapter 1, which examines the cataclysmic bubble burst that left the real estate market in shambles. This is where the origins of the debacle are analyzed to help you get a sharper picture of the terrain you must travel to get out from under water.

Chapter 2 looks at how far the reverberations of the real estate market collapse reached into our current economy. It also puts some numbers on the ripples that continue to roll through today and into the future.

Part II offers expert advice from a number of real estate industry professionals and homeowners who understand firsthand what is going on in the market today. They know because they live and work there every day. That advice begins in Chapter 3 at the front door of a homeowner who spent some of his home's equity to build his business, but the real estate market crash left him without enough equity to qualify to refinance at one of the great rates now available. And he loves his underwater home too much to leave. His story can help you see the ways many responsible homeowners have been trapped by the universal drop in home equity that hit the country.

In Chapter 4, real estate attorney Les R. Kramsky, Esq., offers a legal perspective on the ways underwater homeowners can deal with their housing situations. Kramsky's expertise in the industry was recently recognized when he was appointed executive vice president and general counsel for The Silk Companies, a company that has closed tens of thousands of real estate deals. Kramsky outlines the options that are now available to underwater homeowners.

Next, in Chapter 5, real estate agent Nancy Ringer describes the current conditions in which underwater homeowners must work to turn their homes right side up. Her advice provides a ground view of how real clients are faring in today's market.

In Chapter 6, mortgage broker John Paunan offers homeowners a look at the ways the real estate market has changed since it imploded, and the role Fannie Mae and Freddie Mac play in the lives of millions of underwater homeowners who are seeking relief. His perspective on the mortgage market is invaluable for those looking for answers.

In Chapter 7, another real estate agent offers additional experience from the real estate industry's front lines. This time, real estate agent Dave Watlington offers practical advice on selling an underwater home and the steps an underwater homeowner should take while battling default and foreclosure.

Next, in Chapter 8, real estate agent Michael Milligan rounds out previous lessons with numbers that can help a homeowner understand when negative equity may be tolerable, and how much demands faster action. His anecdotes shed light into reasons why divorced couples stay under one roof and why lenders do not want to foreclose on you.

Utah mortgage broker Brett Stimpson adds another side to the refinancing equation in Chapter 9. Stimpson reviews the top options for underwater homeowners while explaining why refinancing is still your best option if you qualify.

In Chapter 10, nationally recognized real estate expert Brendon DeSimone describes how investing in real estate requires a long-term perspective, why realism must rule the day, and how underwater homeowners can get a grip on the emotional impact of their circumstances.

Chapter 11 is the start of Part III, which provides an overview of the real estate market and where it is headed. This chapter takes the options for underwater homeowners to the macro level by offering them the tips of a real estate economist, John Mulville. As senior vice president for the consulting group at Real Estate Economics, Mulville looks at the big picture every day and spends his time boiling it down to some numbers people can use when planning their future. Underwater homeowners can use his advice to understand valuation, subprime mortgages, how we got into this mess in the first place, and how to recognize the signs of hope on the horizon.

Another advocate of long-term thinking is California State University professor Dr. Rob Wassmer, who teaches underwater homeowners how economists look at real estate. In Chapter 12, Wassmer points out the importance of good counseling, which is often free or low cost. He also teaches underwater homeowners what questions to ask themselves when making a decision about an underwater home, why they should ignore sunk costs, and how ethics play a role.

Chapter 13 features the latest underwater home statistics from CoreLogic, a top provider of data on consumer, financial, and property information and analysis. CoreLogic's chief economist, Mark Fleming, explains what these numbers mean to homeowners and what the numbers tell him about the future.

Part IV focuses on the law of the land and how you can make the most of the many federal programs that are available to underwater homeowners right now. Advice here may save you thousands of dollars in deficiencies, or may help you keep your credit rating intact after your exit from an underwater home.

Chapter 14 explains what every underwater homeowner should know about the mortgage giants Fannie Mae and Freddie Mac, and how these organizations may be the link between you and a better monthly payment.

Next, Chapter 15 investigates the misconduct and lender abuses that took place in the mortgage industry, and describes how the inspectors general of

49 states reached a $25 billion settlement with the biggest banks in the country, and where the money is going.

Chapter 16 then points you in the right direction when you are looking into the offerings available from the U.S. government. Any one of the 12 programs featured in this section could provide you with the break you need after the long 6 years since your home turned upside down.

Last, in Part V, you will find appendices to help you work with the people who understand underwater homes. You will need a decoder for their language, so Appendix A presents a glossary of terms for sorting out the acronyms and jargon so you can understand what everyone in the real estate business is talking about. You will also need real people and programs to help you improve your tough mortgage situation. Your link to them is Appendix B, which lists a number of useful organizations and their Web addresses. These names and numbers can connect you directly to the resources that just may be your key to a brilliant future beyond your underwater home.

Underwater Homes and Upside-Down Mortgages

Mary in California

Mary owned a ranch and home in California for 30 of her 69 years until 2004, when she decided to buy a house to be closer to her children. Two years later, the bottom fell out of the California housing market. This catastrophe left her home worth less than half the loan that she is currently paying off with monthly payments.[1]

Today, some would say Mary's home is underwater; others would say her mortgage is upside down. Whatever it is called, *the amount she owes on her mortgage loan is greater than the current value of her property.*

In addition to the lack of value in her home, Mary is also running into problems with it. Although the house is under full warranty, she is facing many expensive mechanical defects in the house, such as bad wires, an outdated roof, and a questionable furnace. Next she discovers mold. The developer who built the home fixed the mold problem once, but he has since gone out of business and filed for bankruptcy. The repairs required to make her home livable add up to make it an overwhelming burden.

In addition, a recent illness forced Mary to retire from her job. This unanticipated decrease in income makes it hard for her to keep with her monthly mortgage payments, and all those needed repairs remain on the back burner.

With so many difficulties facing her, Mary chooses to sell her home at a loss and move into a rental unit. On the bright side, she is glad she does not have to face all the repair bills. On the other hand, she never imagined herself renting, after being a homeowner for nearly 30 years. Mary is just one of

---

[1] www.aarp.org/money/credit-loans-debt/info-07-2012/nightmare-on-main-street-AARP-ppi-cons-prot.comments.html

millions of underwater homeowners in the United States who are faced with a variety of hard decisions to make regarding their home.

Robert in New Jersey

In 2002, Robert bought his house for $200,000 in a small New Jersey suburb. For many years he has enjoyed his home. He was happy to see its value appreciate every year he lived in it. In 2006, he decided to take advantage of the equity he had accrued during the past 5 years to replace the roof. When he met with a lender to apply for a home equity loan, the lender informed him that he first needed a home appraisal. So, Robert hired an appraiser. After looking over Robert's home, the appraiser turned to him and asked, "How much do you want me to enter on the line that says 'Home Value'?" Robert replied, "$250,000," and that was the number the appraiser entered.

Two years later, the bottom fell out of the housing market. The house next door to Robert's home was still unsold after being on the market for a year. The asking price was $180,000, and buyers were not interested in it. Robert's house was much the same as his neighbor's, but his had a much newer roof and a refurbished kitchen—thanks to the home equity loan he took out in 2006.

The next year, knowing that his house was underwater, Robert sought help from a company that offered to help him refinance his home so his mortgage payments and interest rate would be much lower. He paid the company $3,000 for its services. Robert called the company every week to find out the status of his loan. An agent at the company claimed to be waiting for word from the bank about approval of the loan. Several months passed and the company was no longer answering his phone calls. Robert left message after message, hoping to hear something about his loan application. Six months after paying the company the $3,000, Robert discovered that the company's phone number was no longer in service and the company had folded.

Today, Robert owes $230,000 on his home, which is probably worth about $180,000. Robert and his family live in a home that is underwater. He continues to make his mortgage payments, and loves his house and neighborhood, but he wonders if it is worth the money and effort to continue to stay in his home.

Lisa and Andy in Delaware

For many years, Lisa and Andy wanted to buy a new house in North Wilmington, Delaware. They lived nearby in a small two-bedroom home, but they wanted a larger house in a nicer neighborhood where they could raise their 5-year-old son.

In 2006, they found the perfect house in a lovely neighborhood that was exactly what they wanted. The three-bedroom home was perfect for their family. Their son would have his own bedroom and Lisa could make the third bedroom into a home office for her freelance writing business. Although the sellers were asking $335,000 for their 75-year-old refurbished house, making it the most expensive house in the neighborhood, home prices had been increasing steadily by about $20,000 a year for the past 10 years.

To Lisa and Andy, the investment seemed well worth it and they bought their dream home. When the house needed a new heating and air-conditioning system 2 years later, the couple had little choice but to plunk down $8,000 to ensure they would be comfortable through Delaware's humid summers and cold winters.

Not long thereafter, the bottom fell out of the real estate market. House prices in the neighborhood continued to decrease. Homes sat on the market for more than a year, only to be taken off the market, repriced, and returned to the market to sit for months unsold. Their neighbor's house finally sold in 2010 for $285,000. Lisa and Andy know their home is more desirable, with better upgrades and extensive landscaping, but it is hard to say whether they will ever be able to sell their house for the price they paid for it, let alone the $300,000 they still owe on it. To make matters worse, two houses on their street have recently gone to short sale, which is when the bank agrees to take less than the mortgage, settling the debt, to avoid foreclosure. When neighbors short sell their homes, home values around the neighborhood reflect those lower prices.

Every month when Lisa and Andy pay their mortgage they feel the pressure of being underwater.

Options for Underwater Homeowners

Mary, Robert, and Lisa and Andy (not their real names) are far from being alone with their mortgage difficulties. In December 2011, approximately 22.8

percent of mortgage loans nationwide—one in five—were underwater,[2] and the numbers are not getting better. In July 2012, experts estimated that 11.4 million, or 23.7 percent, of all residential properties in the United States with a mortgage were underwater at the end of the first quarter of 2012.[3] In addition, in June 2012, studies showed that 2.86 million mortgages were delinquent by 12 months or more.[4] These numbers show that there is currently an underwater mortgage crisis taking place in the United States.

This book offers advice and tips from experienced experts to help those whose mortgages are underwater to discover their financial options and find some hope as they face one of the toughest decisions of their lives—stay put and bail out an underwater home or dump it and move on.

THE EFFECTS OF THE MORTGAGE CRISIS ON OLDER PEOPLE

In July 2012, the American Association of Retired Persons (AARP) released the first study[5] to measure the progression of the mortgage crisis and its effect on people age 50 and older. Based on an analysis of nationwide loan-level data for years 2007 to 2011, the study examined loan performance, taking into account borrower age, loan type, and borrower demographics.

As expected, borrowers younger than 50 years have a higher percentage of underwater loans—at 28 percent—compared with 16 percent for borrowers age 50 and older. Among the 50+ population in the United States, the percentage of underwater loans decreases with age, with 18 percent for borrowers age 50 to 64, 14 percent for borrowers age 65 to 74, and 11 percent for borrowers age 75 and older.

In her article for AARP's Public Policy Institute (PPI) titled "Nightmare on Main Street: Older Americans and the Mortgage Market Crisis," Lori Trawinski writes: "Despite the perception that older Americans are more housing secure than younger people, millions of older Americans are carrying more mortgage debt than ever before, and more than three million are at risk of losing their homes."

According to the report, as of December 2011, "approximately 3.5 million loans of people age 50+ were underwater—meaning homeowners owe more than their home is worth, so they

---

[2] Lori A. Trawinski, *Nightmare on Main Street: Older Americans and the Mortgage Market Crisis* AARP Public Policy Institute, 2012), p. 15.

[3] www.corelogic.com/about-us/news/corelogic-reports-negative-equity-decreases-in-first-quarter-of-2012.aspx

[4] http://blogs.reuters.com/great-debate/2012/06/19/a-solution-for-underwater-mortgages-eminent-domain/

[5] Trawinski.

have no equity; 600,000 loans of people age 50+ were in foreclosure, and another 625,000 loans were 90 or more days delinquent. From 2007 to 2011, more than 1.5 million older Americans lost their homes as a result of the mortgage crisis."

The PPI performs public policy research, analysis, and development at AARP. The latest PPI study showed, up to July 2012, "public policy programs designed to stem the progression of the foreclosure crisis have been inadequate, and programs that focus on the unique needs of older Americans are needed."[6]

Note   *Look into government programs.* Although some programs are more successful than others, thousands of underwater homeowners have found relief through federal and state programs.

[6] www.aarp.org/money/credit-loans-debt/info-07-2012/nightmare-on-main-street-AARP-ppi-cons-prot.html

The Real Estate Market and the Underwater Mortgage

The Real Estate Crash

The Bursting of a Bubble

The news in July 2012 showed that recent increases in home sales across the nation dipped once again. Ever since the real estate market bubble—which was inflating like never before in 2005 and 2006—burst, dunking millions of homeowners across the country under water, many of them watch the housing reports closely to determine whether the market is getting any better.

However, the news for home sales in July 2012 was not great. Although the numbers for May 2012 showed that new home sales had reached a 2-year high, the numbers for June were disappointing to many underwater homeowners. On July 25, 2012, the U.S. Census Bureau reported that sales of new single-family houses in June 2012 were at a seasonally adjusted annual rate of 350,000. This number was 8.4 percent less than the revised May rate of 382,000, but was 15.1 percent more than the June 2011 estimate of 304,000.[1] In other words, new home sales were down, but the numbers were better than expected.

How were home prices doing in September 2012? According to the latest numbers from the Census Bureau, the median sale price of new houses sold in September 2012 was $242,400, and the average sale price was $292,400. Both of these numbers were up from July when the median sale price was $232,600; and the average sale price was $273,900. These numbers are a rare breath of fresh air for underwater homeowners, who have been in trouble for six years.

---

[1] www.census.gov/construction/nrs/pdf/newressales.pdf (Retrieved Oct. 27 2012).

When Did the Bubble Burst?

As mentioned, in late 2006, the real estate bubble burst. Prices dropped, home values dropped, and lenders stopped giving loans to homebuyers. More people were out of work and millions of homes were soon under water. Foreclosures began popping up everywhere. The repercussions of the bursting real estate bubble traveled around the country in strange waves that struck some places much sooner than others.

What happened? Economist John Mulville explains:

> Some markets were hit much earlier, some markets were hit much later, but it was generally related to the economy. Employment started to slow down a little. We were having very robust employment prior to that. Unemployment rates were down very, very low. Pretty much anybody who wanted a job had one.[2]

But then things changed. The job market began to dry up, and housing prices dried up with it. Mulville continues, "We got a little bit of a slowdown in the employment in some markets, and that's really where [the economy] started to tumble. So, all of a sudden, if you were unemployed, you couldn't make that [mortgage] payment." This problem began to appear more and more frequently in many areas. When mortgages went unpaid, the real price of homes became apparent. There were no longer subprime borrowers available to buy up houses at previously peak prices. Foreclosure rates started to increase. "Some places were just deeply, deeply hammered by this whole thing," Mulville adds, "and other places didn't really get through scot-free—that would be an understatement—but some places were much less impacted."

By 2008, the whole country was feeling the big drop in the real estate market, but some places were devastated by huge declines in home prices. In addition, in September 2008, Lehman Brothers filed for bankruptcy, Merrill Lynch was bought by Bank of America, and numerous other banks and financial institutions, such as AIG, were "brought to their knees as a result of hundreds of billions of dollars in losses because of bad mortgage finance and real estate investments," according to *The New York Times*.[3] This was the financial meltdown that became known as the *Global Financial Crisis*. Suddenly, homeowners who thought they could simply refinance their way out of an adjustable-rate mortgage, which was now adjusted to a much higher interest rate than ever before, could not find a lender that was willing to give them a loan at a lower rate.

---

[2] Personal interview with John Mulville.

[3] www.nytimes.com/2008/09/15/business/15lehman.html?pagewanted=all (Retrieved July 24, 2012).

Housing Market Crisis

Even before the Global Financial Crisis of 2008, the housing market was in trouble. "There were definitely warning signs," Mulville remarks. "The prices had peaked and mortgage issuances had peaked. . . . Employment had really peaked, which was more important than anything, prior to that. When we hit the whole Lehman [bankruptcy], that was when it really hit home on the financial market."

Before 2006, lenders were practically giving away mortgages, which led to abuses all around. The housing market became so hyperinflated before the bubble burst that the legendary stories told about those days seem almost unreal today. Mulville has a tale of his own from California:

> There is a story out here where one guy, he was a nurse, and he made $55,000 a year, owned 15 homes! He could say whatever he wanted on the loan application and nobody would check it. He got mortgages to buy 15 homes on his income of $55,000 a year: That's how broken-down the underwriting process was.

Lenders were not the only ones who were lax in their policies. Home appraisers from those days were known for asking homeowners, "Well, how much do you think your home is worth? What do you want me to put down for your home's value?" Mulville remarks that this was a typical scenario during the years leading up to the housing market crisis.

Housing Valuation

The trouble with housing valuation today is that appraisers often include local foreclosures and short sales when comparing housing prices in your area to determine the value of your home when you are trying to sell it, which drives the price even lower. (See Figure 1-1 below.) "[Appraisers] are not even using their own definition of market value to set the value on your home," Mulville explains.

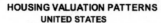

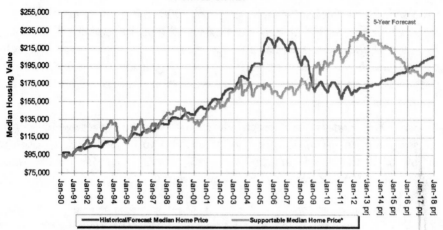

* Over/Under valuation based on value of housing (inclusive of mortgage rates) relative to long-term relationship between housing value & household incomes.
Source: Bureau of Labor Statistics; Census Bureau; National Assoc. of Realtors; Real Estate Economics

Figure 1-1. Real Estate Economics' *Residential Economic Report* from July 2012. Graphic courtesy of Real Estate Economics.

Who Is to Blame for the Crash?

Although many people blame past and present presidents for misguided policy decisions that led to the crash, others point to a variety of other culprits. For example, economist and co-director of the Center for Economic and Policy Research Dean Baker noted that, although others played a part in the debacle, blame should be placed squarely on the shoulders of Alan Greenspan, the economist who served as chairman of the Federal Reserve of the United States from 1987 to 2006.[4]

Why do people point a finger at Alan Greenspan? Many would agree that he did not take the subprime mortgage crisis seriously enough. In January 12, 2012, Zachary A. Goldfarb wrote an article for *The Washington Post* titled, "Fed's Image Tarnished by Newly Released Documents." In his story, Goldfarb wrote:

> In the six years since [the U.S. financial crisis], Greenspan's record—seemingly so sterling when he left the central bank after 18 years—has come under substantial criticism from outside economists and analysts. Many say a range of Fed policies under his watch contributed to the financial crisis, including

---

[4] www.pbs.org/now/shows/412/housing-recession.html (Retrieved October 27, 2012).

keeping interest rates low for too long, failing to take action to stem the housing bubble and allowing inadequate oversight of financial firms.[5]

Greenspan was not the only one at the Federal Reserve who showed a deep misunderstanding of the real estate situation. The next chairman of the Federal Reserve, Ben Shalom Bernanke, who took the helm of the central bank of the United States after Greenspan in February 2006, also seemed misguided during his first few months in office. On January 13, 2012, *The Wall Street Journal* printed an article titled, "Little Alarm Shown at Fed at Dawn of Housing Bust." Reporters Jon Hilsenrath, Lica Di Leo, and Michael S. Derby recalled, "In his second meeting as chairman of the Federal Reserve in May 2006, Ben Bernanke heard a Fed governor warn about the nation's mortgage market. But Mr. Bernanke described the cooling of the housing boom as a 'healthy thing.'"[6] In 2006, Bernanke stated: "So far we are seeing, at worst, an orderly decline in the housing market."[7] The Federal Reserve Chairman's incredible understatement was a strong indication that even the most brilliant economists in charge of the federal banking system, with access to the most important information that was available at the time, were completely unprepared for the federal financial crisis and real estate meltdown that would take place two years later.

The Wall Street Journal reporters went on to reveal that Bernanke's quote came from the 1,197 pages of transcripts released in early 2012 of closed-door Fed meetings from 2006. "The transcripts paint the most detailed picture yet of how top officials at the central bank didn't anticipate the storm about to hit the U.S. economy."[8]

Greenspan Was Not Alone

As mentioned, economist Dean Baker pointed to several others who should also take their fair share of the blame for the housing crisis that led to so many people finding their homes under water. In his March 21, 2008, story for the PBS news show *NOW*, Baker noted:

---

[5] www.washingtonpost.com/business/economy/greenspan-image-tarnished-by-newly-released-documents/2012/01/12/glQAvh0mtP_story.html (Retrieved July 25, 2012).

[6] http://online.wsj.com/article/SB10001424052970204409004577157001537763864.html (Retrieved July 27, 2012).

[7] http://online.wsj.com/article/SB10001424052970204409004577157001537763864.html (Retrieved October 27, 2012).

[8] www.washingtonpost.com/business/economy/greenspan-image-tarnished-by-newly-released-documents/2012/01/12/glQAvh0mtP_story.html (Retrieved October 27, 2012).

> There are literally dozens of federal and state regulatory authorities that could have tried to crack down on the predatory lending practices under their jurisdiction. In fairness, several state regulators did try to crack down, but they were preempted in several cases by federal law.

Baker remarked that others—from president George W. Bush to community leaders—should share blame as well. Rather than work to banish the predatory lending practices that were flourishing at the time, "these people celebrated the growth in homeownership, somehow failing to note that a very high percentage of the new homeowners would soon face foreclosure. The extent to which this celebration was due to a blind commitment to the ideology of homeownership or outright corruption would have to be determined on a case-by-case basis, but it was incredible failure of leadership at all levels,"[9] Baker wrote.

Other culprits, Baker pointed out, included the economists who missed the coming tsunami of foreclosures and underwater mortgages, investors who made millions hedging their bets against the risks involved in subprime lending, bankers who relied on the secondary mortgage market to insure their bad loans, and even the bond rating agencies that could have provided better independent analysis for the banks and financial companies that paid for their ratings.

Innumerable individuals suffered from the implosion of the U.S. real estate bubble more than 6 years ago—a debacle culminating in the mass devaluation of millions of American mortgages. The financial repercussions of that troubled time remain a scar on the American dream, yet the dream often prevails for those who grow wiser and stronger from adversity.

Conclusion

Most homeowners are still feeling the effects of the real estate market crash; however, the time is ripe for recovery. Today is a great day to move beyond financial paralysis. Take matters into your own hands. Fix your personal financial crisis by attacking your own economic issues head on. Start by taking a good look at your entire household situation. Run realistic numbers in your household budget. Gather expert opinions to guide you along the way. Then take the time to make some tough but vital financial decisions. Last, take action. This book provides the information you need to make a powerful, positive change in your real estate situation.

---

[9] www.pbs.org/now/shows/412/housing-recession.html (Retrieved October 27, 2012).

How Bad Is the Underwater Problem?

Those who have suffered since the real estate bubble burst understand all too clearly how devastating the situation was to the national economy and personal fortunes. Many people ready to retire were forced back in to the workforce because retirement plans disappeared with home equity. Many savings funds were tapped or depleted trying to bail out homes with values that plummeted month after month. Millions of Americans were left reeling as they watched their primary asset become their number one liability.

This chapter details the depths of the problem of underwater homes. You might find it at least slightly comforting to know that you are not alone in facing a personal housing crisis. If you find such information cold comfort, skip ahead to the next chapter, which is the first of many to help you get out from under your upside-down mortgage.

According to the 2009 report from the U.S. Census Bureau, "Drowning in Debt: Housing and Households with Underwater Mortgages," written by George R. Carter III and Alfred O. Gottschalck, homeownership rates peaked in the United States in 2004. Home prices peaked 2 years later in 2006.[1] The authors of the report wrote: "Since these peaks, homeownership rates and home prices have fallen at the national level. An increasing number of

---

[1] www.census.gov/housing/ahs/files/Drowning_in_Debt.pdf (Retrieved August 1, 2012).

homeowners are now 'under water' in their mortgages, meaning that they owe more on their mortgages than their homes are worth."

To find out how bad the problem had become, two U.S. Census Bureau surveys were performed in 2009 to collect data on mortgages, making it possible to provide an estimate of the prevalence of underwater mortgages over time. The American Housing Survey (AHS) was used to collect information on the quality of housing in the United States and information on household characteristics. The Survey of Income and Program Participation (SIPP) was used to collect information about income and program participation in the United States; detailed data on taxes, assets, and liabilities; and participation in government transfer programs. The researchers who analyzed the data reported:

> Whereas the AHS follows housing units over time, the SIPP follows individuals and households over time. While the surveys may not collect data on the actual value of the home, both surveys collect owner-estimated home values and data on outstanding principal and interest on mortgages. We use these measures to calculate home equity and to develop an estimate of whether the mortgage is under water.[2]

Using data from the 2003, 2005, 2007, and 2009 AHSs, the researchers explored national and regional trends in underwater mortgages, as well as housing and mortgage characteristics associated with these mortgages. Using two waves of data from the 2004 SIPP panel, they examined tenure transitions of individuals and households whose mortgages are under water. They wrote: "We find across the board increases in underwater mortgages in 2009 and find owners who are underwater or have high housing burdens to be at greater risk of homeownership exit."[3] (According to the research organization the Center for Housing Policy, a household is considered to have a severe housing cost burden if it spends more than 50 percent of its income on housing costs, including utilities.[4])

Survey Results

To ensure the accuracy of the results, both the AHS and the SIPP included self-reported measures of home value and mortgage debt in calculations of home equity. These calculations showed that an estimate of the percentage of underwater mortgages in 2009 in the AHS (11.6 percent) was lower than the

---

[2] Ibid.

[3] Ibid.

[4] http://online.wsj.com/public/resources/documents/Landscape2012.pdf (Retrieved September 18, 2012).

higher reported estimate (23 percent) from the private firm CoreLogic, a leading provider of information, analytics, and business services.

Analysts reported they found percentages of underwater mortgages in the AHS to increase across the board in 2009. In their analyses of the AHSs, the highest percentages of underwater housing units were found

- In the southern United States and in the West in 2007, and the West in 2009

- Among housing units with black-only householders in 2009

- Among Hispanic householders in 2007 and 2009

- Among householders younger than 35 in 2005 and 2007

- Among not-married householders in 2009

- Among householders with a high school education or less in 2003 to 2009

- Among the lowest four income quintiles in 2003 to 2009

- Among units with first-mortgage interests rates more than 8 percent in 2003 to 2009

- Among units with first mortgages that had adjustable rates in 2007 and 2009

- Among multiunit structures and manufactured/mobile homes in 2003 to 2009

- Among first-time homeowners in 2009

Using data from the 2004 SIPP, researchers found underwater status and housing burden to be associated positively with a change in status from owner to renter. The interaction between underwater status and housing burden was not statistically significant. Future research will focus on exploring further the prevalence of underwater mortgages and the effects of underwater mortgages with new data from the SIPP. The first wave of the 2008 SIPP panel housing wealth data was released in 2011 and will allow us to determine whether the 2008 SIPP captured the same changes in underwater status that were captured by the 2009 AHS. The second wave of 2008 SIPP panel housing wealth data will be released in 2012 and will allow us to replicate the owner/renter transition model after the end of the housing boom.

22 Percent of Borrowers Underwater with $689 Billion in Negative Equity

In September 2012, CoreLogic released negative-equity data that showed that 22.3 percent—10.8 million—of all residential properties with a mortgage were in negative equity at the end of the second quarter of 2012, down from 11.4 million (23.7 percent) at the end of the first quarter of 2012.[5]

According to CoreLogic, an additional 2.3 million borrowers had less than 5 percent equity in their home, which is referred to as *near-negative equity*, in the second quarter of 2012. This means that about 600,000 borrowers reached a state of positive equity at the end of the second quarter of 2012. These homeowners joined the other 700,000 borrowers that moved into positive equity in the first quarter of 2012.

Across the United States, CoreLogic reported, negative equity decreased from $691 billion at the end of the first quarter in 2012 to $689 billion at the end of the second quarter. Analysts said the $2 billion decrease in negative equity was the result of better house prices.[6]

Negative equity is synonymous with *underwater* or *upside down* and means that borrowers owe more on their mortgages than their homes are worth. Negative equity can occur because of a decline in the home's value, an increase in mortgage debt, or a combination of both.

Data Highlights of 2012 CoreLogic Study

According to the September 2012 CoreLogic data:[7]

- Nevada had the highest percentage of mortgaged properties in negative equity at 59 percent, followed by Florida (43 percent), Arizona (40 percent), Georgia (36 percent) and Michigan (33 percent). These top five states combined account for 34.1 percent of the total amount of negative equity in the United States.

- Of the total $689 billion in equity, first loans without home equity loans accounted for $339 billion negative equity, while first liens with home equity loans accounted for $353 billion.

---

[5] www.corelogic.com/about-us/news/corelogic-reports-number-of-residential-properties-in-negative-equity-decreases-again-in-second-quarter-of-2012.aspx (Retrieved October 30, 2012).

[6] Ibid.

[7] Ibid.

- About 4.2 million underwater homeowners have both first and second liens. The average mortgage balance for this group of borrowers is $300,000. The average underwater amount is $84,000.

- Most borrowers in negative equity continue to make their mortgage payments.

- Together, negative equity and near-negative equity mortgages accounted for 27 percent of all residential properties with a mortgage.

- The share of borrowers who were underwater and still current on their payments in the second quarter of 2012 was 84.9 percent. This is up from 84.8 percent at the end of the previous quarter.

- At the end of the second quarter in 2012, 1.8 million borrowers were 5 percent underwater.

A Foreclosure Crisis

Is there relief in sight? Probably not in every area of the country, according to reports from around the country. In Alabama, on July 3, 2012, the *Anniston Star* reported, "Foreclosures up, house prices down in Calhoun County." Reporter Patrick McCreless wrote that foreclosures in the county had increased during the previous 3 months, sending house prices down from an average sale price for a home of $102,924 in April to $101,345 in May.[8]

The story is the same in Georgia. *The Champion* in DeKalb County, Georgia, reported on June 29, 2012, that a new wave of foreclosures had hit the county hard even after the initial crisis, when the housing bubble first burst. Reporter Nigel Roberts wrote that there were 1,500 foreclosures in North DeKalb in 2007, and by 2010 that number "more than doubled to 3,988, according to figures from the Atlanta Regional Commission."[9] Even in 2009, Roberts explained, the number of foreclosures continued to accelerate steadily.

The rich are also suffering under the pressure of foreclosure. Recent reports show high-priced homes are seeing the greatest number of foreclosures compared with other categories of houses. According to a February 23, 2012, article on *CNNMoney*, "America's wealthiest families are now losing their

---

[8] http://annistonstar.com/bookmark/19181433 (Retrieved August 2, 2012).
[9] www.championnewspaper.com/news/articles/1849foreclosures-mount-in-north-dekalb--1849.html (Retrieved August 2, 2012).

homes to foreclosure at a faster rate than the rest of the country."[10] Jessica Dickler reported that more than 36,000 homes valued at $1 million or more were foreclosed on in 2011.

According to the *National Foreclosure Report* for May 2012 from CoreLogic, there were 63,000 completed foreclosures in the United States in May 2012 compared with 77,000 in May 2011 and 62,000 in April 2012. CoreLogic reported: "Since the financial crisis began in September 2008, there have been approximately 3.6 million completed foreclosures across the country. Completed foreclosures are an indication of the total number of homes actually lost to foreclosure."[11]

Conclusion

A homeowner suffers significant financial penalties from a foreclosure, and everyone else in an intertwined economy feels its repercussions, too. Each one of those millions of foreclosures touches the homes around it. Nearby home values often decrease when neighboring homeowners allow their bank to take their house, and the negative ripple of so many undervalued homes entering the market reverberates across many neighborhoods and regions.

Unfortunately, foreclosures are only part of the picture. The suffering extends to many underwater homeowners who stay in their home with their families, struggling for years with the hard reality of owning a home that is worth a fraction of its original value.

Options seem few for those bailing out an underwater home, but more options are available than most realize. Real estate experts from around the country can help underwater homeowners find relief. The expert opinions and professional guidance gathered in the following chapters provide underwater homeowners with many answers to their questions. Real estate agents, brokers, lawyers, economists, and other experts share their ideas and tips on how underwater homeowners can improve their lives. And they offer smart perspectives on the past and future of real estate in the United States.

Perhaps the best place to start down the road to personal real estate recovery from the underwater mortgage crisis is to tap in to the expertise of someone who knows about underwater homes firsthand. In the next chapter, we meet an expert whose story and insights offer a valuable starting point toward homeownership healing.

---

[10] http://money.cnn.com/2012/02/23/real_estate/million_dollar_foreclosures/index.htm (Retrieved October 31, 2012).

[11] http://multivu.prnewswire.com/mnr/corelogic/56979/ (Retrieved August 4, 2012).

Expert Advice on Your Underwater Mortgage

Advice from an Underwater Homeowner

Dr. Daniel Fink

When dentist Dr. Daniel Fink bought his house in Kennett Square, Pennsylvania, in 2003, he paid about $650,000. Three years later, noting an appreciable growth in his dental business, Fink decided to refinance his home mortgage and use the equity from his house to acquire a new office space and pay for an assortment of upgrades and improvements. In 2006, his house was appraised for $875,000, which gave him plenty of money to create the perfect facility for his thriving dental practice.

"I wound up getting one of those loans where the rate was floating," Fink said. "Then the market took a tank and everything blew up. My plan had been to refinance into a fixed-rate mortgage, but the housing values dropped. Now I am under water; I owe more than my house is worth."[1]

One way Fink could flip his upside-down mortgage from the red into the black is to refinance, which would allow him to take advantage of the current rock-bottom interest rates. When he first approached his lender about refinancing his mortgage loan, Fink encountered a dead end. His lender told him that the bank would not refinance underwater mortgages like his. For the next 3 years after the real estate market crashed in 2006, nobody at the bank would answer his calls. "For a while, it was very difficult to get a live human being on the phone with Bank of America. Just recently, on one of my last bills, they

---

[1] All quotes from Fink were collected during a personal interview in August 2012.

added a phone number and I was able to call and actually talk to a person. That's when they told me that, basically, I can't do a thing unless I bring $100,000 to the table to get the whole loan down to approximately 80 percent loan-to-value. People like me, I make my payments, but there is no vehicle for me to refinance unless I put a lot of money down to get down to an 80 percent LTV [loan-to-value ratio]. That's where I'm at," he laughs.

Equity Frustration

Although he makes light of his problem, Fink says he is frustrated by the fact that he cannot take advantage of today's low interest rates because he does not have enough equity in his house. On the brighter side, he notes that things are looking better than they were. Prices in his neighborhood are on the rise in 2012. "It's not quite as bad as it was a year ago because my value has come back [up] a little bit."

■ **Tip** *Look on the bright side.* Many signs indicate that today's housing market is improving. Although the rebound is slow in many areas, experts say some areas are recovering fast enough to be back at prehousing crash bubble prices in only a few more years. Keep your eyes on the prize. This attitude can help you get through those frustrating days when it seems like you are sending your monthly mortgage payments into a bottomless black hole.

Mortgages Change Hands

As mentioned at the beginning of the chapter, when Fink first bought his home in 2003, he paid about $650,000 for the house. His mortgage was with Countrywide Financial, the country's biggest mortgage lender at the time. By the end of 2007, the company was suffering financially. Countrywide was bought during the first days of 2008 by Bank of America, when the company was rumored to be on the verge of bankruptcy thanks to a spike in mortgage defaults and foreclosures after the real estate market bubble burst. Many linked those defaults and foreclosures to Countrywide's practice of making subprime loans to borrowers with weak credit.[2]

Today, Bank of America owns Fink's mortgage, which is currently at $814,000. When he recently looked to refinance his home, the bank appraised his house between $725,000 to $800,000. "It's just under water," Fink states. "I'm not

---

[2] www.msnbc.msn.com/id/22606833/ns/business-us_business/t/bank-america-acquire-countrywide/#.UCBnp475Ha4 (Retrieved August 6, 2012).

massively under water." Unfortunately, Fink is stuck with an adjustable-rate mortgage (ARM) with an interest rate that is 6.9 percent, well above the market's currently low rates, which hover around 3.5 percent. "The problem is," Fink remarks about his existing interest rate, "it seems to never go down. It's got an unlimited ceiling, but there's a floor that it will never go below. I'm sitting at 6.9, or something like that. I think it's got a floor of 6.5 percent. So, the hopes of the rate ever really going down [are low]. It's kind of like they trap you because they put these floors in that kick in later, so the rate never really goes back down and you get stuck in this rate."

Trapped in an ARM

Like Fink, many homeowners feel trapped by their ARM that has reached its peak, but that also has a built-in bottom level that kicks in over time. They are stuck with a high-interest mortgage at a time when many others are enjoying the benefits of a market in which interest rates are at an all-time low.

Fink explains, "The problem is, I pay my mortgage on time every month. All I want is a competitive rate. I don't want anyone to hand me money or anything. I would like to just fix my rate at a competitive [level]. You hear about all these people with 3.8 percent and all that stuff. That's what I'd be interested in."

■ **Tip** *Read the fine print.* When you take out any mortgage, whether it is a 30-year fixed mortgage or an ARM, make sure you understand all the fees and the specific interest rate you will be paying. If you do take out an ARM, understand the risks. Sometimes a lender promises that the low initial rate will continue to stay low until you refinance. Nobody, not even your lender, can predict the future. Assume the worst and, hopefully, you will be pleasantly surprised. Most likely, if there is a high limit built into your ARM, be ready to pay that high interest rate for a long time.

Alternatives to an Appraisal

One way to determine the value of your home is to pay a home appraiser around $500 for an appraisal. Another way is to go to your lender, tell the lender that you are interested in refinancing, and ask the lender what the calculations indicate your home is worth. This is what Fink did. "They have some kind of software at the bank where they have a range of what homes are worth. So the guy got on a computer and told me what my home was worth, which was kind of interesting. I had never heard of that before."

What Fink learned is that his home has to be worth much more money before he can refinance his current mortgage. "Right now, there is no way it's going to be worth $1 million, so I've just got to ride it out or hope that I win the lottery or something."

Fink was told by the lender that the Dodd-Frank rules require him to have 20 percent equity in his home before he can take out another mortgage loan. The interest rate for his loan is based on LIBOR, which stands for the London Interbank Offered Rate. (Half of all ARMs in the United States are also based on this reference rate.[3]) Some ARMs are "LIBOR plus four," which make them 4 percentage points higher than whatever the current LIBOR rate is on a specific date. "I don't know if it was in the fine print that I never saw, or after the teaser rate ended, or whatever, but if the LIBOR goes down to 2 or 1.5, Bank of America has a floor on it and it will never go down to what the real rate [is]." Fink feels these kinds of terms on a loan agreement are unfair. "I mean," he notes, "if you're going to play the risk that [the rate is] going to go up, [the lender] should also be able to let it go down too. I think it's ridiculous."

■ **Tip** *Consider an ARM carefully.* ARMs can be risky. Don't be fooled by the word *adjustable.* Be ready to face a much higher interest rate than the starter rate on your ARM. Think of an ARM as an RRM, or rising rate mortgage. The initial low rate of an ARM doesn't last forever, and once it goes up, it generally never comes down near its original level, especially if there is a "floor" built in to the rate as it matures.

Other options are available to Fink, but none of them appeal to him. For example, he could sell his home, but real estate commissions and closing costs are costly. If he were to do a short sale, Fink worries that the risk to his credit is too great. He points out that he is currently financially sound and secure, and he is not willing to harm that status by taking a big hit to his credit score from a short sale. Therefore, he believes that staying in his home until the market rebounds is his best option.

Many Wait for Real Estate Market to Rise

Fink is not alone in his real estate woes. According to the latest numbers from CoreLogic, a company that tracks consumer, financial, and property information, 10.8 million, or 22.3 percent, of all residential properties in the

---

[3] www.nytimes.com/2012/08/07/opinion/libor-naked-and-exposed.html (Retrieved August 6, 2012).

United States with a mortgage were under water (or in negative equity) at the end of the second quarter of 2012.[4]

Fink watches the market and hopes that the recent increase in home prices in his region will continue to build upward momentum. "In a couple of years, home values will go back up and then it will be easier to refinance without bringing a whole lot of money to the table. However, I don't know how long that's going to take. And in the meantime, I'm paying a pretty noncompetitive rate."

■ **Tip** *Be patient and ignore the media and the stories about how it's now time to refinance and take advantage of low, low rates.* If home prices continue their slow ascent, homes that are only slightly under water should gain equity along the way. The real estate market is in the middle of a slow correction that will take some time. Enjoy your house for all of the other great things it offers and try to avoid thinking about the frustratingly long time it may take for it to return to its former equity.

Fink takes full responsibility for his current situation. He would like the bank to recognize that he is a great customer who never misses a payment. He simply wants a lower interest rate. "It's my own decision," Fink says. "I realize that. I wasn't hoodwinked, but it would just be nice if there were some vehicle for people who actually pay their bills [to get a mortgage at a lower interest rate]. This [is] a factor of the whole real estate crash."

Most people whose mortgages are under water do not have the kind of money available that their lender wants them to put on the table to refinance. As mentioned, Fink needs to plunk down a cool $100,000 to be eligible for a new loan, but he says he cannot do it. Would he pay the money if he had it available? "It would depend. What I would do is crunch the numbers of how long I plan on staying [in his home], and if the savings in my monthly payments [are more] than the $100,000 over the amount of time that I plan on staying in the house, then, yeah; it's worth it."

Fink notes that he loves his house and plans to stay there for a long time. He and his wife are raising their two sons there, and they are happy to stay there for the rest of their lives. This makes the option of selling seem much less attractive than simply continuing to make monthly payments on his current mortgage.

---

[4] www.corelogic.com/about-us/news/corelogic-reports-number-of-residential-properties-in-negative-equity-decreases-again-in-second-quarter-of-2012.aspx (Retrieved October 31, 2012).

▓ **Tip**   *Crunch the numbers.* If you are trying to figure out whether it is worth it to take money out of your savings to give to your bank to qualify for a refinanced mortgage, look closely at the math.

Five Strategic Steps for Underwater Homeowners

Here are five strategic steps every underwater homeowner should take when deciding on a plan to proceed:

1. First, take a realistic view of how long you plan to stay in the house. What factors will keep you there? Why would you move?

2. Talk to a mortgage broker (you'll learn more about them and what they do in later chapters) to find out whether your LTV ratio permits refinancing at a lower rate or whether you qualify for a government program designed to help underwater homeowners.

3. Next, talk to another mortgage broker to figure out what kind of a competitive rate you can get. Maybe it's better than the first one offered. Are there points (basically, the bank's fee) you have to pay to get the loan? Factor these into your calculations.

4. Then, compare the savings of the new loan with the lower interest rate with your current loan and its higher interest rate. Compare the difference of the principal in any offer. Your mortgage broker will be happy to do this math for you.

5. Finally, make a decision whether this new investment is worth it to you. If you cannot say that you will stay in the house long enough to make the investment worthwhile, then save the money and choose another path.

Staying Financially Sound and Secure

What kind of advice would Fink offer to somebody else who is in a similar situation? He doesn't think one piece of advice fits everybody: "For some people, a short sale works. For some people, it's better to ride it out and wait for the market to come back. Some people, if they have some other asset they can sell to pay the mortgage down in order to refinance it, [can afford to refinance]. So, it's kind of an individual thing. I don't know that there is one piece of advice, one-size-fits-all, which I think is part of the problem."

▨ **Tip**   *Open your eyes.* Every investment comes with risks. Do not ignore the risks when making important decisions. Get good advice about those risks. Sometimes good advice comes at a price, but in the case of the biggest investment you will probably ever make, that price is just a drop in the bucket.

Many times, especially when it comes to large investments, risks are unpredictable. "I knew the risks," Fink said. "The problem is that what happened was so largely unforeseen and out of my control, I think it's a little bit unfair. No one could foresee that we'd be in the worst economy in 100 years. Who foresaw that coming?" What did he learn from his experience? "Know your risks," says Fink. "Be prepared to deal with them."

▨ **Tip**   *If it looks too good to be true, it probably is.* Although this phrase applies to a lot of things in life, it is certainly apropos to real estate. Markets rise and fall. Every steady rise ends. Read the fine print in every contract and be prepared to walk away from every negotiation.

Conclusion

Fink has chosen to put his underwater status aside so that he can enjoy the rest of his life, his beautiful home, and the people he loves who live there. "I work hard, pay the note, and wait for the day when I can refinance. That's all I can do."

In other words, stay put and be happy. Wise words for all who can continue to pay their mortgage.

Now let's turn to the advice of a real estate attorney who will explain the options for those who can't ride out the storm in their own home.

Advice from a Real Estate Attorney

Les Kramsky

Although other underwater homeowners are valuable sources of good advice about dealing with an underwater mortgage, a real estate attorney offers more legal opinions and options. Les R. Kramsky, Esq. is a real estate attorney who represents clients in New Jersey and in New York. Kramsky's firm represents purchasers, sellers, borrowers, lenders, banks, and mortgage companies in purchases, sales, and refinance transactions. Unlike many law firms that handle numerous different types of legal matters, Kramsky's firm prides itself on concentrating in the area of residential and commercial real estate. In September 2012, Kramsky was appointed executive vice president and general counsel at The Silk Companies, a real estate services firm. This chapter covers the options underwater homeowners can take, presented from a real estate attorney's perspective.

You're Under Water: When to Contact a Real Estate Attorney

First things first. Why would a homeowner with an underwater mortgage pay for the services of an attorney rather than simply going to see a mortgage broker in the hope of a refinance? Kramsky, who has been in the real estate industry for more than 20 years, says there are many advantages to working with an attorney: "If the [mortgage] is under water, there is a very good chance that nothing could be done with a mortgage broker unless [the homeowner] qualifies for a [Home Affordable Refinance Program (HARP)] loan. Basically, a real estate attorney can give options to an underwater homeowner [about] the different things that they can do."[1] Let's take a quick look at each option, then get into greater depth later in this chapter.

Loan Modification

According to Kramsky, "The first thing [homeowners] can do is to try to modify their loan. Today, it is more and more prevalent that you have underwater mortgages, so the lenders are more and more willing to work with the borrowers and/or their attorneys to try to get a loan modified if they qualify for the modification and they feel that they would still be able to afford the mortgage. So, I think that's the most important reason [to get an attorney involved]. I think it's always best to go to a real estate attorney if you're going to try to modify your mortgage."

What is a loan modification? It is one of the best ways to deal with an underwater mortgage. Basically, a loan modification is a permanent change to one or more of the terms of the borrower's loan. The modification also allows the loan to be reinstated, with the wonderful result for borrowers that they now have payments they can afford.

Beware of Unscrupulous Loan Modification Companies!

Kramsky warns, "One thing you should never do, in my opinion, is go to one of these loan modification companies. [There are], unfortunately, a lot of unscrupulous companies. I've heard of a lot of horror stories of clients who come to me afterwards where they gave thousands of dollars to a loan modification company that would promise them the world and then, in the end, they find out that the company didn't do anything, won't give them a refund, and it's too late by the time they get to me in terms of getting their money back. By that time, [these companies] have shut their doors or are under investigation."

Kramsky adds, "Not . . . all companies are scam companies, but there are a lot of companies out there, and you have to be careful. My opinion is, you're better off going to a real estate attorney before you go to any type of loan modification company."

---

[1] All quotes from Kramsky were collected during a personal interview in July 2012.

Short Sale

Another alternative that a real estate attorney can assist with is completing a short sale. In essence, the homeowner decides to sell the house for less than what is owed on the mortgage. "Today, mortgage companies are more and more willing to settle on accepting a lower amount," Kramsky comments. "If you're able to come up with the difference, then it will not affect your credit. But most people are unwilling or unable to come up with the difference, which could be $10,000, $50,000, $100,000. So, it will affect your credit score. It will be reported by the lender. However, that is something you can explain if you need to apply for a mortgage within a couple of years."

Kramsky adds that this is a popular alternative today. "A lot of deals I do are short sales."

So, if you have an underwater mortgage and decide to do a short sale, and you sell your home for $50,000 less than what you owe on the mortgage, you may be required by the bank to pay the deficiency of $50,000 if you have money in your savings or if you have a 401K plan worth more than the deficiency. "The bank is going to want to see your financials," Kramsky explains. "[It is] going to know all of your assets. And if [it sees] there is enough money there, [it's] not going to approve the short sale unless you pay the deficiency."

But in many situations, he continues, there aren't enough assets to make it worthwhile. "The bank just wants the short sale to go through and get whatever money [it] can. [It owns] too many properties. There are too many problems out there, so [the bank will] approve it and . . . just not pursue a deficiency."

If you cannot pay the difference between what your house sells for and what you owe on your mortgage, your credit score and ability to buy another house in the near future will be affected. Kramsky remarks, "If [the bank does] not pursue the deficiency and you do not pay the deficiency, your credit score will take a hit. It won't be a devastating hit, but it will be reported as a short sale, so . . . your credit score [will take a hit]."

Tip *Get help for a short sale.* If your mortgage is are under water, you have no assets, and you want to get out of your house, go see a real estate attorney to help you with a short sale. With the help of a real estate attorney, you could possibly end up never having to pay the deficiency or have a deficiency judgment made against you. As mentioned, your credit score may drop temporarily, but if you continue to pay your other bills and act responsibly with your money, that score will rise over the next few years so that you will then be eligible to take out another mortgage to buy another house. This process may take a few years, but you will have escaped thousands of dollars in bills for the difference between the selling price and what you owe on your mortgage.

If your lender will not approve of a short sale, then another option you should explore is some form of foreclosure.

Foreclosure: Strategic Default

In a foreclosure, the lender takes steps to repossess your home to then sell it to satisfy at least part of the debt that is owed. If the lender has to remove you forcibly from the home, it can get ugly.

However, there's a less-harsh version of foreclosure called a *strategic default*. According to Kramsky, "Basically, a homeowner looks at [his or her situation] and says, 'Wow. I have no equity in this house, and it would be OK to stop paying my mortgage and just walk away from this whole debt.' Obviously, it's going to affect your credit, but a lot of people today, unfortunately, don't have great credit. And the other risk is that the lender can come after you for a deficiency for what's left over after they sell the house. But today, most of the major lenders are not pursuing those deficiency judgments against the borrowers. So I do see a lot of people just walking away from their house."

Some don't walk away, but stay put. "If you stop paying the mortgage, you can live [in your house] and save up money for 1 or 2 even 3 years until the foreclosure action actually goes through," notes Kramsky.

Shop Locally

Of course, not every state in the country has as many foreclosures on the books as New Jersey, so talk to a real estate attorney in your particular area before you count on being able to live in your home and save your money before the foreclosure action is complete and you are evicted. In some states there is a large gap in time between the time that a foreclosure is filed and the time a homeowner is served with an eviction notice. Homeowners can use states with long foreclosure timelines to their advantage. Kramsky explains, "New Jersey is one of the worst states in terms of [time period], for a lender to foreclose. If you do hire a foreclosure defense attorney, there are ways that [she] can defend the homeowner with different strategies to stall, and sometimes you can even end up in a modification because the lender doesn't want the property."

Although a loan modification is a positive repercussion from a strategic default scenario, homeowners who choose this option also face potential negative effects to their credit score that could keep them from buying another home in the near future.

"Some people, if they qualify, also file a bankruptcy, Chapter 7," Kramsky says. "So this way, the lender will not come after them for a deficiency, but [they] will be able to buy a house within a few years after [their] default on a mortgage. Today, mortgage companies understand the marketplace, so people will be able, in 3 years, to qualify for a mortgage again. And other people, if they need to get a mortgage sooner, are getting others—family, friends, relatives—to cosign for them."

FORECLOSURE TIMELINES

According to RealtyTrac, a firm that publishes the country's largest database of foreclosures, auction, and bank-owned homes, different states have different timelines for the foreclosure process. For example, in Texas, a foreclosure only takes about 27 days. In Tennessee, the foreclosure process should only take about 40 to 45 days. Virginia's foreclosure timeline is also around 45 days. Maryland's foreclosure process takes about 46 days.

On the other hand, some states are so bogged down with foreclosures that their processes take months. For example, in Delaware, the foreclosure process can take anywhere from 170 to 210 days. In New Jersey and Pennsylvania, RealtyTrac reports that the timeline for both states is 270 days. In Wisconsin, the foreclosure timeline is 290 days.[2]

Knowing these timelines can help an underwater mortgage holder prepare for the next step.

HARP: Better Than a Strategic Default

According to Kramsky, strategic default is really a last-resort option, but some homeowners do it because they feel they are in too deep. He adds, "And they can live in their house without paying the mortgage and just save money for a while—for months, or years even, in some places. For them, that might be the better option, knowing that they're going to take a big hit on their credit."

But there are alternatives. Refinancing is extremely difficult for those with underwater mortgages because lenders usually require homeowners to have equity in the home to pursue this option. Kramsky explains that the HARP program "allows [those] with a Fannie Mae or Freddie Mac mortgage to have the ability, even if they're under water, to refinance and get that lower interest rate. And if [their] payment comes down a couple hundred dollars or more, that may be the difference for [those who are] struggling with their mortgage to allow them to continue to pay their mortgage."

[2] www.realtytrac.com/foreclosure-laws/foreclosure-laws-comparison.asp (Retrieved July 16, 2012).

A real estate attorney, along with a mortgage broker, can help you determine whether you qualify for the HARP 2.0 program. In addition to having a Fannie Mae– or Freddie Mac–owned mortgage, your credit must be good and, adds Kramsky, "[t]here's a long-term qualification: You can't have a default in your mortgage in the past 6 months and you can only have defaulted once in the past year. [If you qualify for the HARP 2.0], then your interest rate will be at a much lower rate than what you have now."

WATCH FOR HARP 3.0

Homeowners with underwater mortgages should keep their eyes open for the next version of HARP: HARP 3.0. According to a press release issued July 12, 2012, nearly 30 million new borrowers could qualify for the expanded program, which as of this writing has not been approved by Congress.

Obama administration officials say HARP will save homeowners an average of $250 a month in mortgage payments, and that HARP overall will help an anticipated 4 million to 5 million underwater homeowners. An administration spokesperson stated, "Senate bill 3085, introduced by U.S. Senators Robert Menendez (D-NJ) and Barbara Boxer (D-CA), would expand and streamline refinancing opportunities under the existing Home Affordable Refinance Program (HARP). Research from Manhattan's Columbia Business School at Columbia University estimates this new legislation would increase the total number of homeowners who refinance under HARP to up to 13 million and produce total potential savings of $35 billion a year."[3]

Mortgage Brokers Can Help with HARP

If you are struggling with an underwater mortgage, you have never missed a payment for your mortgage, and your mortgage loan is owned by Freddie Mac or Fannie Mae, go see a mortgage broker. The broker can offer you free advice at the outset, and probably only charges you if you actually take out the loan. Even then, that charge comes out of the interest rate you pay for your reduced monthly mortgage payment. If your mortgage broker tries to ask for an up-front, nonrefundable fee to help you with your refinancing or your loan modification, go find another mortgage broker!

Kramsky advises, "If you qualify for the HARP 2.0 program, then of course go to your mortgage broker, but I would go to a real estate attorney first." He explains that, because a person's home is usually the biggest asset he or she owns, getting a lawyer's advice before taking out a new mortgage can provide the homeowner with a greater level of security. "Even if it costs you a little bit

---

[3] www.prweb.com/releases/prwebharp_approval/30/prweb9684520.htm (Retrieved July 15, 2012).

of money, it's well worth it to get the right advice, have someone lead you in the right direction, and [lay out] all the options for you."

▓ **Tip** *Hire a real estate attorney.* If you qualify for HARP, you may be able to refinance your mortgage. A mortgage broker can do this for you, but hire a real estate attorney, too. A good real estate attorney can point you in the right direction toward a reputable mortgage broker and can help you make one of the biggest decisions of your life.

THE *WALL STREET JOURNAL* RATE

The first option for any homeowner who is under water who is intent on staying in the home is a refinance deal. Today, mortgage rates can be found for their lowest interest rates in recent memory. The *Wall Street Journal*, for the past year, has reported a prime rate of 3.25 percent.

The prime rate, according to a recent *Wall Street Journal* bank survey, is perhaps the most widely used benchmark when banks set their home equity lines of credit and credit card rates.[4]

The *Wall Street Journal* surveys the 30 largest banks, and when three quarters of them (23 banks) change, the newspaper changes its rate, effective on the day the *Wall Street Journal* publishes the new rate. It's the most widely quoted measure of the prime rate, which is the rate at which banks will lend money to their most-favored customers. The prime rate will move up or down according to changes by the Federal Reserve Board.[5]

Options for Homeowners

Let's look at some of these options in greater depth.

1. Refinance

Refinancing means you pay off an existing mortgage loan with the money you receive from a new loan for the same amount of money that you owe, but the new loan comes with better terms, such as a lower interest rate or lower monthly payments. The house remains the collateral for the loan. By refinancing, homeowners who are under water can reduce their monthly bills, which makes it much easier to stay in the house.

---

[4] www.bankrate.com/rates/interest-rates/prime-rate.aspx#ixzz20oh8I9UV (Retrieved July 17, 2012).

[5] www.bankrate.com/rates/interest-rates/wall-street-prime-rate.aspx (Retrieved July 17, 2012).

Anyone interested in refinancing should start off looking at the HARP 2.0 program (and, if it passes through the U.S. Congress, HARP 3.0). HARP 2.0 is a valuable tool for homeowners who have kept up with their mortgage payments. Les Kramsky says, "From what I understand, it's the most popular, and [it's] because they are allowing more and more people to qualify by loosening the creditor qualifications. You don't need to get an appraisal anymore or pay for an appraisal. I think that's the first thing to check to see if you qualify for that."

The best way to determine whether you qualify for HARP 2.0 is first to go online and see whether Fannie Mae or Freddie Mac own your mortgage. You can find out whether Fannie Mae owns your mortgage by going to www. fanniemae.com/loanlookup/. Similarly, you can determine whether Freddie Mac owns your mortgage by going to www.freddiemac.com/corporate/. Or, you can call your lender. Talking to your lender directly can help you determine the types of refinancing options available to you. So many programs are becoming available these days, it pays to contact your lender if you have not spoken to him or her recently.

■ **Tip**   *Stay in touch with your lender.* Make sure you have the most up-to-date information from your lender about refinancing before you pursue other options. New programs become available all of the time. Ask your lender about its latest programs for underwater homeowners. Making regular phone calls to your lender is the best way to learn what you can do to improve the terms of your loan.

---

2. Modify Your Loan

A loan modification is an opportunity to change the terms and conditions of the loan that you already have by going to your lender and petitioning for better terms. If your mortgage is under water and you want to get better terms for your loan, you can request that your lender lower your monthly payments or reduce your interest rate. Sometimes a loan modification involves extending the duration of the loan, which may mean an additional cost to the borrower in the long run for some savings in monthly payments.

A lender may accept your petition for a loan modification or reject it, but you will never know unless you try. Talking with your lender directly helps you get all the paperwork together that you need to petition properly for a loan modification.

Les Kramsky advises homeowners to hire an attorney when attempting to get a loan modification. "It's definitely very hard for a borrower to do it on their own. Each lender has [its] own qualifications and [its] own paperwork that they need filled out. Unfortunately, they don't make it easy. I find they lose documents all the time."

Other issues that many borrowers run into when seeking a loan modification include personnel changes. The loan modification process at most banks takes a long period of time. Because people at banks are often moved from one office to another, the person with whom you are communicating to complete your loan modification may not be there to see it through to the end. Kramsky adds, "You're dealing with one person, then you have a new person assigned to the modification, so you need to be persistent. [Getting a new loan is] not going to happen overnight. They are going to call you for updates all the time. But if you do qualify, and your income shows that you are able to afford the modified mortgage, it can happen."

Complicated Maze of Paperwork

Kramsky explains that he thinks it is always best to use an attorney for this complicated maze of paperwork, although homeowners can do this on their own with the right attention to detail and persistence. Kramsky comments, "In my experience, [getting a modified loan] is a viable option. Not everyone is going to get approved, but a lot of people will."

One of the difficulties homeowners face when attempting to complete a loan modification is that banks often bundle the mortgages they own and sell those portfolios to other banks. This process can make it difficult for borrowers who are working with one lender to get a loan modification petition approved, because suddenly that lender no longer owns the mortgage. This may mean that borrowers have to start the entire process all over again with the new owner of the mortgage. This is when persistence is key. Kramsky notes that scenario is quite common. "I received approval on one [loan modification. Then] they sold the home loan and I had to start over. So, yes, that definitely is a potential problem. You never know about the timing of your modification."

How long does the average loan modification take to go through? Some take a month; others take a year or more. Patience is also key.

There May Be Hope on the Horizon

Even if homeowners who apply for a loan modification get denied, sometimes only a missing piece of paperwork may stand between approval and denial. This is when remaining persistent, patient, and hopeful work to the benefit for underwater mortgage holders. Kramsky adds, "Sometimes you get denied and then you resubmit paperwork and then you get approved for that. That can stretch [the approval process] out 6 months, 8 months, 9 months, a year. Be persistent."

Sometimes the obstacles that stand in the way of an underwater homeowner preventing a loan modification from being approved are easily remedied. Stay in constant contact with a representative from the lender to keep obstacles from becoming overwhelming. This is also when having a good attorney can pay off: The attorney spends his or her time ensuring that all the appropriate paperwork has been submitted and received by the lender.

One hurdle that can prevent a loan modification from being approved is shoddy accounting. Make sure you account for all your income and your expenses when applying for a loan modification. This is when the itemized budget you've kept and tracked for several months (perhaps with Quicken or another tax software that can help you track income and expenses) pays off. Problems with accounting can lead to petitions for loan modifications being rejected.

"A lot of [the loan approval process] has to do with the accounting," Kramsky explains, "knowing all your income and expenses, and being able to lay it out for the lender and knowing what the lender is actually looking for, because you can't show too much income and you can't show too little income. So, you have to be just right to get approved."

■ **Tip**   *Check your work.* Be thorough when doing your accounting and submitting your paperwork to your lender for a loan modification. Be truthful. Be accurate. Be thorough.

Kramsky adds, "You want to be truthful, and you want to do all your research, because I've had people who've shown too much income and then I would say, 'Well, what about your dry cleaning expenses? Did you include your grocery shopping or shopping for your children?' And [then my clients say], 'Oh no! Oh no!' Then, boom, next thing you know they [include that information] and then they qualify."

■ **Tip**   *Do your budget!* This cannot be stressed enough. Knowing how much you make and how much you spend each month is one of the most valuable things you can learn about yourself when trying to improve your financial situation. Understanding your budget inside and out will help you complete the paperwork for a loan modification and save you much time and energy in the long run. Don't rely on estimates; look at your receipts and bank statements.

A lender who is deciding whether you qualify for their loan modification program looks at your application or petition and judges all your expenses and incomes. The more proof you have of them, including bank statements, receipts, credit card bills, utility bills, pay stubs, and tax returns, the better off you will be when applying for a loan modification. If you are a W2 employee, keep 3 to 4 months of your pay stubs to verify your income to your lender, Kramsky suggests.

Regarding receipts, Kramsky says, "I'd keep everything for at least 6 months, to have everything documented to show. It's not that much that you really need to show, but you do need your standard financial stuff. I would go back at least 6 months."

Pay off Your Mortgage Insurance

Another tip for homeowners who are anticipating a loan modification application in their near future: Get rid of your mortgage insurance, also known as private mortgage insurance (PMI); it is another barrier between you and a possible loan modification.

What is PMI? Basically, when you originally bought your home, if you could not make a down payment of 20 percent or more, you had to buy PMI. This insurance protected your lender from default on your loan. If you agreed to pay a higher interest rate, you may have avoided paying PMI.

PMI charges vary depending on the size of the down payment and the loan, but they typically amount to about 0.5 percent of the loan, according to the Mortgage Bankers Association of America.[6]

Mortgage lenders cannot modify your loan before you have paid off your first 20 percent of your house, so you need to do that, eliminating your PMI, before you are eligible for a loan modification. "That's very important," Kramsky notes. "Also, if you have other mortgages, if you're doing a home equity loan or any other second mortgage, those have to be subordinated." This means that you need to obtain a document from your second mortgage or your home equity lender that says that mortgage will be subordinated to the primary mortgage loan. Kramsky explains that this is not difficult to do in today's market. "Today, [the second mortgage or home equity lenders] are in second position already, so it shouldn't be [difficult]. [The eligibility requirements apply] more to a HARP 2.0 and anything to do with a HARP 2.0 refinance. [Your primary lender] always wants to see a document. If you have a second [mortgage] or if you have a home equity [loan], [your primary

---

[6] www.bankrate.com/finance/mortgages/the-basics-of-private-mortgage-insurance-pmi.aspx (Retrieved July 16, 2012).

lender] will want to see a document to make sure that subordination will be recorded, stating that [your second mortgage lender understands it] will still be in second position."

■ **Tip** *You are not alone.* Ask for help from those people around you with the knowledge to get you over hurdles. Your mortgage broker can help you get a document from your secondary lender that allows you to subordinate your second loan to the first loan you are trying to refinance or modify.

Kramsky says that many people do not realize how much help is available to them. "Some people don't realize that. They're like, 'You know what? I'm so under water. My first [mortgage] is under water. Then I have a second; [forget] my third.' Luckily, under HARP, you can still refinance if you qualify."

■ **Tip** *Think twice.* Don't think a second loan on your home disqualifies you from help. Some mortgage modification and refinance programs offer ways to help you even if you have more than one loan on your house outstanding.

---

3. Go For a Short Sale

First you tried to refinance and you were shot down by your lender. Then you tried to get a loan modification from your lender, but you were found to be unqualified for any program. Now what? Your next course of action is probably a short sale—an opportunity to sell your house for less than you owe on your mortgage. As mentioned, one of the benefits of this option is that you may find out that you do not have to pay the difference between what the price your house sells for and what you owe on your mortgage. On the other hand, one of the possible downsides of this scenario is that your credit score could take a hit, making it hard for you to buy your next house during the next few years. These two sides of this option need to be considered seriously.

The short sale is a common choice these days for underwater homeowners. Kramsky remarks, "It's a popular option because in today's real estate market, the value of their house is such that they are not able to pay what they owe on their mortgage [if they sell]. Whether a person wants to do a short sale, or needs to do a short sale, or just wants to sell their house because they're relocating, they're retiring, they'll do a short sale."

When a homeowner gets an offer to buy the home, it becomes a short sale when the amount the person is willing to buy the home for is less than what the homeowner owes to the bank for the mortgage. Sometimes homeowners take money out of their savings or retirement funds to pay the difference between the selling price and the mortgage amount that is due. This type of transaction has no negative influence on sellers' credit score, so they are able to buy another home without delay. Kramsky explains, "Whether you're going to come up with whatever deficiency amount will determine whether you're going to take a hit on your credit or not."

A Hit to Your Credit

If your lender decides to pay off your deficiency, you will suffer the negative effects to your credit score, which will hinder your ability to buy your next home for the next 2 to 3 years.

In her column for *The Washington Post* titled, "What's worse for credit score—foreclosure, short sale or deed in lieu?" on August 30, 2011, columnist Michelle Singletary wrote: "This is not true — turns out there's no significant difference in [Fair Isaac Corporation (FICO)] score impact among foreclosures, short sales, or deeds in lieu of foreclosure, said Bradley Graham, senior director of scores product management at FICO, which is the trademark credit scoring model created by Fair Isaac Corp," and is the most widely used credit scoring system in the country.[7] (Note: Deeds in lieu of foreclosure are explained later.)

COSIGNING OPTION

Getting somebody who is close to you to cosign for your next mortgage is one way to get around a lousy credit score, which could be preventing you from getting a loan. Then, you can work on establishing a better credit score with which you can either transfer that loan over to your own name or refinance the loan at a future date.

"It will take anywhere from 2 to 4 years to build your credit up again," Kramsky points out. "Hopefully it's only your mortgage that's showing a default and you don't have any unexplainable defaults, and not just everything went bad. So you can build [your credit] up in 2 to 4 years, and if you want to buy a house sooner with a cosigner, a lot of times people will use their parents or a sibling, hoping they can buy on their credit alone."

Working with a real estate attorney, homeowners can decide which option will allow them to buy their next home in a reasonable amount of time after getting out of an underwater mortgage.

---

[7] www.washingtonpost.com/business/economy/whats-worse-for-credit-score--foreclosure-short-sale-or-deed-in-lieu/2011/08/30/glQAbnTaqJ_story.html (Retrieved June 16, 2012).

FICO Score Impacts

According to the experts at FICO, as far as your FICO score is concerned, there is no difference between foreclosures and short sales or deeds in lieu of foreclosures. Each of these actions is considered an account that was "not paid as agreed" and has the same affect on your FICO score.

FICO experts also point out that it's a common misconception that a foreclosure makes it impossible to rebuild your credit. In fact, they add that if you keep all of your other credit obligations in good standing, there's a good chance that your FICO score could begin to rebound in just 2 years.[8]

Kramsky says there is only a negative effect to your credit score if you fail to pay off the deficiency after the short sale. One option for homeowners, he points out, is to borrow money to pay off the deficiency. This is another way to avoid a hit to your credit score. If you cannot pay off your deficiency, then you probably have to rent your next home for the next few years or look for somebody, such as a relative or close friend to cosign for your next mortgage.

Deficiency Judgment

When a bank goes after homeowners for a deficiency after a short sale, the lender can sue to obtain a deficiency judgment. To prevent the chance of having the bank pursue a deficiency judgment and impact your credit negatively, you can pay off the deficiency at the closing of the short sale. Kramsky says, "You can make a deal with the bank and pay it off. You borrow the money from someone, a family member, whatever, and then basically it's a clean deal. The bank doesn't care; they're paid in full. Then you have no hit on your credit."

If there is a deficiency, then the bank often charges that to the home seller after the house is sold. "Here's the thing," explains Kramsky, "Let's say there's a deficiency of $20,000. With a major lender, there's a good chance they are not going to pursue the borrower for the deficiency, but it will still affect your credit."

■ **Tip** *Do not assume the worst.* Never start with the assumption that you have to pay the entire deficiency yourself. Hire an attorney who can plead your case with your lender or talk to your lender directly. It is really up to the lender's discretion whether the bank requires the seller doing a short sale to pay off the difference between the selling price and the money owed on the seller's

---

[8] www.myfico.com/crediteducation/questions/foreclosure-credit-score.aspx (Retrieved June 16, 2012).

mortgage. Talk to someone at the bank that holds your mortgage loan and find out whether you can get a better deal than having to pay off the entire deficiency yourself. Sometimes banks forgive the entire deficiency. It all depends on your specific financial circumstances and the size of your lender.

Wait to Declare Bankruptcy

Declaring bankruptcy may be another way to avoid a tremendous debt, since some types of bankruptcies will discharge a mortgage debt. The downside of a bankruptcy is that you will be unable to buy your next home for at least 7 years, rather than the 2 or 3 years you will have to wait if you simply pay off a deficiency judgment or if your bank forgives your deficiency.

"Some people," notes Kramsky, "knowing that they're a candidate for bankruptcy, will wait to see, on a strategic default or on a short sale, if the lender's going to pursue them. If it doesn't, they're fine, but if the lender does, then they'll file for bankruptcy and get a discharge."

Different kinds of bankruptcies have different levels of discharge. If you reach this level of debt, your real estate attorney can help you decide what kind of bankruptcy is right for you. According to LawFirms.com, a mortgage debt is completely dischargeable in a Chapter 7 Bankruptcy. "However, the debtor will not be able to keep the home, as the collateral will revert to the bank or mortgage company as compensation for the deficiency owed by the debtor. In a Chapter 13 Bankruptcy, the automatic stay entered by the Bankruptcy Court can prevent a foreclosure until the debtor can negotiate a payment plan with the bank and resume paying his regular mortgage."[9]

▨ **Tip** *Consider waiting to pay any deficiency on your short sale.* Many banks forgive the deficiency, so wait to determine whether the lender pursues a deficiency judgment against you— keeping in mind that, if you do wait, it will affect your credit score negatively. If you do, declaring bankruptcy may be another way to avoid a tremendous debt, since some types of bankruptcies will discharge a mortgage debt.

4. Deed in Lieu of Foreclosure

Another option for underwater mortgage holders, after a short sale, is a deed in lieu of foreclosure, which is simply a voluntary foreclosure. In a deed in lieu,

[9] www.lawfirms.com/resources/bankruptcy/debt-relief/discharge-debt-bankruptcy.htm (Retrieved July 17, 2012).

an underwater homeowners simply make a deal with the lender to return the house back to the lender in good condition. Homeowners also sign the deed over to the lender.

Kramsky says he doesn't handle many deeds in lieu of foreclosures. "I've seen it; I don't think it's that popular of an option. It's basically, the homeowner just says, 'You know what? I don't want to do this. I just want to leave. Here's the deed.' And [he] just [signs] it over to the bank. For the bank, it makes the process of foreclosure less expensive and quicker. I don't really see that as a popular option today. I would never really recommend [a deed in lieu of foreclosure] because if you are going to do that, you're probably better off looking at a short sale or doing a strategic default. I think those are better options, strategically, for a borrower."

Kramsky adds, "Deed in lieu is basically really just helping the lender keep their foreclosure costs down, giving them a quicker resolution for the foreclosure process." He believes that the deed in lieu of foreclosure has more benefits for the bank than the borrower because the effects of a deed in lieu on a borrower's credit are the same as the effects of a standard foreclosure.

5. Foreclosure

When you have run out of other options, your last choice is to go to foreclosure. This process involves the lender repossessing your home and selling it to the highest bidder at a sheriff's auction.

When you are unable to pay your monthly mortgage payment for whatever reason, you default on your mortgage payments. After a couple of months, you will have lost your opportunity to take advantage of the previous four options and foreclosure is imminent. What can you do?

Rent back is one way to go. Sometimes a lender offers a rent-back option, which may allow you to stay in your home for a year or two while the bank sorts out the foreclosure process. A rent-back situation allows you to continue to stay in the home, but instead of making monthly mortgage payments, you pay rent on a 1- or 2-year lease. Usually these rent payments are less than the mortgage payments you were once paying. If you want to continue to stay in your house even after you determine that foreclosure is your only option, ask your lender about any rent-back program that might be available.

▨ Note According to Kramsky, there is a difference between how soon you will be able to buy your next home after going through a foreclosure or a short sale: "The nation's two largest mortgage investors, Fannie Mae and Freddie Mac, with certain exceptions, won't lend to you again for 5 years (foreclosure) and 2 years (short sale)."

Be Strategic

Kramsky says that one bit of advice he would give to anyone facing foreclosure is to "use it to your advantage. Make it strategic. Do not make any payments. Save your money so you can go somewhere and rent a place or move in with someone—whatever you're doing. I would stay in the place for as long as you possibly can. Most foreclosures in most states take a very, very long time. Just stay rent free, mortgage free, and save your money."

Staying in a house that is being foreclosed is full of uncertainty, because it is hard to predict when the foreclosure will be finalized, but it is an option for those who need a place to stay while making plans for the future. A bank cannot throw homeowners out of their foreclosed house until the foreclosure process is complete, and then there is an eviction process, which stake another month or two. Use this time wisely. Do not wait passively until you are evicted to decide what you will do next. Save your money. Search out a rental unit somewhere that you can afford. Pay off your other bills so you can recover more easily from the hit your credit score takes from the foreclosure action. Take an active role in your future and use this time to improve your financial situation down the road. Educate yourself on the timelines for foreclosure and eviction in your area.

6. Bankruptcy

Bankruptcy is really the last option for those who have lost everything, including their underwater mortgage, to a foreclosure. Kramsky points out that this is not something most people will have to consider.

Talk to your real estate attorney before filing for bankruptcy. If you do file, it will be another 7 years before you can buy your next home. Check out your options. There are several different kinds of bankruptcy. Have an attorney walk you through the possibilities of each kind of bankruptcy, if the weight of your debt is crushing you.

According to U.S. courts, "Bankruptcy laws help people who can no longer pay their creditors get a fresh start—by liquidating assets to pay their debts or by creating a repayment plan. Bankruptcy laws also protect troubled businesses and provide for orderly distributions to business creditors through reorganization or liquidation." The federal judiciary points out that most cases in the United States are filed under the three main chapters of the Bankruptcy Code — Chapter 7, Chapter 11, and Chapter 13.[10]

▨ **Note** Federal courts have exclusive jurisdiction over bankruptcy cases. This means that a bankruptcy case cannot be filed in a state court.

What to Do If You Are Considering Bankruptcy

If you are considering bankruptcy as an option, the first action you must take is to file a petition with the bankruptcy court. Hire a bankruptcy attorney to help you do this.

There are several ways to file. For example, you can file your petition as an individual or as a husband and wife together. Another option is to file as a corporation or other entity. You will then be required to file statements listing all your assets, income, liabilities, and the names and addresses of all your creditors, as well as how much you owe to each of them.

When you file a petition, this automatically prevents, or *stays,* all debt collection actions against you and your property. According to the U.S. courts: "As long as the stay remains in effect, creditors cannot bring or continue lawsuits, make wage garnishments, or even make telephone calls demanding payment." Each of the people or organizations to whom you owe money receive a notice from the clerk of the court that you have filed a bankruptcy petition.

Some people file bankruptcy to reorganize and establish a plan to repay their creditors whereas others are simply trying to liquidate their property. In most cases when homeowners are trying to liquidate their property, there is usually little or no money available from the estate to pay creditors. As a result, there are usually few issues or disputes and homeowners are normally granted a discharge of most debts without objection. "This means you will no longer be personally liable for repaying the debts."[11]

---

[10] www.uscourts.gov/FederalCourts/Bankruptcy.aspx (Retrieved July 19, 2012).

[11] www.uscourts.gov/FederalCourts/UnderstandingtheFederalCourts/ HowCourtsWork/ BankruptcyCases.aspx (Retrieved July 19, 2012).

Questions in a Bankruptcy Case

According to U.S. laws, conflicts between lenders and borrowers may turn into a lawsuit in a bankruptcy case over who owns certain property, how it should be used, what the property is worth, how much is owed on a debt, whether the person declaring bankruptcy should be discharged from certain debts, or how much money should be paid to lawyers, accountants, auctioneers, and any other professional who gets involved. Litigation in the bankruptcy court is conducted in nearly the same way that civil cases are handled in the district court. There could also be discovery, pretrial proceedings, settlement efforts, and a trial.[12] On the bright side, this is not a common occurrence. Kramsky notes that lenders just want the house.

■ **Tip** *Wait to file bankruptcy.* You may not be pursued by your lender for the difference between what you owe on your mortgage and the selling price of your home at foreclosure. You may not be as under water and financially impacted as you imagine. Let time, and a good real estate attorney, tell you when bankruptcy is your final option. Wait and see whether the bank forces your hand. There is always the possibility they will drop the deficiency.

---

7. Stay Put

Of course, there is always a final option available to homeowners whose mortgage is under water. Keep paying your mortgage payments, stay in your home, and wait for the real estate market to rebound. If you live in an area where there are jobs, chances are the market will recover in the near future. You may have to wait 3, 5, or even 10 years, but you may find yourself with a home that is worth more than what you owe to your mortgage lender after home prices bounce back to what they were when you bought your home.

Stick with the Plan

Those with a steady income and those whose homes are only 5 percent or 10 percent under water have the option of looking at their homes as a long-term investment rather than a short-term investment that is currently under water. You simply look at your home as you did when you signed your 30-year mortgage in the first place: This is a long-term deal. You agreed to pay off your house at the price it was at the time, so you stick with the plan, stop looking on Zillow.com and other web sites that show your home has decreased in value, and enjoy the home you bought.

---

[12] www.gamb.uscourts.gov/USCourts/understanding-bankruptcy (Retrieved August 10, 2012).

One way to make this option even more appealing is to remember that a home is more than a monetary investment. It is a lifestyle. It gives you shelter. It provides your family and friends a place to enjoy each other. It offers you a neighborhood and neighbors you have come to love and appreciate, and the schools your children attend. It offers you the place you live. It is more than a stock or bond. It offers many intangible qualities that, when remembered and appreciated, make owning a home that is under water something that has more value than the price tag indicates.

For many people, this is the least painful choice to make regarding their underwater mortgage. In addition, their credit score remains high, so when they want to sell their home several years down the road, lenders will offer them the best loans available. Underwater homeowners should not forget that there are many wonderful benefits to staying in a home that is under water. Kramsky agrees. "[These homeowners] are making decent money and they get to have a nice house that has gone down in value, which a lot of them have. What are you going to do? You don't qualify for any programs, you don't want to move, . . . you just continue to pay [your mortgage]."

Long-Term Investing

Looking at your home as a long-term investment instead of a short-term investment can help you avoid the anxiety that comes with daily calculations of your home's monetary value. Open your eyes to the larger picture. Widen your purview to include all the other good things that owning your home brings to you. Market fluctuations have distracted many people from the less-tangible things that make life worth living. A 30-year mortgage *is* a long-term investment. So is a 15-year mortgage. When you stop seeing it as such, you open yourself up to the worried angst of a disgruntled short-term investor rather than the calm satisfaction of a long-term investor. In 10 years, you may be living in a home that will sell for much more than you paid for it.

"It's Not the End of the World"

Kramsky concludes by advising homeowners whose mortgages are under water not to let their real estate situation ruin their lives. "There's a lot of people out there in foreclosure, a lot of people out there who have underwater mortgages. My best advice is to go to a real estate attorney, let them lay out your options, and make a decision. Like anything else, it's not the end of the world. It's not a big deal. I have clients that come to me crying, hysterical, but it's just a house, and there's a lot of options out there for people with underwater mortgages."

▨ **Tip** *Make your mortgage payments.* No matter what anyone tells you, make your payments. Even if your lender tells you to stop paying so you can qualify for a loan modification, don't do it. This is bad advice from your lender.

LOAN MODIFICATION ADVICE: STOP MAKING PAYMENTS OR NOT?

Some people whose home mortgages are under water encounter a paradox. They are told that the number one thing they must do to retain good credit is to make sure they continue to pay their mortgage payments on time, but then they call their creditor looking for a loan modification, and their lender tells them they have to miss some mortgage payments before they are eligible to get a loan modification. The trouble is that when they do not get the loan modification, they are hit with a blow to their credit score for their missed payments, and they still have to pay their missed mortgage payments along with any penalties and interest they may have accrued over the time they stopped making their payments. What should homeowners do? Listen to the lender who says to stop making payments so they will be eligible for the loan modification but risk foreclosure because they defaulted on their mortgage payments? Or continue to make payments but lose the option of a loan modification?

Kramsky says he runs into this dilemma a lot in his practice. "I've heard that advice, not recently, but more like 2 years ago. I don't think it's something that happens now. From my experience, today, [lenders are] not telling people that they have to default on their loan in order to qualify for the loan modification. They used to, absolutely; they used to. But I would *never* tell a client that. Most real estate attorneys—good real estate attorneys—wouldn't advise their clients to default on their mortgage if they have the means to pay it or want to pay it. For that very reason, I think it's important to try to continue to make the payments on your mortgage if you still should be able to qualify, if you do qualify for a loan modification."

▨ **Tip** *Look to the future.* Enjoy your home as a lifestyle choice. Even if your mortgage is under water, it is still your home. Make it a good one. Stop looking at it as a number and see it for what it is: *your home.* This is where you live your life; it's not just a figure in a stock portfolio. "No matter how dreary and gray our homes are, we people of flesh and blood would rather live there than in any other country, be it ever so beautiful," wrote L. Frank Baum in *The Wonderful Wizard of Oz.* "There is no place like home."[13]

---

[13] Frank L. Baum, *The Wonderful Wizard of Oz* (Simon & Brown, 2012), p. 23.

Conclusion

Kramsky has walked us through the various options for underwater homeowners through the eyes of an attorney. Next we'll look at some of the same options, but through the eyes of a real estate agent. As you'll see, loan modifications, short sales, deeds in lieu of foreclosure, and other possibilities can help hoist you free of the housing anchor now weighing you down.

Advice from a Real Estate Agent

Nancy Ringer

Experienced real estate agents have been on the front lines of the real estate industry through the good times and the bad. None were left unscathed when the real estate bubble burst. Those who made it through understand the intrinsic and extrinsic values of a home. Working during the days of plummeting prices, and with worried banks and frightened consumers, the world of the real estate agent was rocked to its core. Although the recovery is slow, many agents continue to work with bankers, lawyers, brokers, homeowners, contractors, and others in the industry, which gives them a broad perspective on the field. Don't take their advice lightly.

No matter what options underwater homeowners choose when dealing with their mortgage situation, multiple perspectives on those options can help them make the best decision. Here is some advice from the perspective of a real estate agent, Nancy Ringer, who has helped many homeowners avoid foreclosure. [1]

Just as attorneys have their own perspective on the law, real estate agents have their own take on the issues surrounding the real estate industry and what homeowners should do with their current and future homes. Although some agents have expertise in the relatively new option of short sales, others know more about deeds in lieu of foreclosure because their clients have

---

[1] All quotes from Ringer were collected during personal interviews in June and July 2012.

decided that is their best option. The best real estate agents, like Ringer, understand all the options for homeowners and advise their clients to make the best decision while considering all the variables at play when selling or buying a home.

When you are ready to get some expert advice, sometimes the least expensive option is to talk to a real estate agent. Because they are usually paid a commission from each purchase or sale, their advice is free until a deal is closed. This means that those seeking advice about their options have one source that can help them get multiple perspectives on a complex situation from several seasoned experts for free.

Smart homeowners write down a list of the questions they have about their options. They then call a half dozen or more real estate agents, ask them the same questions, and write down all the advice and points of view. One benefit of this tactic toward turning a home right side up is the vast store of knowledge many real estate agents have to impart. Another benefit is a clear view of which real estate agent is right for you if you choose to sell your home. However, until you talk to a knowledgeable real estate agent, you will never know all your options. These professionals know more about your market than just about anyone.

Before we get into the options available to most underwater mortgage holders, remember: Your best option of all is to refinance your current loan at a lower interest rate and better terms. Your current lender is a good place to start to find out what is available to you, but other refinancing options are available. Big banks are only one type of option. Credit unions and other smaller, local lenders are out there, too.

REFINANCING BASICS

Although a mortgage modification is an adjustment of the terms of a borrower's current loan, a refinance replaces the existing mortgage altogether with a new loan. This new loan has a lower rate or more favorable terms. For example, an example of a better term might be a fixed-rate loan that replaces an adjustable one.

Of course, if underwater homeowners could simply refinance their loan with better terms or a lower rate, this would be a great way to improve their chances of getting out from an underwater mortgage. The trouble is, most banks will not refinance an underwater mortgage. Most lenders want a home to have about 20 percent equity before refinancing. Although most lenders will not refinance underwater homes, some homeowners are eligible for a mortgage refinance through HARP, the government program.

First Step: Pay a Visit to a Real Estate Agent

Ringer says, "I have watched too many people panic because they have not gathered enough information regarding their options and the market as it pertains to their specific location. They are paralyzed with fear and indecision and stop making their mortgage payments. Some of those people could have refinanced when they were solvent and could have sold their house with little out-of-pocket money." Every day, new conditions shift home values and lender options. Instead of making a bad decision in haste, talk to a local real estate agent or two. Or three.

Real estate agents have much to offer a borrower who is sitting on the edge of an underwater mortgage. If you think you might not be able to afford your home, start to take action by contacting a local real estate agent to schedule a listing appointment. This appointment is free of charge, so the price is right. Plus, it does not obligate you to list your home. A real estate agent can tell you how much nearby properties are selling for and have sold for, and can give you an estimate of your home's current value. A real estate agent may even give you a solid referral or two for good lenders.

■ **Tip** *Not all lenders are equal.* You have a choice of lenders when you refinance; credit unions, investors, and banks are just a few of your options. Today's interest rates are historically low, so many people are refinancing. If you have not looked lately, always shop around for a good lender. Compare good-faith estimates from lenders. Deals among them may differ, so research what is available.

According to Ringer, "If you know that you can no longer afford to make payments on your property, get it listed first, before you go into default, and contact your lender to ask what your options are." A refinance is possible, in some cases. If you do not qualify for refinancing and you default on your mortgage loan, then there are at least four options you must explore before making a decision and taking action on your underwater home: loan modification, short sale, deed in lieu of foreclosure, and foreclosure. Banks call these *mortgage default services.* Let's start by taking another look at loan modifications.

Option 1: Modify Your Loan

After you have defaulted, your lender will want you first to consider loan modification, a permanent change in one or more of the terms of your loan.

A modification allows the loan to be reinstated at different, more palatable terms, and results in a payment you can afford.

Loan modification is available to some people who have not been keeping up with their payments and want to stay in their home. Waiting out the market offers hope that eventually the house's market value will go up over time, slowly drawing the mortgage out from under water, so you can eventually sell it and get some equity back out of the house. At the same time, with a loan modification, the lender keeps a customer and eventually gets its money back. This is the best possible option for homeowners and the bank if homeowners have fallen behind on their mortgage payments.

Are Loan Modifications Difficult to Get?

How hard is it to get a loan modification? Nancy Ringer has worked as a realtor selling homes around the mid-Atlantic states for more than a decade. Ringer explains that, before 2008, it was often quite difficult for an underwater homeowner to get a mortgage modification because "people couldn't get to the banks quick enough, couldn't get all of their information in quick enough, and banks were so overwhelmed they couldn't process things." She adds that this was often the case during the first 2 years after the real estate market crashed. "The problem is many borrowers purchased at the height of the market, with little to no cash. Many of those people could not afford their loans in the beginning and still can't afford their loan even with the loan modification." Today, loan modifications are not as difficult for homeowners to get because lenders have more experience working with underwater borrowers.

The Making Home Affordable Program

One reason it's easier to modify a loan is the result of a $75 billion mortgage modification program provided by the Obama administration. It has helped some of the more than 5 million homeowners who are behind in paying their mortgage and are facing a foreclosure. The program, called *Making Home Affordable,* has been criticized by many experts because it helped fewer people than it originally intended, and only tens of thousands of people were helped out of the more than 650,000 people who took part in the program through November 2009.[2] In August 2010, critics pointed out that the program had a

---

[2] www.nytimes.com/2009/11/29/business/economy/29modify.html?_r=1. (Retrieved November 2, 2012

very high dropout rate: More than 616,000 trial modification offers had been canceled by lenders.[3]

To learn more about the Making Home Affordable program, head to www.makinghomeaffordable.gov. The Home Affordable Modification Program[4]—HAMP—is the main component of the MHA program. HAMP is designed specifically to help underwater homeowners lower their mortgage payments. Even if you missed a mortgage payment or are at imminent risk of defaulting on your mortgage, HAMP can help you lower your monthly payments.

ANSWERS TO LOAN MODIFICATION QUESTIONS

Because real estate conditions, rules, and laws change constantly, navigating the loan modification process can be confusing. Understanding the legal obstacles placed on lenders can help you choose whether loan modification is a viable option. One place to find guidance is the U.S. Department of Housing and Urban Development (HUD). Here are answers to frequently asked questions about loan modification from the experts at HUD:

Question: *If I choose the loan modification option, will my lender include all fees in the new mortgage?*
Answer: Legal fees and related foreclosure costs for work actually completed and applicable to the current default episode may be included in your new principal balance.

Question: *Can my lender come in and inspect my property if they have concerns about property condition?*
Answer: Yes. Your lender may conduct any review it deems necessary to verify that the property has no physical conditions that negatively affect your continued ability to support the modified mortgage payment as a borrower.

Question: *Can my lender include late charges in a loan modification?*
Answer: The goal in providing you with a loan modification is to bring the delinquent mortgage current and to give you a new start; therefore, your lender should waive all accrued late fees.

Question: *When giving me a loan modification, do banks pay an escrow advance for homeowner's association (HOA) fees?*
Answer: The HUD Handbook states: "Lenders must also escrow funds for those items which, if not paid, would create liens on the property positioned ahead of the HUD-insured mortgage."[5]

---

[3] www.nytimes.com/2010/08/21/business/economy/21housing.html?_r=0 (Retrieved November 1, 2012).

[4] www.makinghomeaffordable.gov/programs/lower-payments/Pages/hamp.aspx).

[5] www.hud.gov/offices/adm/hudclips/handbooks/hsgh/4330.1/43301c2HSGH.pdf (Retrieved November 1, 2012).

Question: *Is there a new base interest rate that lenders may assess when completing a loan modification?*
Answer: Yes. The lender reduces the loan modification note rate to the current market rate.

Question: *Are lenders required to reamortize the total amount due over a 360-month period?*
Answer: Yes. The lender must reamortize the total unpaid amount due over a 360-month period from the due date of the first installment required under the modified mortgage.

Question: *What date is used when determining the correct interest rate for a loan modification?*
Answer: The date the lender approves the loan modification (all verification completed and servicing notes documented, reported to the Single Family Default Monitoring System) is the date that lenders must use in determining the interest rate.

Question: *Can a lender do a loan modification when the borrower is unemployed, the spouse is employed, but the spouse's name is not on the mortgage?*
Answer: Based upon this scenario, the lender should conduct a financial review of the household income and expenses to determine whether surplus income is sufficient to meet the new modified mortgage payment, but insufficient to pay back the overdue payments (arrearage). After this process has been completed, the lender should then consult with its legal counsel to determine whether the asset is eligible for a loan modification because the spouse is not on the original mortgage.[6]

The only way to know whether you qualify for a loan modification is to have a conversation with your lender or mortgage servicer. These professionals can give advice and have knowledge of the latest government or institutional programs that may help you.

According to Ringer, if you try for a loan modification, "The bank first says to you, 'Is there any way we can keep you in this house and honoring the agreement that you made?' If you can't do that, then a lot of investor guidelines dictate that you have listed that house for at least 90 days to try and sell it on the open market. That would be the short sale. Investor guidelines drive all of it. You would do a loan modification prior to listing the house."

Option 2: Short Sale

A short sale, as you may recall, means that the homeowner actively lists the house on the open market in an effort to get a sales agreement. The property is sold for less than the balance of the mortgage. The bank accepts the amount negotiated and discharges the loan.

According to MakingHomeAffordable.gov, in a short sale, the lender allows you to list and sell your mortgaged property with the understanding that the

---

[6] www.nytimes.com/2010/03/08/business/08short.html?_r=1&pagewanted=all (Retrieved August 8, 2012).

net proceeds from the sale may be less than the total amount due on the first mortgage. In general, if you make a good-faith effort to sell the property but are not successful, your lender may then consider a deed in lieu of foreclosure (discussed later).

If you decide to pursue a short sale, the federal Home Affordable Foreclosure Alternatives (HAFA) program[7] currently provides a number of options that may help you avoid a costly foreclosure. These options offer incentives to you, your lender, and investors who use a short sale or deed in lieu to avoid foreclosure. These HAFA alternatives are available to all HAMP-eligible borrowers who request a short sale or deed in lieu of foreclosure. Those who have missed two consecutive payments during a HAMP modification are also eligible, as well as those who do not qualify for other HAMP programs.

Do Lenders Waive Deficiencies?

Today, more often than not, the bank will waive the deficiency, which is the difference between the selling price and what is owed on the loan. Before 2010, however, most banks did not waive the deficiency if the property was used as an investment property or a second home, such as a vacation property.

Thankfully, in April 2010, the new HAFA program took effect. The program aimed to help hundreds of thousands of delinquent borrowers who were not assisted by the loan modification program. This new Federal Housing Administration (FHA) program focused on helping homeowners complete the process of the short sale. According to David Streitfeld's article, "Program Will Pay Homeowners to Sell at a Loss," in *The New York Times* on March 7, 2010, "Lenders will be compelled to accept that arrangement, forgiving the difference between the market price of the property and what they are owed. Seth Wheeler, a senior adviser to the U.S. Treasury Department, commented, "We want to streamline and standardize the short sale process to make it much easier on the borrower and much easier on the lender." In his story, Streitfeld wrote: "Under the new program, the servicing bank, as with all modifications, will get $1,000. Another $1,000 can go toward a second loan, if there is one. And for the first time the government would give money to the distressed homeowners themselves. They will get $1,500 in 'relocation assistance.'"[8]

---

[7] www.makinghomeaffordable.gov/programs/exit-gracefully/Pages/hafa.aspx (Retrieved November 2, 2012).

[8] http://www.nytimes.com/2010/03/08/business/08short.html?pagewanted=all (Retrieved August 8, 2012).

These types of arrangements expanded in early 2012 when the FHA announced a new program offering $3,000 in relocation incentives to homeowners who do a short sale. Meanwhile, many banks offer their own financial incentives to complete short sales. For example, in May 2012, Bank of America offered homeowners up to $30,000 to sell their home in a short sale.

ANSWERS TO COMMON SHORT SALE QUESTIONS

Question: *What are the benefits of a short sale?*
Ringer: The benefit is [that] it has less impact on your credit [than a foreclosure].

Question: *Will you be able to buy another house immediately?*
Ringer: Probably not right away. But it's less of a loss for the bank. The house is not going to sit vacant, and the bank is not going to have to bring that house into the bank's inventory to babysit it. [In contrast,] it takes a year by the time the deed in lieu is done, and then it goes into REO[9] and goes on the open market. It can be a year before that property resells again. So you've got a property that just got vacant. You can have environmental issues come up. Mold can take over [a] house within 3 or 4 days in a house that has had its utilities turned off and no sump pump running. The financial impact of a property sitting vacant—it's unbelievable until people start to see it with their own eyes.

Question: *Why are so many people having trouble getting loans today compared to just a few years ago?*
Ringer: It is harder to get a mortgage because [a few years ago] banks let too many people buy houses who never had any blood, sweat, or tears in that property. When you don't put 20 percent down, it creates a greater risk.

Option 3: Deed in Lieu of Foreclosure

Deed in lieu of foreclosure is another term for *voluntary foreclosure*. It is an option for homeowners when they can no longer handle the payments on their house and agree to work with the bank to turn the house back over to the bank. In this way, the bank does not have to proceed with a formal foreclosure proceeding.

When underwater homeowners go through with a deed in lieu of foreclosure, they give the property voluntarily to the lender, and the lender cancels the loan in exchange for the deed to the property. With a deed in lieu, the lender promises not to initiate foreclosure proceedings and to terminate any foreclosure proceedings already underway. In many deed in lieu transfers, the

[9] An REO, or real estate owned, is a bank-owned property up for sale.

lender agrees to forgive the deficiency balance that results from the sale of the property.[10]

The popularity of deed in lieu of foreclosure is a fairly new phenomenon, although the idea of voluntary transfers of property ownership from borrowers to creditors goes way back to the first time a borrower gave up a house to a bank after defaulting on a loan. The idea resurfaced in 2009 when the Obama administration included deeds in lieu of foreclosure as an option in its HAFA program, and mortgage giant Fannie Mae cut the "penalty box" time for homeowners who use the technique from 4 years to 2 before they can qualify for another home mortgage.

■ **Tip** *Consider a deed in lieu of foreclosure before foreclosing.* This option allows you to purchase a new home a few years sooner than if you go through the foreclosure process.

In June 2010, the *Los Angeles Times* reported that "One of the largest servicers, Bank of America, has mailed out 100,000 deed-in-lieu solicitations to customers in the last 60 days, and its volume of completed transactions is breaking company records, according to officials."[11]

According to Bank of America, a deed in lieu prevents foreclosure for borrowers who can no longer make their mortgage payments. "While it will not allow you to keep your property, it will help you to avoid the public sale or auction of your house. A deed in lieu also allows you to start rebuilding your credit sooner than if you went through a foreclosure."[12]

Who Qualifies for Deed in Lieu?

Different banks have different rules, of course, but let's look at Bank of America's rules. In its view, you may be eligible for a deed in lieu of foreclosure if one or more of the following conditions apply:

- You are going through a hardship (for example, a job loss, divorce, or medical emergency).
- You are unable to afford your current mortgage payment.

---

[10] www.bills.com/a-deed-in-lieu-of-foreclosure-vs-a-short-sale/ (Retrieved August 12, 2012).

[11] http://articles.latimes.com/2010/jun/27/business/la-fi-harney-20100627-5 (Retrieved July 25, 2012).

[12] http://homeloanhelp.bankofamerica.com/en/deed-in-lieu.html (Retrieved July 25, 2012).

- You are unable to modify your current mortgage to make it affordable.

- You tried to sell your property at fair market value with a licensed real estate agent for at least 90 to 120 days and were unsuccessful.

Depending on your loan type, when you complete a deed in lieu of foreclosure, up to $3,000 may be available for your relocation expenses. You may also be eligible for up to $6,000 to help settle obligations such as your home equity loan or line of credit. A deed in lieu effectively ends your home loan, and in some cases means you are not required to pay any remaining amount owed on your loan (also known as the *deficiency*, which we discussed earlier).

Although a deed in lieu of foreclosure has a negative effect on your credit, by going through a deed in lieu, you can avoid selling your house at a sheriff's sale and can begin rebuilding your credit sooner. If you go through a deed in lieu, your lender reports your loan status as a "deed received in lieu of foreclosure on a defaulted mortgage and resolved by acceptance of a deed in lieu of foreclosure."

■ **Tip** *Don't start here.* A deed in lieu should only be considered after you have explored all other options, including a loan modification or a short sale.

QUESTIONS AND ANSWERS ABOUT
DEED IN LIEU OF FORECLOSURE

Here are some straightforward answers from Ringer about several common questions regarding a deed in lieu of foreclosure:

Question: *How does doing a deed in lieu of (voluntary) foreclosure affect a person's credit score and ability to buy a house in the future?*

Ringer: It has a lesser impact [than an outright foreclosure]. A person's credit would show that [the] home equity line or loan would be closed "deed in lieu of foreclosure," and that would have a lesser impact [depending on your initial credit score] with a 3-year recovery where you can begin again to get another house compared to a regular foreclosure, which would take you a good 7 years.

The other big thing to remember is investors: A large bank is often the servicer for tens of thousands of other investors. Each investor has a guideline, a requirement for lending money, so the public forgets that the servicer is just the messenger. The investors want their money.

And if they're not going to get their money, they're taking losses of hundreds of thousands of dollars, sometimes per property. It's not just like a $10,000 loss on a property; there are hundreds [of thousands of dollars] on up. So these investors, by doing deed in lieu of foreclosure, quite often waive the borrower's deficiency [the difference between what they can get for the house and the original loan amount]. Whereas, if you don't take responsibility for turning your house back over, and [the bank does] a regular foreclosure, you could face a deficiency, which means that investors will pursue you until you are dead to get their money back.

Question: *Do banks start off trying to help homeowners do a short sale instead of a deed in lieu of foreclosure?*
Ringer: Banks want a short sale first. A short sale is very responsible and the . . . best [option] for everybody, because if you think about it, the bank doesn't have to take that property back into its inventory. With a short sale, the borrower lives in the house, puts it on the market, the bank agrees to take less, and then the new owner moves in, and the bank can avoid all of the expenses from deed in lieu and then REO [real estate-owned] selling.

Question: *What are some benefits of acting now to solve my real estate dilemma?*
Ringer: One thing is so basic, but people overlook it. Let's say you are getting a divorce, your husband is moving out and he is not going to pay that mortgage, [and you conclude that, before long,] there is no way you can pay it. Here are a couple things to keep in mind:

- No realtor is going to put your house on the market if [she knows] you are behind on your payment.

- The bank wants you to have [the house] on the market for 3 months to see if you can sell it before [it] will do a voluntary deed in lieu of foreclosure.

So, as I recently told a client, if you go to a real estate agent and you tell her that you are moving and [ask her to] put [your] house on the market, and your payments are current, you are not lying. You are not lying on your disclosure. You are being very ethical and moral. It doesn't mean that you can't go back to that agent and say, "My life has changed. I'm making a decision not to pay this. We're going to have to do a short sale." Or, you don't have to say anything and you just drop your price. In other words, get your house on the market as soon as possible.

More of the banks are doing "approved" short sales. They are approving you for a short sale before you list the house because they are making it as easy as they can [for you to get out of your underwater mortgage]. You then want to get a third-party authorization form, so that you can get your real estate agent in touch with your bank and anybody else that you need to help with the process, and then, if the house sells, which it may or may not, you're done. You walk away. You can recover in a couple of years, a whole lot quicker.

■ **Tip** *Get started now.* Find and fill out the paperwork or online forms to help you move forward. An approval for a short sale may take time, and time means money when you are paying a mortgage for a house you cannot afford. Putting your home on the market is also a lengthy process, so start that process early, too.

Be Patient!

Many borrowers get angry when the deed in lieu doesn't happen as quickly as they expect. They move out, as asked, but when the process continues, they say they would have stayed in the house while the bank wrapped up the paperwork. At the closing table, the message from banks is, "You pay, you stay." When homeowners stop paying the mortgage, they lose the rights to stay in the house unless some kind of rent-back agreement has been signed. According to HUD, a deed in lieu of foreclosure must be completed within 90 days of initiation of the process.[13]

"With voluntary foreclosure, the minute you sign paperwork and sign your deed over to the bank, even though they haven't had it recorded, they've put a lock on your house," Ringer explains. "You've agreed to move out, so the bank will come to you and say, 'We want you to move out in 10 days or 2 weeks. Can you do this?' And the bank sends someone out to lock the door, and then the bank finishes getting their paperwork recorded."

But it's worth playing by the bank's rules. By working with the lender to pursue a deed in lieu of foreclosure, homeowners can avoid the much longer negative effects of a foreclosure on their credit. In addition, the lender may also be willing to pay the homeowner thousands of dollars in relocation costs. Plus, homeowners can move on with their lives faster than if they pursue a short sale, which can take many more months to complete.

■ **Tip** *Negotiate!* Before agreeing to a deed in lieu of foreclosure, negotiate for relocation costs. Do not leave the deal empty handed! For example, the HAFA program provides $3,000 in "relocation assistance" for those doing a short sale or a deed in lieu.

---

[13] http://portal.hud.gov/hudportal/HUD?src=/program_offices/housing/sfh/nsc/faqdil (Retrieved August 12, 2012).

Consider Renting Back

Renting back is an option for people who want to stay in their home, yet cannot afford to continue to make high mortgage payments. Formally, a rent-back program is an arrangement between the bank and the borrower who may be involved in a deed in lieu of foreclosure. It occurs when homeowners are allowed to stay in their home and agree to live there at a rent that is more reasonable than the previous underwater mortgage payment. Homeowners live in the house, take care of it, and keep the utilities running for a year or two. Basically, if you want to stay in your home, the bank lets you do that at the going rate for rentals in your area for a couple of years while you make other living arrangements. Why do banks do this? Ringer explains, "Banks have so many foreclosures, they don't want any more!"

Tip   *Ask about a rent-back program.* This is important to bring up during the initial negotiations with the bank when considering options. While doing a deed in lieu of foreclosure, underwater homeowners who want to stay in their home for a longer period of time should always ask about any available rent-back program the bank may offer.

Option 4: Foreclosure

For homeowners who hope to retain the ability to buy another home in the near future, a foreclosure is the worst possible scenario. A foreclosure is a forced process during which the bank eventually takes over the house, kicks out the occupants (sometimes with assistance from police), and seals the house with locks. If this happens to you, you will not be able to buy another house for at least 7 years. If you are able to go the route of the deed in lieu of foreclosure, or voluntary foreclosure, you only have to wait 3 years before you are eligible to buy another home.

Banks Do Not Want to Foreclose

Although many underwater homeowners fear that lenders will not try to help them avoid a foreclosure, this is usually not the case. Other options are not only better for the homeowner, but these options—such as modifications, short sales, and deeds in lieu of foreclosure—benefit lenders as well.

Ringer explains, "You have to remember the whole concept is for the bank to take people through what is called *the waterfall of mortgage default services.* The bank will first see if there is any way to keep [the homeowners] in the house. The bank doesn't want to take back the house. The bank doesn't want a whole bunch of assets; they're depreciating, deteriorating assets. They're liabilities, so the bank wants to see how it can keep people in their house. . . . . The other thing is, there is such a glut of houses out there on the market sitting vacant, that the bank just doesn't want more. It just further erodes the values overall throughout communities. And a vacant listing is subject to vandalism, mold and mildew, [other] environmental issues, just a number of things can happen once people move out."

Because values are constantly decreasing after a house is no longer occupied by the homeowner, it is in the best interest of lenders to keep people in their home as long as possible, rather than let the house sit vacant and become a target for any number of problems that can leach value from it.

NEGOTIATE FOR CASH

One of the first things a bank will do when a house is foreclosed is take possession of the house and send a property preservation representative out to the house to change the locks. When you leave, place the keys for the old locks on the kitchen counter along with the garage door opener. Leave the front curtains or blinds open so property preservation people can look inside the house.

Note that any unwanted possessions do not help the bank recoup its costs for the lost mortgage. Some homeowners leave boats and cars on the property, expecting to get some kind of reimbursement from the bank, but the bank sees these objects as yet another hassle to deal with. Removing personal belongings that are left on or in the property costs a bank thousands of dollars in extra fees, which may be passed along to the former owner.

According to a recent *Wall Street Journal* article titled "Buyers' Revenge: Trash the House After Foreclosure," some banks are paying homeowners thousands of dollars to return their foreclosed homes to the bank in good condition.[14]

Remember, the bank simply wants the money it loaned to the homeowner to buy the house. That's it. When a homeowner moves out, the bank expects it to be left in "broom-swept" condition, with all paint cans, trash, and personal belongings removed. Making a deal with the bank to do this can mean money in your pocket.

■ **Tip** *Keep it clean.* Some banks offer homeowners cash when they clean a foreclosed house before handing over the keys. If a bank offers you a few hundred dollars to clean the house before leaving, negotiate! A former homeowner described in the *Wall Street Journal* story negotiated a $300 offer into a $2,800 check that he received when he handed over his keys to his clean, foreclosed house to the bank's agent.

[14] http://online.wsj.com/article/SB120665586667656988l.html (Retrieved August 12, 2012).

Are *You* Under Water, Too?

Your mortgage can be under water, but you can also be personally under water when your income does not cover all your monthly, quarterly, and yearly bills. If you are personally under water, it's time to look at your budget and reconsider the daily choices that are holding you under. Talking to a bank to help you consolidate your credit card bills and your other monthly costs can be a step in the right direction. Another vital step is to look at all those bills and try to eliminate any expenses that are pulling you under water.

If your mortgage is under water, you have options from which to choose. However, if your personal finances are also under water and there is no way that you can pay your monthly mortgage bill, then your only real choice is foreclosure.

Of course, how you deal with your underwater mortgage depends on the state in which you live. For example, California passed a law that enhances HAFA's financial incentives to underwater homeowners and lenders who do short sales and deeds in lieu to avoid foreclosure. Because many people who did short sales ended up faring worse than those who did foreclosures, California's law ensures underwater homeowners do not have more financial liability after a short sale than they would after a foreclosure.[15]

Bankruptcy is another option. The bankruptcy forgives the debt against a house, but the homeowner still has to turn the deed over for the house. Nancy Ringer says, "Most people don't know that. They do a bankruptcy, they think they're done—the debt against their house is wiped out. But, they still have to do a voluntary foreclosure and give the deed back."

You Must Transfer Ownership to the Lender

In every state, even if you go through a bankruptcy, you still need to take additional actions to settle your housing situation. A bankruptcy leaves your house in limbo. Ringer explains, "Remember: There are two things that are key in real estate. You have ownership of the property, but then you have the mortgage against it. So you need to have your mortgages, your HOA fees, everything satisfied [to complete the bankruptcy], and you're released of all your responsibilities, plus the title transfer. This is the transfer of ownership from the homeowner to the bank or lender."

In other words, a title transfer is not included in a bankruptcy, so homeowners must go through a deed in lieu of foreclosure as well as the bankruptcy if this

---

[15] www.leginfo.ca.gov/pub/09-10/bill/sen/sb_0901-0950/sb_931_cfa_20100503_115327_sen_comm.html (Retrieved October 14, 2012).

is the route they decide to take on the way toward fixing their financial mess. However, Ringer cautions against walking away without telling anyone. She notes, "What you have is a mentality where people are fleeing neighborhoods and walking away from their homes saying, 'We'll never, ever, ever be able to resell this for what we owe, so we are consciously making a decision to walk away.'"

When homeowners make this kind of financial decision, they never truly get away from the mistake. It will continue to haunt their credit history until they deal with it.

■ **Tip** *Deal with it.* Even if a short sale or foreclosure is going to affect your credit, go through the motions to close the process so you can get started on the rest of your life. When you follow through with whatever procedure you choose, your credit score will begin to inch up again, and in 3 to 7 years, you will be back to a point where you can buy another home.

Conclusion

A real estate agent is an adviser, salesperson, counselor, psychologist, confidante, representative, and friend. These agents know how to work a contact list. The rest of the housing industry is at their fingertips, and homeowners can benefit from their professional and personal experiences. Some of the people on that contact list are mortgage brokers, who also come in contact with a large variety of professionals while making a living in the real estate market. Mortgage brokers have a valuable perspective honed on the many financial transactions they broker every day. In the next chapter, a midwestern mortgage broker presents helpful explanations of the past and present of the real estate industry, and provides a realistic look at the future.

Advice from a Mortgage Broker

John Paunan

John Paunan is a mortgage broker and president at Integrity Mortgage Corp., a small mortgage brokerage firm that operates in Illinois. The company has been in operation since 1998 and Paunan has been running it since 2005. He has been around the real estate market long enough to see it rise and fall and struggle to rise again. Although the housing market in Illinois is doing better than many other places around the country, such as Nevada and California, he says Illinois still has a way to go before it sees a full recovery of its home prices.

"In 2005/2006 it was kind of the absolute pinnacle," he explains. "And in terms of activity—since we are a transaction-based market when it comes to residential real estate—that was also the height of value. When things did pop, it did dramatically affect the Chicago market the same way it did most of the markets, [but] not to the extent that it hit Florida or Nevada's Las Vegas area. Those were *really* devastated by what happened in real estate, with all the speculation. Obviously, Chicago had its fair share of speculators, but not to the extent as those other markets."[1]

Despite the devastating effects of the bursting of the real estate market bubble in Chicago and other parts of Illinois, Paunan says things are beginning to look up.

---

[1] All quotes from Paunan were collected during a personal interview in July 2012.

Regaining a Foothold

Real estate "is slowly starting to regain footing here," Paunan reflects. "I'd say I think we're kind of at the point where things are leveling off at the bottom. Certain communities have actually already started to increase. Those are the areas that generally have held their values. Some other areas, you know, they're still hard hit because they're waiting for providers to come back in."

Paunan notes that he is seeing a slight increase in home prices lately, but those prices are nowhere near the heights they were reaching when he first started working as a mortgage broker in 2005, when the real estate market was red hot. Loans were being generated like never before. "The guidelines at that time were quite different from what we have now," Paunan remarks. "Now, you see articles about Freddie Mac and Fannie Mae and how the quality of loans that are coming through are now really high quality. The fault rates on them are really low. But what was happening in 2005, 2006—[lenders and borrowers] were speculating on loans. People could essentially buy investment properties with zero down and that, in and of itself, probably had the highest impact in terms of possible foreclosure, possible default."

Back to the Past

Many years ago, a distinct separation existed between residential properties and investment properties that served an important purpose. Paunan explains: "Historically speaking, there's a reason why we treat investment properties differently from residential. Back in 2005 and 2006, because the market was so red hot, lenders took it upon themselves to be as competitive as they possibly could [and that meant saying to someone], 'We're going to give you a loan to buy an investment property, one that you're not even going to live in, and do it with no skin in the game.' That was a recipe for disaster."

Things have moved back to the way it used to be: People need to put down a solid down payment to get a mortgage loan. Tough new requirements make it hard for many borrowers to buy one of the millions of homes now on the market, so the entire real estate industry waits for buyers to get jobs so they can make down payments. Meanwhile, borrowers wait for lenders to loosen lending criteria. These sluggish processes create an extremely slow recovery for real estate across the country.

Writing on the Wall

Paunan says he saw the writing on the wall when he first got involved in the real estate business. His background in law helped him realize right away that something was askew: "I was actually practicing law up in Wisconsin . . . when I first started taking over operations [at Integrity Mortgage Corp.]. It's a family business. I bought two houses before [the crash], but they were all with what you would call vanilla loans. I had the down payments; I was buying them as my primary residences so everything was like a regular loan about them. So I didn't know, frankly, what was happening in the financial markets, when I first got into [the real estate business]. That was in 2005. That was still the day of the stated loan [when borrowers stated their income but offered no proof], or the no-ratio loan [when lenders didn't verify debt-to-income ratio]. A lot of the crazy [types of loans] were out there."

Many mortgage brokers could not believe what was going on in the lending industry, and Paunan was one of them. He recalls, "I was really taken aback by some of the things that were happening. And I kind of foresaw or anticipated [that] there was going to be a reckoning." As subprime lending became more and more popular, many professionals in the real estate industry worried about what would happen when too many people with high-risk loans entered the market.

What Is a Subprime Loan?

In real estate jargon, *subprime* means *substandard*. When people talk about subprime loans, generally they are talking about loans that are given to people who have below-average credit. Despite their credit risk, some banks were willing to lend to those people. Most often, these were the loans that were not protected by Fannie May or Freddie Mac—organizations designed to help homebuyers with good credit scores and the money to make solid down payments.

Paunan explains that the subprime market "was created for people with poor credit. In some instances, some lenders became very creative, very risky. They had an affinity for the risk, to take on more competitive advantage. They were willing to offer [a loan] to someone with a low minimum credit score— something like low 600 or below 500—or no score." Paunan notes that some banks didn't look at credit profiles at all, as long as they had a down payment.

To many, this lack of credit review seemed like a recipe for disaster. "Obviously, [borrowers'] history with credit is a pretty good indicator of how they'll deal with it in the future," Paunan remarks. "But that wasn't really a consideration for [these lenders] because they thought that if [people were] going to put down that much money, then they would be unwilling to walk away." Now this reasoning may hold true if the market stays steady or continues to increase, but what happens in a market when values decrease? Then, the equity homeowners are counting on, equity that banks are willing to protect, is no longer there, and borrowers are going to walk away. This is one of the major factors that burst the real estate market bubble.

The Trouble with Stated Income Loans

One type of loan that many lenders were offering in the years leading up to the real estate bubble crash was something called a *stated income loan* or a *stated loan*. A stated loan allows a borrower to take out a loan by simply stating his or her income, a number which is not verified by the lender. This practice made little sense to those who had always believed in the importance of credit checks, income verification, and solid collateral when making loans to homebuyers.

John Paunan says customers began to inquire about these financial products. "I do recall when I first started . . . getting phone calls from people [asking], 'Do you do stated loans?' And I thought that was kind of an odd thing to ask right away. [With a stated loan, brokers were not supposed to verify their income.] We were supposed to then ask [customers] what they make. That's it." Based on this limited amount of information, some mortgage brokers were willing to offer borrowers a stated loan. And many borrowers were claiming that their income was much more than the guidelines said someone in their profession would make. If one mortgage broker refused, then the borrower would simply go to another who was willing to provide a loan. Paunan notes that this was a common practice at the time. After the real estate bubble burst, stated loans became less and less popular with lenders. Paunan recalls, "Illinois was probably one of the first states that, 3 years ago, essentially just outlawed [stated loans] altogether."

Plenty of Blame to Go Around

Some experts claim banks started the trouble by creating risky loans that confused investors into taking loans they could not afford. Others blame lawmakers for sowing the seeds of catastrophe with policies that were too lax. Still others say borrowers played a role as well. Blame and excuses flow daily through the media as the recovery slowly tries to regain traction.

Who is to blame for the eventual collapse of the real estate market 5 or 6 years ago? Paunan says many people and organizations must take some of the credit for an unrealistic situation finally coming to light. "It's wholesale," he remarks, meaning there was as much risk taking on the lender's side as on the borrower's side of the market. "Yes, there's a lot of blame on lenders, a lot of blame on brokers, blame on realtors, attorneys. There was all kind of fraud happening there."

Many played a role in the debacle that overwhelmed the real estate market, driving it into the ground. "Setting the outright fraud aside, there [is] still a lot of blame to go around when it comes to borrowers and lenders," Paunan continues. On one side of the coin, lenders were "willing to offer quick, easy money to people that historically have not shown a propensity for paying back their debt." But on the other side, Paunan explains, there were "also borrowers willing to take the risk because they're thinking, Hey, everyone else did it. I want to get in to the free money game as well."

▧ **Tip** *There is no such thing as free money.* If the deal seems too good to be true, there is always a catch. Never discount the risk involved in an investment that looks too easy.

Underwater Home Owners and HARP

Today, Paunan says he works every day with people whose mortgages are under water. "It's part of the landscape," he remarks. The people he can help are those who qualify for the Home Affordable Refinance Program or HARP. This program is designed to assist homeowners in refinancing their mortgages even if they owe more than their home's current value. As noted in Chapter 4, to qualify for this program, you must meet the following criteria:

- The mortgage must be owned or guaranteed by Freddie Mac or Fannie Mae.

- The mortgage must have been sold to Fannie Mae or Freddie Mac on or before May 31, 2009.

- The mortgage cannot have been refinanced under HARP previously unless it is a Fannie Mae loan that was refinanced under HARP from March to May 2009.

- The current LTV ratio must be more than 80 percent.

- Homeowners must be current on the mortgage at the time of the refinance, with a good payment history for the past 12 months.

The HARP 2.0 program expires at the end of 2013.

Paunan says he cannot help those who do not qualify for HARP because their mortgages are not guaranteed by Freddie Mac or Fannie Mae. "The first generation of it was called *Refi Plus* or *HARP*, which was the FreddyMac version," he explained. "Those programs were released 3 years ago, and most recently have been upgraded—and they've increased the qualifications for them—with the HARP 2.0."

Although many more people qualify for the HARP 2.0 program than the original incarnation of HARP, there are still many other borrowers who do not qualify based on the program's changed restrictions. For example, loans purchased by Fannie Mae on or after June 1, 2009, are not eligible for HARP's DU Refi Plus, which has different verification requirement than Refi Plus. Although homeowners with government mortgages may not be eligible for DU Refi Plus, there are other refinance options available from Fannie Mae and Freddie Mac.

Fannie Mae and Freddie Mac Hurdles

There are a few things that can mess up a refinance through the HARP program, including mortgage insurance and lender overlays.

Mortgage Insurance

One hurdle that once prevented many people from refinancing a Fannie Mae or Freddie Mac mortgage was the issue of mortgage insurance on the loan. Paunan explains that this is no longer such a large obstacle. "Under the original program, nothing could be done because those mortgage insurance contracts were with private companies," he recalls. "So they can't tell a private company, 'Please reinsure this loan,' which now is technically under water. A lot of them were not willing to do that."

Today, the situation has changed. Paunan notes that many people are getting what's called *recertification* from mortgage insurance companies, which allows homeowners to refinance. But, he says, some companies don't allow this. He concludes, "[T]here's still a lot of hurdles to get over for the average borrower. If you have mortgage insurance, your [refinance] is going to be harder to do."

Lender Overlays

Another obstacle that can stand in the way of a Freddie Mac or Fannie Mae refinance through HARP is something called a *lender overlay*. An overlay is any extra rule a lender applies to any current list of rules connected to your loan. This factor is part of the guidelines that say who gets a new loan. For example, an overlay could be a specific LTV ratio. It could also be a minimum down payment for the loan. The most common is the credit score overlay,[2] which requires a minimum score.

---

[2] www.zillow.com/blog/2010-03-18/what-are-lender-overlays/ (Retrieved August 10, 2012).

Paunan explains that many lenders have their own overlays. Even if the loan qualifies technically, the lender may want the loan to value to be, say, between 105 percent and 115 percent. Essentially, an overlay is a lender's additional restriction. So, the bad news for underwater homeowners is that, even if homeowners believe they are qualified for a refinance, a lender may have other restrictions that go beyond the Freddie Mac and Fannie Mae requirements. These restrictions make it harder for underwater homeowners to refinance. Paunan adds, "Any lender can have [its] own overlay. [Lenders watch] their own amount of exposure and don't want to take everyone under the auspices of the program."

Streamline Your FHA Mortgage

There is a unique refinancing option available for homeowners who have a mortgage that is guaranteed by the Federal Housing Administration (FHA). It is called a *streamline refinance*. The basic requirements of a streamline refinance are as follows:

- The mortgage to be refinanced must already be FHA insured.

- The mortgage to be refinanced should be current (not delinquent).

- The refinance results in a lowering of the borrower's monthly principal and interest payments or, under certain circumstances, the conversion of an ARM to a fixed-rate mortgage.

- No cash may be taken out on mortgages refinanced using the streamline refinance process.

Lenders may offer streamline refinances in several ways. Some lenders offer no-cost refinances (actually, no out-of-pocket expenses to the borrower) by charging a higher rate of interest on the new loan than if the borrower financed or paid the closing costs in cash. From this premium, the lender pays any closing costs that are incurred on the transaction. The FHA does not allow lenders to include closing costs in the new mortgage amount of a streamline refinance. Investment properties (properties that borrowers do not occupy as their principal residence) may only be refinanced without an appraisal.[3]

---

[3] http://portal.hud.gov/hudportal/HUD?src=/program_offices/housing/fhahistory (Retrieved August 10, 2012).

According to Paunan, "Essentially, what that means is if you've been current on your FHA loan, no delinquency within the past 12 months, no late payments, then you can do [a streamline. If your credit score is about 640 or above], then you can do an FHA streamline, and [the lender is] not going to reverify your income. All they're going to make sure is that you're still employed in the same field, that you're current on your debt, and that you're able to reduce your old loan payment. That's [reducing] principal, taxes, and insurance plus mortgage insurance on the new loan by 5 percent. As long as there's a 5 percent improvement, you can streamline your FHA loan. It's another great program."

The FHA has permitted streamline refinances on insured mortgages since the early 1980s. *Streamline refinance* refers only to the amount of documentation and underwriting that the lender must perform; it does not mean that there are no costs involved in the transaction.

Options for Other Underwater Homeowners

For homeowners with underwater mortgages that are not FHA loans or those owned by Freddie Mac or Fannie Mae, there are still many other options available to help them rise above the surface of their negative equity. Nevertheless, those options are dependent on the lender who owns the loan. Therefore, the best place for these homeowners to find these options, Paunan points out, is to go directly to their lender. "[Homeowners] can throw themselves at the mercy of the lender in hopes that that lender has a loss mitigation program," he advises. "That's essentially what it is. The borrower says, 'Hey, you know what? This loan is under water. I've been current. I'd like to get some relief the way everyone else is.' You would think the lender would say, 'Yeah, absolutely. That makes sense for us to give you some relief and ensure that you'll be paying that mortgage over the long term.'"

It doesn't always work out this way, of course. After homeowners describe their financial situation, it's up to the lender to decide whether keeping those homeowner as customers with better loan terms is worth the investment. On the one hand, most borrowers don't want to ruin their credit by walking away, but many consider doing so if they are deep under water. Lenders, who don't want to lose a customer paying on time, recognize this. Says Paunan, "The lender doesn't want to lose a borrower who's paying everything on time. And then there's the borrower who is making mortgage payments on essentially something that has a negative value. So I see a balance on either side. I would assume lenders are willing to give some relief." And many do, but only if you ask.

The Trouble with Leviathans

Many underwater homeowners who have tried to get through to their lenders to discuss refinancing their home or making a mortgage modification say that they have found it extremely difficult to get through to a living person on the other end of the telephone. Lenders often have automated phone message recordings that make it hard to talk to a real customer service representative who can help.

Paunan explains, "Most loans are essentially owned by the big five banks. And if you do want to contact any of them—Wells Fargo, Chase, Citi—and try to get answers from them, it's going to be very hard, because they are leviathans. And you know leviathans don't respond to you. You'd be better off, you know, if your loan does qualify under one of the programs, to try to contact one of the small companies, like a broker, for instance. We can look at the guidelines each one of those lenders issues and see if the loan can be sent back to that same lender or even sent to a different lender that has friendlier guidelines."

■ **Tip** *Go to a broker first.* A great place for free advice about the status of your loan is a mortgage broker. Brokers help to point you in the right direction. Even if you have, eventually, to call a larger bank for help with your mortgage, starting with a broker can help you learn more about your loan, which helps you in the long run when you finally get through to the larger lender.

How Mortgage Brokers Help Underwater Homeowners

There are several ways a mortgage broker can help an underwater homeowner. For example, Paunan explains that if you want to find out whether you qualify for a program, "apply with a broker, the same way you would apply with a lender. And then that broker [does] the legwork and [sees] if there's a lender out there willing to lend" based on your situation. For example, "if the person has a Fanny Mae loan currently, and they fall within a 105 to 115 loan-to-value, then that broker will go and look at what lenders are open to lending on that scenario."

One of the benefits of working with a mortgage broker is the fact that a licensed mortgage broker cannot charge you twice for the same services. "As of last year, May of 2011," Paunan notes, "the Federal Reserve actually changed the rules as to how mortgage brokers can get compensated. The way it was before, a broker could be compensated by both the borrower, upfront—they could pay them a fee—and the lender. So they could actually get paid from both sides. And, as part of the negotiations between the broker and the lender, the broker would come up with whatever compensation level they wanted to get from either the borrower or from the lender. But with the Federal Reserve change, it's one or the other. They can get paid from the borrower or get paid from the lender, in the form of a rebate. Essentially, part of the compensation is based on the interest rate, so it's one or the other now."

■ **Tip** *Shop around for a mortgage broker.* When you shop around for a broker, first find out whether the broker is going to charge a fee. If the broker does not charge a fee, this means that the rate should be the lowest that's available, because the broker cannot get compensation from both the borrower and the lender. Beware of upfront fees, because good mortgage brokers make their money from closed loans, not upfront fees.

HOW MORTGAGE BROKERS MAKE THEIR MONEY

Most mortgage brokers make their money by taking a percentage from the lender. If you pay the broker directly upfront, you might save a quarter point on the interest rates. "If you look at the costs," notes Paunan, "and the additional cost of the loan itself, it doesn't make sense [for a borrower to pay a broker] because you're saving on the interest rate. It would take you years to recapture that additional cost. So you'd be better off just taking what's called the *lender paid option*." In this case, the lender is "compensating the broker and paying the third-party fees or even [giving] a rebate to help pay some of those closing costs."

Today, the options for a borrower are better than ever before. "There's a lot of controversy around [the new rule limiting how mortgage brokers are paid][4] because brokers didn't like the fact that they were losing the opportunity to get paid by both [the borrower and the lender]," Paunan says. "Some brokers probably made more money that way. But now I can quote to a borrower, 'Here's an interest rate and here's also a rebate you can use toward closing costs.' So it makes it actually doubly beneficial to a borrower and makes me more competitive in the market. So, it's actually been a very good thing, I'd say, for business."

What Underwater Homeowners Should Know about Rebates

Where does the rebate that goes to the borrower originate? Paunan says it is based on the interest rate paid by the borrower.

"So let's say the lender is selling a particular interest rate with a certain rebate attached to it. The higher the interest rate attached to it, the more money

---

[4] www.federalreserve.gov/bankinforeg/regzcg.htm (Retrieved November 1, 2012).

the lender will end up making over the long run. [The lender is] willing to compensate both the broker and the borrower for that higher interest rate." By accepting the higher interest rate, the borrower can use that money to reduce the closing costs of the loan. Today, the rebate from the lender is just an incentive for the borrower to choose that lender's loan.

In the past, the rebate was used as an incentive for the broker to sell a higher rate because the broker would get paid more by that lender. But according to the new rules, "the compensation is fixed [and] we can't make any more or any less on any particular loan. We make a fixed amount. So the incentive for us to sell at a higher rate isn't there. But the incentive is there for the borrower, which is to get more money to use for closing costs."

Now, for example, borrowers have two options: (1) they can take a 3.5 percent loan, which is the lowest rate available, and pay closing costs or (2) they can take a 3.625 percent loan, which wipes out any closing costs. By taking the second option, the borrower's closing costs are paid by the rebate from the lender.

■ **Tip** *Ask about a rebate.* If you are short on cash, a rebate can help you pay for the closing costs of the loan.

Look for the License

Today, mortgage brokers are heavily regulated by the National Mortgage Licensing System (NMLS). All brokers have to get a license. They also have to pass national exams to get certified on a yearly basis.

Paunan says that employees of big banks do not have to pass these tests, "theoretically because they have their own qualification system that they make their employees go through." When borrowers talk to representatives of the big banks, they often do not realize that the person on the other end of the telephone is not a licensed mortgage broker. "They're there to collect information. They don't have the ability to give the advice nor [do they] know the guidelines the way that someone who, every day, is looking at the guidelines. That's why it kind of does make sense to go approach a broker."

■ **Tip** *Talk to a professional.* When seeking professional advice about your real estate options, go to your mortgage broker first because he or she offers good, free advice about your situation. Then, if he or she thinks you need more expert advice from somebody who has deeper legal skills, then that broker will tell you whether you need to see an attorney.

■ **Tip** *Get more than one opinion.* While shopping around for free advice, go to several mortgage brokers and find out what kinds of rates other people can offer you. This kind of due diligence saves you money in the long run. Then, if you need a lawyer, you are better informed when asking questions, which saves you even more money, because you will probably pay your attorney by the hour.

"Skin in the Game"

Most real estate experts agree that having some personal investment in a home keeps most people from walking away the moment they face economic problems. The borrowers who purchased their homes with stated loans and no money down were the first to walk away when the real estate market tanked.

Although many homeowners with subprime loans walked away from their homes, choosing foreclosure over the difficult struggle of keeping up payments on an underwater mortgage, many who put large down payments into their homes have stayed to reap equity from their homes at a later date. This is one of the benefits of keeping borrowers in the "conventional market" instead of the subprime market. Borrowers with equity, Paunan explains, are, generally, the best risk for lenders. "If they've got skin in the game, they'll stay on top of the mortgage."

Conclusion

So far you have gathered another underwater homeowner, an attorney, a real estate agent, and a mortgage broker to add to your team of advisers and counselors. By bringing several perspectives to the table, you are better able to get a realistic perspective on the matter at hand: Stabilizing your housing situation by making a series of crucial decisions that will have a major impact on your future finances.

In the next chapter, East Coast real estate agent Dave Watlington offers homeowners another look at the ways their situation is shaped by a variety of forces that have been at work for many years. He also presents the nuts and bolts of how an underwater home can be sold in today's real estate market, including how to protect your credit score when selling an underwater home, how to petition your lender for a short sale, and why you may need a short sale negotiator to ease you through the process. Along the way, he also points out how to take advantage of HARP, the dangers of short sale scams, and why you should know your "front end ratio."

Advice from a Real Estate Agent

Dave Watlington

Dave Watlington is a real estate agent who sells houses in Delaware, Maryland, and Pennsylvania. Watlington was working in the industry while home prices went sky high during the years before the real estate market bubble burst. He then felt the effects of their rapid descent when the bottom dropped out of the market. Today, he continues to help homebuyers find the home of their dreams, and homeowners to sell their homes as the market slowly recovers.

While working as a real estate agent during some of the market's most volatile years, Watlington says he has helped many people with underwater mortgages. People whose mortgages are upside down usually try to make the most of their situation. Watlington notes that many of the people he knows who are in this situation stay in their home by acknowledging that whatever happened in the market created their current circumstances. "If they're able to still maintain their mortgage and enjoy the home," he explains, "then they just look at it as a time frame that will soon pass, and down the road there will be appreciation."[1]

---

[1] All quotes from Watlington were collected during a personal interview in July 2012.

Waiting Game

Underwater homeowners often survive by playing a difficult waiting game. While they wait, Watlington points out, many people continue to see their homes decrease in value. He says this is the result of "the artificial appreciation that occurred last decade being balanced out by the decline that we're seeing in the last 5 years."

Like many real estate professionals, Watlington sees what happened to the market as a "perfect storm" that caught many homeowners by surprise. He helps people who come to him for advice about their underwater mortgages by reminding them they did nothing wrong. They were simply victims of larger forces that were out of their control.

"Many people who were buying and selling when the market was hot, they were riding the wave," he explains. Things were good and people weren't concerned about the future or things like ARMs changing. "And then the mortgages started to adjust and the values declined and they weren't able to refinance like they hoped they'd be able to. That's where some of those people got themselves in trouble."

The increase in home prices that preceded the real estate market crash was the result of housing appreciation gone wild. Strong demand combined with lower inventory and the promise of easy money, and too many people did not realize the risks of going into such an out-of-control market.

Post–9/11 Real Estate Boom

Watlington says he believes the market bubble started to expand shortly after 9/11. That was when the boom began. "It was silent for a week or two immediately upon the aftermath of [the terrorist attack,] then all of a sudden real estate became a very hot commodity. And it just grew and grew and grew. And a lot of the secondary home market grew as well. That made up like 40 percent of all transactions during the boom."

By 2008, the real estate market was facing its worst crisis in years. Foreclosures clogged the market in the best and worst neighborhoods in many areas. Nearly everyone who owned a home lost equity as the real estate bubble burst. Today, many homeowners still feel the repercussions of the industry's collapse.

Underwater homeowners continue to feel the reverberations of that catastrophe every month when they make another payment on an underwater mortgage. Some love their home so much they will wait out the real estate recovery. Others put their home on the market. Many of these people have no option but to sell their home.

■ **Tip** *Determine the real value of your home.* Whether you plan to stay in your home or move away, putting your home on the market is the best way to determine its real worth.

Selling an Underwater Home

What can you do if you have no choice but to sell your home? What happens when you must relocate for your job? If this is the case, playing the waiting game is not an option. There is no more time to wait for the market to rebound so you can get some equity from your home. A sale must occur. This is when the advice and expertise of a good real estate agent can be helpful.

Dave Watlington points out that there are four options available when homeowners want to sell a home that is under water:

1. Bring money to the table. Sell the house on the open market and pay off the deficiency. One way to do this is by signing a promissory note with the bank. Get an attorney to help you with this process. This option should entail no damage to a credit score (when the promissory note is repaid).

2. Go for a short sale. Make an arrangement with the lender and sell the house at a loss. Sometimes banks forgive the deficiency; sometimes the owner is responsible for the deficiency. This option causes homeowners to take a large hit on their credit score.

3. Choose a deed in lieu of foreclosure. Sign the deed and return the house to the lender. This arrangement "expedites the foreclosure process," Watlington explains. Although home-owners' credit will take a hit, they could get some money from the lender for relocation costs when they hand over the keys and sign the deed over to the bank.

4. Foreclose. Allow the bank to repossess the home and sell it at a sheriff's auction. Although this might be the easiest option for homeowners, it leaves a large blot on their credit score for 7 years. In addition, a lender looks at the decision to walk away from a home as a sign of a poor credit risk, which can result in the need to pay a much larger down payment on the next home

purchased. For example, the lender may require a 30 percent down payment or more.[2]

Options 3 and 4 have been explored elsewhere in this book, so let's look at the first two from the perspective of a realtor.

Option 1: Put Money on the Table

People with enough money in savings or tucked away somewhere else will sometimes sell their home at a loss, but make up for that loss with their own money. These underwater homeowners believe it is worth the extra cash to be done with a mortgage that is upside down. They also do not want to suffer the consequences of taking a hit to their credit score.

If, for example, homeowners need to come up with $50,000 of their own money to make the transaction and pay off the lien holder, and they're willing and able to do that, then that is an option. Watlington notes that this choice "[avoids] the impact of what a short sale may do to them from a credit-worthiness standpoint."

One way that some homeowners avoid the hit to their credit score that a short sale or foreclosure would entail is by withdrawing money from a retirement fund or 401K to keep the underwater home sale from becoming a short sale. This option allows homeowners to buy another home at a lower interest rate, which will save them money over the long term.

Option 2: Petition for a Short Sale

Although bringing money to the table is a great option for those with the cash, this is not usually an option that is available to most sellers with deeply underwater mortgages. "The short sale itself is perceived as the better option because it's believed that it's not going to have as great an impact on someone's credit," Watlington comments. "[Homeowners] would be able to buy [another home] potentially sooner than if they did go to foreclosure."

The biggest advantage of the short sale is the contract between the lien holder and the seller that says the homeowner is not responsible for paying the difference between the selling price and what is owed on the mortgage. Watlington explains, "So if they owe $300,000 on their mortgage but they're only able to sell the house for $265,000 minus expenses, and the bank only

---

[2] http://money.cnn.com/2010/05/28/real_estate/homebuying_after_foreclosure/index.htm (Retrieved August 14, 2012).

gets $230,000, there's a $70,000 deficiency. The bank is forgiving the homeowner of any liability for that $70,000."

Note Of course, unless the Mortgage Debt Relief Act of 2007 is reinstated by Congress, homeowners who complete a short sale after December 31, 2012, have to pay taxes on that deficiency even if the deficiency is forgiven by the lender.

Goal: Deficiency Forgiveness

When attempting to get a short sale, the seller's attorney petitions the lender in an effort to get a signed document that states the deficiency will be forgiven. If the lender signs the agreement, excellent. But, Watlington says, an attorney might instead tell you, "They've actually provided a promissory note or a deficiency judgment for you to sign that says you're going to pay them back that $70,000."

In Watlington's view, this option is not in the best interest of the seller. Why do a short sale if the bank does not cover the deficiency? The benefit of the short sale is the forgiveness of the deficiency. So, this is a situation in which the seller should continue to negotiate. Bottom line: If you're going to do a short sale, look for full forgiveness, not a requirement or obligation to pay the money back.

Petitioning the Lender

A borrower has to petition the lender to get a short sale. How does this process work? Watlington remarks there are two ways this can happen. First, "you can petition the lender for the short sale process. And typically what [the lender does] is instruct you on what [it's] going to need." You can often find out what you need to do on a lender's web site. For example, Wells Fargo offers assistance at www.wellsfargo.com/homeassist/shortsale, and Bank of America provides numerous tips and information on short sales on its web site at homeloanhelp.bankofamerica.com/en/short-sale.html.

The other way to petition a lender for the option of doing a short sale is to meet with a real estate agent. "What likely will occur is that the property will be listed and the value determined from a marketing standpoint," Watlington explains. If you're successful in getting an offer and coming to terms, "then that contract is submitted to the lender for their approval. There's not much that can be done on a short sale until you actually have a ready, willing, and able buyer. So, a big part of the process is having a contract to be able to submit to the bank so [it] can review all the documentation required by the seller, as well as the contract."

The next step in this process is to obtain a preliminary settlement sheet so the lender can see what proceeds it is going to receive if it accepts the short sale contract. The contract is then reviewed by the bank's negotiators. The bank does its own appraisal of the property to ensure that the appraiser either supports the contracted price or finds that the offer is significantly lower than the potential value of the property. Watlington says, "In that case, sometimes the bank will counteroffer the buyer and say, 'We appreciate your offer of $230,000, but our appraisers are telling us that the value is more like $250,000.' They say, 'This is the value we're willing to accept.'"

If the appraised price is reasonable, then sometimes the deal is made at that price. Or, maybe there's another round of negotiations and the house might sell for, say, $240,000. If the bank and the buyer can't come to terms, the house goes back on the market.

Beware of Short Sale Scams

According to Fannie Mae, the perpetrator of a short sale scam profits by concealing parties to the transaction or connected transactions, or falsifying material information including the true value of the property so the servicer cannot make an informed short sale decision.[3] For example, in June 2012, agents with the Federal Bureau of Investigation (FBI) and U.S. Secret Service arrested three men who were named in federal indictments that allege they defrauded homeowners, financial institutions, and real estate investors in schemes that targeted the distressed homeowner market and allegedly caused more than $10 million in losses.

According to court documents, the defendants used a variety of schemes, at least two of which centered on fraudulent short sale approval letters purportedly issued by a bank. Many of the properties used in the schemes were distressed homes. In some cases, the defendants claimed to have insiders working at the bank who, in exchange for cash, would authorize short sales for far less than the fair market value. This allowed the defendants to "flip" the house for a significant profit.

In some cases, the defendants used short sale approval letters that had been entirely fabricated to carry out their schemes. As a result, homebuyers and investors purchased homes they thought had a clear title but were actually devalued and subject to hundreds of thousands of dollars worth of liens. In some instances, individuals would assume the identities of property owners

---

[3] www.efanniemae.com/utility/legal/pdf/fraudschchar.pdf (Retrieved August 14, 2012).

and then sell or refinance the relevant properties without authority. In one case, a home owned by individuals who reside in Saudi Arabia was transferred multiple times and resulted in more than $1 million in losses.[4] Although million-dollar scams are rare, they are not unheard of.

■ **Tip** *Do your homework.* Learn everything you can before you go to a short sale. As this option gets more traction from use, more people become familiar with its ins and outs. Talk to more than one person. Find out what your options are. If you have not talked to an attorney, find a good one and discuss your options. If you cannot afford an attorney, seek out a mediator who can give you some advice about the best way to proceed. Real estate agents who have been involved in many short sales can also offer you some good advice for free.

Finding the Best Option

Watlington says he works with people to try to identify their best option. He explains, "Typically, when I'm meeting with them, I'm out there to discuss the marketability of their property. I say in that interview process or in my preliminary research, I've determined the value of their home is less than what they owe on the property. Then, I [tell] them, 'Either bring cash to the table, or an alternative option is a short sale, if that's something you want to consider.'"

The problem with a short sale is that it is likely to affect your credit because it's going to show the settlement account as not paid off. "That's the negative of doing that process," Watlington adds. "If there's anything beyond that usually I refer them to an attorney to determine what would be the best course of action for them in regard to their property."

Benefits of a Short Sale

If you cannot get together enough money to pay off the difference between the amount owed on the mortgage and the selling price of the home, then a short sale is, as mentioned, your next best option. The benefits of a short sale, rather than going through foreclosure, include the avoidance of an eviction process, and the house is not sold at a public sale or auction.

Bank of America has a program called the *Cooperative Short Sale Program,* which is also called a *preapproved price short sale.* One benefit of this program

---

[4] www.fbi.gov/losangeles/press-releases/2012/three-arrested-in-los-angeles-and-orange-county-for-fraud-involving-short-sale-real-estate-transactions (Retrieved August 14, 2012).

is the possibility of monetary relocation assistance, which can net sellers between $2,500 and $30,000.[5]

Negative Impact of a Short Sale

What kind of an impact does a short sale have on your credit and your ability to buy another home? A big impact, according to Fair Isaac, the company responsible for creating the FICO score, the leading credit-scoring formula.

According to the article "Credit scores will plummet with a short sale" published in the *Los Angeles Times*: "Fair Isaac recently released a chart showing the effects of various credit score blows, from a missed mortgage payment to a foreclosure or a short sale with a deficiency balance (the difference between the home sale proceeds and what you owe). Someone with FICO scores in the 780 range would lose 90 to 110 points with a single skipped payment. A short sale or foreclosure would trim 140 to 160 points from that 780 score."[6]

A credit score that suffers such a big hit will take a few years to return to previous levels. If you can do a short sale and have your deficiency forgiven by your lender, then it may be worth suffering the credit score consequences of a short sale. You must make your own decision about preserving or depleting your credit score. Although this number will affect your timeline for buying another home, moving out of your home may be more of an imperative than protecting your credit score.

How Long Will It Take?

One thing that homeowners must keep in mind is that a short sale is not a fast process. Patience is a requirement when choosing this option. Watlington says he has seen dramatic variations in the time span of different short sales. He notes, "The shortest one I had was 45 days. I've had some that had been going 6 months before getting any response from the bank as to whether they would accept the offer or not. And this is probably going back 2 years." Low prices motivate patient purchasers to wait out the protracted process.

Watlington comments that he is not alone when it comes to long delays in short sales. "I've had colleagues where literally the offer was written on St.

---

[5] http://homeloanhelp.bankofamerica.com/en/short-sale.html?cm_mmc=Cre-ForeclosureAlternative-_-Google-PS-_-bank%20of%20america%20short%20sale-_-Short%20Sale (Retrieved August 11, 2012).

[6] http://articles.latimes.com/2011/apr/10/business/la-fi-montalk-20110410 (Retrieved August 11, 2012).

Patrick's Day and by Halloween it hadn't closed yet," Watlington recalls. "So it really all depends on what's involved."

Today, many lenders are beginning to improve how well they deal with their customers. For example, some are beginning to offer consumers direct telephone numbers to real, live human beings who can discuss their mortgage options. Still, others lag behind.

Watlington says his experiences have taught him that some banks are better than others when it comes to improving customer service. "There are some that are more diligent, more receptive to getting it done and others who, maybe because of volume, aren't as diligent or efficient with the process."

The recent improvements in customer service at banks may be attributed to the time that has passed between the bursting of the real estate bubble and today. "You need to remember, banks weren't dealing with short sales, either, until the market fell out and started to decline," Watlington explains. "So they had to hire people to train them on what they wanted them to do in order to deal with a short sale. So we aren't dealing with people who went to school for 4 years to deal with short sales." Because banks have had time to learn how to deal with the giant volume of short sales and foreclosures entering their system, perhaps they have gained the institutional intelligence that has made them better at working with customers to complete those transactions.

Processes Take Time

How long will the process take? This depends on your lender and how many liens you have on your home, as well as whether you just have a primary mortgage or if you have a first and second home equity loan. Having two or more lien holders slows down the process.

Watlington explains, "So, if somebody got a first and a second [mortgage] with their lender, then that would go quicker than somebody who has a first and a second with two separate lenders. The quickest approval that I obtained had been about 45 days from contract acceptance. However, I did have the assistance of a short sale negotiator in our marketplace. So, I did the typical realtor thing: I marketed the property, found a buyer for the property, and then, once we had a contract, the short sale negotiator took the process from there in terms of trying to expedite the approval from the lender."

▓ **Tip** *Get a short sale negotiator involved.* A short sale negotiator is a problem solver who works on behalf of sellers to help them get the best deal they can and reach a short sale settlement with the bank. Having a third party negotiate between the bank and seller helps to improve the outcome.

Although a short sale negotiator may be a licensed real estate agent who has successful experience in completing short sales, a real estate attorney is the best person for this role. Anyone without a license should be avoided.

Short Sale Negotiators

There are many benefits to hiring a licensed short sale negotiator rather than trying to manage the process yourself. A seasoned short sale negotiator, whether an attorney or an experienced real estate agent, knows what the bank wants in terms of documents, how it wants to receive them, and in what order. In addition, these people understand how to communicate with the lender's negotiators.

"The negotiators actually seem to be more accessible to [the bank] than they are for us," Watlington explains. "There seems to be a layer of insulation, or at least there was at one point, where we would call and follow up on the status of things and you'd get kind of a call center rep. He'd say, 'Well, the system tells me a negotiator hasn't been assigned yet. Please call back in a week.' Whereas, it seems that the negotiators have developed some sort of rapport [with the bank] because of their success in doing things the way they want them. They have a better process to seeing the short sale through."

Hiring an attorney as a short sale negotiator will cost you a fee. Some licensed real estate agents will do this job as part of their commission for selling the house.

Tip *Shop around for a negotiator.* When you find someone who has a track record for completing successful short sales, ask for references. Talk to past clients about the negotiator, then make sure you know who will be paying for the negotiator's services, and how much.

Who Pays for the Negotiator?

Sometimes the negotiator's fees can be wrapped up in the settlement contract. Says Watlington, "Basically, when you get to settlement, the lender for the seller has approved all the fees on the settlement sheet. Oftentimes, it includes fees related to the short sale negotiator."

Although sellers have to pay for their attorney out of pocket, lenders often pay the commission of a licensed real estate agent who serves as a short sale negotiator.

■ **Tip** *Negotiate with the lender for the short sale negotiator's fee.* If you use a licensed real estate agent as your short sale negotiator, the bank will often pay commissions and closing costs. Make sure your settlement contract includes the payment for the negotiator.

Brokers and the Secondary Market

Getting more people involved in your short sale can improve your chances of success if those people are licensed professionals with good referrals. The real estate market changes daily, heaving and contracting on its slow procession to recovery. As the housing situation in your area shifts with the changing tide of rules and regulations, getting the latest advice from your support team can help you avoid missing alterations in processes and laws that apply to you.

A real estate agent should be just one of your valuable sources of free advice about a short sale or a foreclosure. A mortgage broker also has much knowledge and expertise to offer. When is it best to get a mortgage broker involved in this process?

Watlington explains, "Typically they come in on the buying side of the transaction. I mean, buyers are using mortgage brokers for the purposes of obtaining financing to purchase a property." Refinancing a home through HARP is the primary reason an underwater homeowner would want to contact a mortgage broker.

Lenders' Learning Curve

At many banks, there was a huge learning curve for those dealing with so many foreclosures and short sales for the first time. And if it was hard for the banks to cope with such a huge bulk of these types of sales, it was even more difficult for real estate agents to keep up with the new ways of working with those banks.

Watlington says that short sales seemed to be a new phenomenon and that even agents who'd been in the marketplace for 20 to 30 years hadn't experienced them before. "That's where the market went, so it's part of the market. At first, there was a lot of resistance from the agents wanting to deal with short sales because they are very labor intensive."

When real estate agents finally realized that a large percentage of their business would revolve around short sales, they began to take on more of them. After all, Watlington adds, "You're trying to help [sellers] accomplish what they want or need to do with their property."

Today, more guidelines and more requirements for all lenders have bogged down the process at large and small lenders alike. Watlington agrees. "As far as I can tell, for the most part, they all have about the same processing time. There are a few that are a lot slower, but most of them are pretty much on the same [slow] schedule."

Although these new regulations may add some extra time to the refinancing process for underwater mortgage holders, the new rules help to protect all homeowners. Watlington says he believes the Dodd-Frank Act leveled the playing field in several ways because it mandates what Fannie Mae and Freddie Mac require in terms of purchasing mortgages in the secondary mortgage market. "If you don't meet the guidelines that were implemented," he adds, "then you're not going to be able to sell the loan in the secondary mortgage market unless you met all those requirements."

This means mortgage companies on the front end are more diligent about verifying your information, and they have more guidelines to follow to make sure that, when they do go to sell this loan on the secondary market, they don't have any resistance. What exactly is this "secondary mortgage market?" It is the market for the securities and bonds that are backed up by the value of a group of mortgage loans. Basically, lenders bundle a bunch of their mortgages and sell them to other firms that specialize in servicing these loans. For example, Fannie Mae and Freddie Mac operate in the secondary mortgage market and, in fact, buy half the mortgages in the country. Rather than making home loans directly to consumers, both organizations work with mortgage lenders to help ensure they have funds to lend to homebuyers at affordable rates.[7] They do this by buying mortgages from the loan originators, giving lenders more funds they can then use to help more people finance their home purchases.

FANNIE MAE, FREDDIE MAC, AND THE SECONDARY MORTGAGE MARKET

Four decades ago, congressional charters set up Fannie Mae and Freddie Mac as government-sponsored enterprises (GSEs)—privately owned financial institutions established by the government to fulfill a public mission. The two GSEs were created to provide a stable source of funding for residential mortgages across the country, including loans on housing for low- and moderate-income families. Fannie Mae and Freddie Mac carry out that mission through their operations in the secondary mortgage market. They purchase mortgages that meet certain standards from banks and other originators, pool those loans into mortgage-backed securities (MBSs) that they guarantee against losses from defaults on the underlying mortgages, and sell

---

[7] www.cunastrategicservices.com/Fannie_Mae_103.html (Retrieved August 11, 2012).

the securities to investors—a process referred to as *securitization*. In addition, they buy mortgages and MBSs (both each other's and those issued by private companies) to hold in their portfolios. They fund those portfolio holdings by issuing debt obligations, known as *agency securities*, which are sold to investors.

The enactment of the Housing and Economic Recovery Act of 2008 established the Federal Housing Finance Agency and gave it the authority to place Fannie Mae and Freddie Mac in conservatorship—a step it took in September 2008. This was necessary because Fannie and Freddie, like others who had securitized mortgages, held many bad loans and were in danger of going under.

The U.S. Treasury was granted the authority to provide the GSEs with unlimited capital (by purchasing their stock) to maintain their solvency through 2012. Those actions gave the government control over the two institutions and effectively made the government's backing of their debt securities and MBS guarantees explicit.

As a result of that aid and the explicit federal guarantee, Fannie Mae and Freddie Mac were able to continue channeling funds to the mortgage market, even as private financial institutions were faltering. Consequently, in 2009, the two GSEs owned or guaranteed roughly half of all outstanding mortgages in the United States (including a significant share of subprime mortgages), and they financed three quarters of new mortgages originated that year. Including the 20 percent of home loans insured by federal agencies, such as the FHA, more than 90 percent of new mortgages made in 2009 carried a federal guarantee.[8]

How Much Should a Homebuyer Spend?

Mortgages are tricky business. Figuring out how much you can afford is an important part of determining your options for your next house. What should you pay for your home? Any lender can help you look at your budget and decide what price range you should be investigating the next time around, after you have shed your underwater burden. Reviewing options from a number of lenders, including big banks, small banks, and credit unions, can help you decide what is right for your financial situation.

When buyers ask Watlington how much they should spend on their new home, he tells them to look closely at their earnings and their expenses.

"Basically, I refer them to the experts in that field," he explains. "So I'll say, 'Before we go shopping, what you'll need to do is speak with a mortgage lender to determine what your qualifications are. That way you'll know that you're shopping for houses that are within your budget.' I don't typically tell them what they can afford, especially with all the new guidelines."

---

[8] www.cbo.gov/publication/21992 (Retrieved August 11, 2012).

Without looking closely at buyers' budgets, there is no way to determine effectively how much they should spend on a home. For example, Watlington says, "Someone might tell me [he makes] $100,000, but [he's] a contractor and [he has] expenses. Then, after [he speaks] with a lender, [he finds] [he only makes] $50,000. So, usually I have a mortgage lender speak to [buyers] first to evaluate their circumstance. [The lender] determines they can buy a house for up to $300,000. They say, 'You can buy a house up to $300,000, and your payment's going to be $1,500 a month if you buy a $300,000 house. Are you comfortable with that?' If they say yes, then we'll work up to $300,000. If they say, 'No. I'd really like to make my payment be closer to $1,200, then I do the math to figure [it] out [and say], 'OK, then we need to stay under this price to make sure that we stay within your budget.'" It's essential to know your price range going in, and that's something a lender can figure out for you.

Front-End Ratio

What's the ideal percentage of income that homebuyers should allow for monthly mortgage payments? Watlington says, "This number has changed over time, but typically the mortgage is principal and interest, taxes and insurance: This should be 28 percent of your gross [pretax] income."

When a married couple is buying a house, some people who are financially conservative say that this percentage should be based on the gross income of only the primary earner in the house. Others say that this percentage should be based on the gross income of both the husband and wife.

"It depends on who's applying for the mortgage," Watlington notes. "So if it's husband and wife, or just husband or just wife or just individual, it's 28 percent of what your gross income is."

To calculate this housing expense ratio, or front-end ratio, simply multiply your gross annual salary by 0.28, then divide by 12 (months). The answer is the most you should spend on your monthly mortgage payment.[9]

Lenders also look at homebuyers' credit score when deciding whether they qualify for a loan.

▨ **Tip** *Before buying anything, determine your front-end ratio.* If your estimated monthly mortgage payment is more than 28 percent of your monthly income, find a new loan or a new house.

---

[9] www.bankrate.com/finance/mortgages/how-much-house-can-you-buy--1.aspx (Retrieved August 11, 2012).

Are Lenders Tougher Than Before?

Although some homeowners claim it is harder to deal with lenders now than before the real estate market bubble burst, Watlington says he does not see a difference. "I think it all comes down to the individual and the company, the service they provide."

Many new guidelines for lenders have been put in place to protect consumers, which has led to some increases in wait times for processes that were once much faster. For example, Watlington notes that refinances are taking longer to process than they did several years ago. "I think they may take a little longer than they used to. I know when I refinanced in 2003, it took, like, two and a half weeks, but now it can take more than a month." Many homeowners complain that refinancing a mortgage can now take several months.

Take Advantage of HARP If You Qualify

Watlington was able to save 1.125 percent on his interest rate when he refinanced his home through HARP.[10] He was able to capitalize on HARP because his mortgage was in excess of the value of his property. "When you refinance, the appraisal needs to support the value of your home to allow for you to be able to refi. So, [the law] made a provision that said, as long as you had put 20 percent down, you could refinance with your current lender using a government product. Basically it was [about] a 105 percent [loan-to-value] threshold. So, if you're refinancing $367,000 and the appraisal came in at $350,000, then they would allow you to do the refi."

Today, homeowners must have a current LTV ratio that is more than 80 percent to qualify for HARP. In addition, borrowers must be current on their mortgage payments and have a good payment history during the past year. In addition, the home must be owned or guaranteed by Freddie Mac or Fannie Mae; it must have been sold to Fannie Mae or Freddie Mac on or before May 31, 2009; and it cannot have been refinanced under HARP previously unless it is a Fannie Mae loan that was refinanced under HARP from March to May 2009.

Watlington notes that anyone who might qualify for the program should look into it. "[If homeowners aren't] going anywhere, they can save themselves hundreds of dollars per month by doing that refinance. So it certainly would be something I would make aware to [people] if they were considering it."

---

[10] www.makinghomeaffordable.gov/programs/lower-rates/Pages/harp.aspx (Retrieved November 3, 2012).

▓ **Tip** *Watch the news.* Watch for new federal and state programs for people with underwater mortgages. Many banks also have new programs to help homeowners. Talk to your lender about what might be available. Contact a counselor who knows about the latest programs. Although you may not be able to bail out your home completely, you may find yourself able at least to refinance and reduce the amount by which you are under water. A partial bailout is better than none at all!

Conclusion

The real estate market continues to shift slowly as it recovers. Watching the news and studying the media can add to the one-on-one advice you receive from real estate agents, mortgage brokers, attorneys, other homeowners, and even economists. Each voice adds another layer of protection to the arsenal the underwater homeowner needs to fight negative equity. More layers of expertise help them find more powerful solutions to their problems.

In the next chapter, real estate agent Michael Milligan presents a different view of the real estate market covered by previous experts. Milligan also helps those who are under water determine which option is best for them. Although he shares his experiences in the field and the expertise he has gained along the way, he also focuses on those who are under added financial pressures, such as a divorce or other hardships, and presents ways they can get through these tough times.

Advice from a Real Estate Agent

Michael Milligan

When dealing with a doctor, lawyer, or any professional, it is always best to get a second opinion. Get a third if you can afford it. The same advice applies to real estate. All realtors have their own area of expertise, so seek out more than one. Add up the experiences and anecdotes from a variety of agents before you make a decision.

When reaching out to professionals in the real estate industry, the majority of the ones who are making a living by helping homeowners buy and sell their homes are real estate agents. These are the people out there opening lockboxes and turning keys inside the homes that are on the market today. One real estate agent who is helping East Coast homeowners buy and sell their homes is Michael Milligan, an agent for the firm Keller Williams.

Milligan has been selling houses in Delaware and Pennsylvania since 2009. Although he has been a real estate agent for only 3 years, before that he was on the other side of the table; he worked as a real estate inspector and landlord for many years. He also bought and sold a few houses of his own before he became a full-time real estate sales agent. In this chapter, Milligan offers an experienced perspective on the short sale process, the numbers involved in owning and selling a home, the trust needed to make the best real estate decisions, and a number of other important areas underwater homeowners must consider.

Milligan's first clients in 2009 were underwater homeowners, so short sales were the first kinds of sales in which he was involved. "The reasons why [homeowners] were under water varied," Milligan explains. "Some people bought at the height of the market. Some people continued to borrow against the equity of their home, and the value went down. If they defaulted on their mortgage in some way and they have to sell, then they have to petition their bank in order to call it a hardship and have [their situation] approved by the bank in order to sell [their home] for less than they owe."[1]

A mortgage default service, like a short sale, is an option that is intended to help you avoid foreclosure, whether you have missed a payment or are at risk of imminent default because of some kind of hardship. You can do a short sale even if you miss a payment, but you should not let that happen before you look into the short sale option. By getting the short sale process underway early, you have more time to make the short sale happen. Remember, you can still do a short sale even if the foreclosure process is underway. On its web site, Wells Fargo states that a short sale can help you avoid a foreclosure sale and may be considered even if the foreclosure process has started.[2] According to Bank of America, homeowners can do a short sale all the way up until the day of foreclosure.[3]

Today, Milligan sees the real estate market stabilizing and fewer people in default. "In 2009, the reason I got into the short sale part of that business was somewhat because you have to fish where the fish are. That's when the economy was really going south and there was a large, large volume of people [who] were getting out of their homes because they were under water." Many of these people, who would often default on their mortgage payments, were turning to short sales. "People were losing their jobs and they really couldn't afford to pay for their home anymore." In 2009, the drop in the employment numbers were hitting many people where they lived.

Typical Scenarios

The typical scenarios for underwater homeowners at that time included either the loss of a job or a divorce. "A lot of times divorce follows job loss," Milligan points out. "Financial strain on an already strained relationship pushes it to the brink, and I've noticed that a lot with a lot of the clients I deal with."

What does Milligan tell those people when they come to him and ask him for advice about their underwater homes? He says there are different kinds of

---

[1] All quotes from Milligan were collected during a personal interview in July 2012.

[2] www.wellsfargo.com/homeassist/shortsale (Retrieved October 7, 2012).

[3] http://homeloanhelp.bankofamerica.com/en/short-sale.html (Retrieved October 6, 2012).

people who come to him these days. "In this market, there are those that want to sell. They have to sell for a certain [price]." For example, a family that bought in 2005 at the peak of the market wants to sell its house in 2012. "It's not worth as much as it was, but, they say, 'We bought it for *this* and now we have to sell it for *that* in order to break even.' And the conversation's very difficult because you can get the home appraised and find out that it's not worth what they need to sell it for. So there really needs to be a difficult conversation about: Do you need to stay in your home, why are you moving, where are you trying to get to, and, really, what are you trying to accomplish?"

▓ **Tip**   *Ask yourself the hard questions.* What are your motivations for selling your home? What are the benefits of staying? What are the benefits of selling the house? Are you willing to take a loss? Are you willing to take a drop in your credit score? How much do you love your house? What will you be losing if you move? One suggestion that may help you make a decision is simply to draw a line down the center of a piece of paper. On one side list the reasons to stay and on the other list the reasons to go. Balancing these two choices can help you make your decision with your eyes wide open.

When is it best to stay in your home? Milligan notes he will sometimes advise people to stay. This solution is often spurred by the math. "When they absolutely, positively need to sell for a specific number, I can do some market analysis for their area and determine if that's in the ballpark of where things are selling." He explains that he also looks at the condition of the home as well as the prices of nearby homes to determine the likelihood of selling their house.

Numbers Game

Sometimes, the numbers just don't add up. Milligan explains, "This happens very, very frequently. As a matter of fact, last week, someone had to sell for $400,000. They couldn't go any lower. But homes in their neighborhood were selling for $350,000, so I told them that no one can sell their home for $400,000. In fact, if someone were going to buy their home for $400,000, no bank would give them a mortgage, because you can't get a $400,000 mortgage on a $350,000 house these days."

This is the type of scenario that keeps people in their home. Milligan advises homeowners to stay in the home until the market recovers. He estimates that will happen in 4 to 7 years.

Although a real estate agent can lay out the facts of the situation, it is up to you to decide what you will ultimately do with that information. So the questions become: Do you cash out and sell your home for less? Do you bring money to the table and pay off the remainder of your loan so you're not at default with the bank? Do you take money out of an IRA, 401K, or other investment to put down on your new home and try to start over?

On the bright side, we are now living in a buyer's market, so the market may work in your favor. Milligan adds, "You'll be where you want to be, and you're buying at the bottom of the market and, [maybe,] selling back when the market does recover. You'll have that equity back."

When a homeowner sells a $400,000 home with no equity for $350,000, there is a $50,000 deficiency with which he must contend. How much is too much of a deficiency to pay off with your life's savings? Milligan explains that each person must make this decision for him- or herself. "It's a case-by-case basis. For some people, a $50,000 gap is not a big deal. To other people, $50,000 is just something they'll never recover from, so they just have to stay. I know of a couple right now that's been divorced for 3 years and they're still living in the house together, divorced, because they can't afford to move on. It's a shame, and I know how unhappy they both are, but they are both holding on to the asset that has lost so much value. Neither one of them can move on to another house. It's a terrible situation, but that's just what they have to do, because [the amount of the deficiency] is just too great for them."

Living Together after a Divorce?

The couple just described by Milligan is not alone. Many others have had to make a tough decision because of the state of the real estate market and the lack of equity in their home. Many times, the reason why a family wants to sell its house is because of a divorce. With some minor modifications, a couple can turn a single-family house of the right size into a place where the two divorced people can live comfortably. Strong people in the right situation can do many difficult things when they put their mind to it.

"[This option is] not something I would advise," Milligan comments. "Happiness comes in many forms, and if you're not happy, and you have to go to a home that you are not happy in every day, it will start to weigh on you psychologically. But that's not a decision I could make for [these couples]. That's where I leave my real estate expertise at the door and say, 'These are the numbers. You need to decide what is best for you.'"

Reporter Gerri L. Elder's recent article posted on TotalDivorce.com describes this exact situation. She wrote: "A recent report by Law.com discussed a growing trend of divorcing couples who simply do not have the option to sell their homes and are thus making the decision to keep the marital home as a joint investment during and after the divorce. The spouses then become roommates and attempt to ride out the rough housing market together yet apart. If the housing market eventually bounces back, the ex-spouses can then sell the home and split a larger profit."

Elder goes on to explain that this type of living arrangement can be tough on couples. If the couple can live together separately, and there is no abuse involved in the relationship, perhaps this is an option. Although it might not be easy.[4]

▨ **Tip** *Decide for yourself.* Your living situation is your decision. After you have listened to all the experts, lawyers, counselors, real estate agents, mortgage brokers, and so on, you are still the one who has to live with the ramifications of your decision. Think for yourself and do what is best for *you*. Ask yourself: What is important to me? Is my credit score more important than my daily happiness? Does my happiness override my need for having equity in my home? Only you can answer these questions.

Short Sale Option

As noted in earlier chapters, one option that divorced couples, or anyone with an underwater mortgage, may have at their disposal is the short sale. As we've learned, a short sale is when the house is sold for less than what is owed on the mortgage (it is a sale that is "short" some money).

In 2010, there were 354,000 short sales in the United States. The next year, there were 380,000 short sales in the United States. These numbers represent a giant increase in this type of activity compared with the 105,000 short sales that took place in 2008.[5]

Letter of Hardship

After you decide that you can no longer afford your house, your next step is to write a letter of hardship. Whether you are looking for a mortgage modification, a short sale, or a deed in lieu of foreclosure, you need to inform your bank about your situation in a well-worded letter. Don't go overboard; simply state your hardship. Some hardships that a bank recognizes as legitimate include the loss of a job, a job relocation, or extreme medical expenses. Be specific, include numbers, and be truthful and realistic. Then, put yourself in

---

[4] www.totaldivorce.com/news/articles/society/housing-market.aspx (Retrieved July 24, 2012).

[5] www.statisticbrain.com/foreclosure-home-sales-statistics/ (Retrieved July 24, 2012).

your lender's shoes. Ask yourself this question: Why is it in the lender's best interest to give me what I want? Answer this question in your letter by spelling out specifically the benefits that the lender will realize by giving you an affordable solution to the situation rather than a foreclosure.

■ **Tip**   *Be polite.* In a letter of hardship, get to the point. Include all your contact information as well as the contact information for your attorney or your real estate agent, or both. Contact your lender so you know exactly to whom the letter should be sent and the preferred way to send it. Then, hope for the best.

Why would a lender want to give you a modification or permit a short sale? Think about it: The bank does not want your house. The bank does not want to be a landlord. The bank wants to get paid. When a bank forecloses on a house, it has yet another property to worry about. Foreclosed homes are subject to break-ins, pests, weather damage, mold, fire, and so on. Money is much less messy than the upkeep of a derelict house.

Another thing the bank does not want is homeowners who stop paying their bills. Milligan explains, "Since the short sale process began a couple of years ago, the one thing that the banks have guarded against is selective default, which is people determining that their house is worth less than it was, but they just don't want to pay it back, so they are just selectively defaulting." He continues, "They didn't lose their job. They still have the same income. They can still afford to pay. They just feel like they're paying on a depreciating asset and they choose not to." A bank wants to avoid this type of situation, which will end in yet another foreclosure and another home without an occupant. This is why the short sale is often a better option for everyone involved.

Decision Time: To Sell Short or Not to Sell Short

The first step is to decide whether a short sale is right for you. This is when the process begins. The next step includes working to get the approval of your lender to do a short sale.

"To do a short sale, you petition the bank," explains Milligan. "You have a deficiency in your income caused by whatever scenario. I've seen widows who aren't . . . receiving any income. I have seen people lose their jobs. People take a downgrade in position and they are in a place they can't afford. Self-employed people who aren't working as much as they used to—a lot of that happened back [during the crash]—they have to provide a hardship letter to the bank and show them that they used to make *this* and now they are making *this*."

Even if you think you have a great reason to do a short sale, the bank could disagree and choose to deny you the short sale option. Why would they shoot you down? If the bank does not want to pay for the loss of the deficiency, then the bank could deny the short sale. But, if the bank is willing to forgive the deficiency, then a short sale is a wonderful option that beats having to go through a foreclosure. Although a short sale can be a long shot, it is an option worth trying for homeowners who have the time to go through the lengthy short sale process. An attorney can help homeowners speed up this process.

If the short sale option falls through, homeowners may have to consider some kind of foreclosure, including a deed in lieu of foreclosure. "The option is, you can stop paying on your mortgage and it will go into foreclosure, which is very similar to a bankruptcy, where you won't be able to buy a home for 5 to 7 years. You won't be able to [take out a loan to] buy a car. You can't go buy anything at that point: Your credit isn't any good," comments Milligan. It may take up to 7 years to recover from such a big blow to your credit score. But on the bright side, after that time is up, you can put all your bad luck behind you and go into your next home investment with your eyes wide open to the reality of taking out a loan.

Credit Score Hits

Many people wonder how bad their credit will be affected by a short sale or a foreclosure. According to columnist Michelle Singletary's article in *The Washington Post* in August 2011 titled "What's worse for credit score—foreclosure, short sale or deed in lieu?": "If you apply for a loan in the future, certain lenders may look more favorably at a short sale than at a foreclosure, but the credit scoring system sees all these defaults as equally bad."[6]

Short Sale Approval Process

Lenders analyze the homeowner's petition. Every lender employs risk mitigators, who decide whether the petitioner can do a short sale. Milligan says: "They take a week to get back to the borrowers and tell them, 'Yes, you are approved. You can sell the house for less.' And they'll tell them the price point to begin at. 'We're not going to take half the value, but we want to be competitive. And we understand that your debt will not fully be repaid.'" These are the types of instructions that will come back to a homeowner when a lender approves a short sale.

---

[6] www.washingtonpost.com/business/economy/whats-worse-for-credit-score--foreclosure-short-sale-or-deed-in-lieu/2011/08/30/glQAbnTaqJ_story.html (Retrieved July 25, 2012).

What are the repercussions of a short sale? Some states allow lenders to render deficiency judgments against a borrower who did not pay off a mortgage completely as a result of a short sale or foreclosure. Others lenders do not. By looking online, you should be able to find resources that indicate whether your state allows deficiency judgments. Try looking at www. foreclosurefish.com/blog/index.php?id=994 to determine whether you might be facing a deficiency judgment.

More Lenders Seek Mortgage Debt Repayment

According to writer Jessica Silver-Greenberg of the *Wall Street Journal,* "Forty-one states and the District of Columbia permit lenders to sue borrowers for mortgage debt still left after a foreclosure sale. The economics of today's battered housing market mean that lenders are doing so more and more."

If you are unlucky enough to have a deficiency judgment against you, keep in mind that the amount of your debt will only grow, because some of these judgments also carry interest, often at a rate of around 8 percent.

"Florida is among the biggest deficiency judgment states. Since the start of 2007, it has had more foreclosures than any other state that allows deficiency judgments—more than 9 percent of the U.S. total, according to research firm Lender Processing Services Inc.," wrote Jessica Silver-Greenberg wrote in "House Is Gone but Debt Lives On."[7]

Will the bank come after you for the deficiency from a short sale? Maybe. To find out what your chances are, ask your local real estate professionals how other people in your state have fared after a short sale. If you live in a state that allows lenders to pursue a deficiency judgment, petition your lender to get a signed letter stating the lender will not pursue your deficiency. Getting a real estate attorney involved in the process can help you navigate the real estate laws and processes in your state.

■ **Tip** *Determine whether you live in a state that renders deficiency judgments.* Whether lenders can pursue previous mortgage holders for the difference between the selling price and the amount that was owed on the mortgage depends on the state in which you live. Knowing this information can help you decide whether you want to pursue a short sale or a foreclosure.

---

[7] http://online.wsj.com/article/SB10001424053111904060604576572532029526792.html (Retrieved July 25, 2012).

No Profit from a Short Sale

Besides coming after you for the deficiency, which may or may not happen, the bank requires a few things from your short sale. Milligan points out, "As a short sale borrower, you are not allowed to make any money on the sale of this house because the bank is taking a loss already. Any proceeds you receive go to the bank."

The bank often states this clearly in the agreement the borrower signs before the short sale is approved. Why? "Because some people try to finagle [the sale] in a way so they sell [the house] for $175,000 when it's worth $250,000, but they receive $5,000 at the settlement from the buyer, and [that $5,000] is not allowed to change hands like that," Milligan explains. This is just one way that lenders protect themselves and it is crucial for sellers to read the fine print in their lender agreement so they don't get into trouble by breaking the rules of the contract. Bottom line: If you are doing a short sale, don't expect to get anything from the sale of your house. Simply enjoy the fact that your lender has (hopefully) forgiven a debt that could have cost you thousands of dollars.

Another thing to expect after a short sale is a blow to your credit. Milligan explains: "The borrower will receive a nominal hit to their credit score, which is, I think, between 50 and 60 points that it will go down. And they are not allowed to buy a house for 2 years."

According to law experts at Cornell University Law School, consumer credit guidelines are primarily governed by federal and state statutes, such as the Uniform Consumer Credit Code, which has been adopted in 11 states and Guam, and the federal Consumer Credit Protection Act.[8]

Lease–Purchase Agreements

Although some people who have been through the short sale are suddenly restricted from buying a new house for the next 2 years, there are ways that people have found to move into another house before those 2 years are up. For example, there is something called a *lease purchase* that people choose to do when they locate the next house of their dreams. This option is something that Milligan says is becoming more popular.

"So, what you see now in the market are a lot of folks trying to do lease purchases. They've short sold their house. The husband or wife has now found another job. Their income level is back and a little more stable, but they

---

[8] www.law.cornell.edu/wex/consumer_credit. (Retrieved September 30, 2012).

can't buy a house for 2 years. They have the income, so they find the house that they like and they try to negotiate with the seller to lease it for a year or a year and a half or however long it will take for them to be out of the short sale scenario." The couple can live in the home as renters on a lease until their time limit from the short sale has passed, then they work to buy the home after the moratorium has ended.

Milligan explains, "They go to the seller and say, 'I can't purchase your house right now because of my situation. However, we will lease it for a year. Then, when a year's up, we can discuss purchasing the home, or we can do a lease purchase now.'

He continues, "The advice that I give my sellers always is, 'Don't get involved in the lease–purchase agreement. Just lease the house if you want to rent it and then, when the lease is up, revisit the idea of buying the home, because you don't know what the value is going to be. You don't want to be locked in to a value now for the future."

Flipping this advice around, people whose mortgages are under water can also learn from this situation. If you are trying to sell your house, but the price keeps going lower and lower, you may want to consider renting out the house with a lease agreement. "From sellers' perspective, sometimes they're trying to sell [their home] for $400,000, and they can't. And the price is going down and down and down. And then they say, 'I don't want to take this big of a loss, so I'm just going to rent it out.' I have a client doing that right now," Milligan recalls. "They were trying to sell a year ago. They weren't getting their price, so they decided to lease it. And now the lease is about to end and they want to pursue selling it again."

■ **Tip** *Consider renting out your property.* If you cannot get your selling price on your home, you may want to consider renting it to a tenant for a year. This gives you some time to allow the market to recover before you move to the option of selling. While you wait, you have the benefits of a steady income to pay your mortgage, and perhaps other expenses, while you consider what you may do in the future.

Everyone Is Concerned about Value

Milligan notes that about 10 percent of the people with whom he works have mortgages that are under water, but 100 percent of his clients are concerned about value. There is one thing that must also be remembered by all the people who are selling their homes who are concerned about the low prices they are being offered by purchasers: Value works both ways. Today, the entire market is down. When you are selling your house in a normal sale these days, you may get much less than you want, but when you are buying, there are amazing bargains to be had. Milligan comments that this is something he tells all his clients. "All the prices are down. If you're going to sell your home for $50,000 less, you're going to buy your home for $50,000 less, too." He says he asks his clients, "'Would you rather make $100,000 more and buy your new home for $100,000 more? In the end, isn't it the same thing?'"

■ **Tip** *Look to the future.* When you sell your home at the bottom of the market you may recoup all the money you lost when you buy a new home at the bottom of the market. Stay focused on the bright side of the topsy-turvy real estate market. It works both ways.

■ **Tip** *Feeling alone? Look to the past.* If you think you are the only one who has lost value in your home, ask your realtor to show you what the house you would like to buy was worth before the real estate market tanked. That should give you a better perspective on how much value everyone lost when the bubble burst.

Buyers' Market

Milligan has a great example of how the real estate situation is now a buyer's market. He has a client who sold a house earlier this year. The home was appraised at $425,000 and his client had an eye on a house that was $890,000. Milligan recalls, "He sold his house for $400,000 the first day it went on the market. He purposefully listed it for under [the] appraised value because he was going to put in an offer on this new house that was $140,000 below what that homeowner was asking. And it all worked out. My client sold his home really fast, and he bought another home at a discount severely under what it was listed for on the market." Milligan's client had enough equity in their home that they could sell it for $25,000 less and still have funds to put down on the new home. "It really just became an exercise in motivation. He was motivated to move into this other house, and he was willing to sell his house quickly, and the seller of the other house was willing to sell it for $750,000. . . . The $890,000 home was on the market for a very long time. It had come down from $1 million. It was a situation where [the other homeowner] was ready to take whatever offer came back."

▨ **Tip**   *Watch your credit score.* The buyer's market scenario is a good example of the power of good credit and keeping your credit score nice and high. The people who were able to buy a better house and pick up a house for $140,000 under the selling price were able to do so only because they had the credit that allowed them to be preapproved for the house. Without their good credit, they could not have benefited from the buyer's market.

How Long Does It Take to Sell a Home?

If you are trying to sell your home, don't expect the 1-day turnaround experienced by the homeowner in Milligan's example. He notes that the areas where he works have 7 months of inventory, which means the current trend is that the average house sits on the market for about 7 months before it is sold. "If all of the buyers now, who are looking for a home, bought homes that are on the market, it would take them 7 months to do so," he explains. He adds that the homes he encounters are typically on the market for 90 to 100 days, but there are so many variables that it is difficult to provide anyone a hard-and-fast number about how long it takes to sell a home.

Milligan also points out that there are two parallel markets. "There's the retail market, where people have equity in their home and can sell it for whatever the market wants and it looks nice, and they just want to sell it, and they want to move on with something else. And then the secondary market is all of these distressed properties: short sales, foreclosures. They'll sit on the market for a year or a year and a half."

▨ **Tip**   *Be patient.* Selling your home does not happen overnight, especially if you are going through a short sale. Be prepared for it to take a long time to sell your home. After you have been approved for a short sale, then expect it to take a year or two before the home will sell. This is why it is so important to get started now. Contact your lender immediately if you think the short sale is the right option for you.

Milligan says, "I have short sales that have sat on the market for anywhere from 6 months to 2 years, but I have other retail sales homes where the bank is really not involved, other than receiving a mortgage payoff at settlement, and that could land anywhere from a week to 90 days."

Advice for the Underwater Homeowner

Every real estate sales agent has his or her own experiences in the marketplace, so individual words of advice vary from person to person, which is why it is important to talk to as many people in the industry as possible about your situation, especially if your mortgage is under water. After you talk to a variety of experts, pick one that you can work well with if you decide you are ready to sell. One reason why this is crucial to an underwater homeowner is because the process of selling your home in a short sale is a long one. Choose wisely; this will be a long relationship.

■ **Tip** *Trust is essential.* Work with a real estate agent you trust. You will rely on this individual for sound advice. Get references. Meet face to face. Spend some time with this person to get a feel for his or her experiences and personal style. Be truthful about your situation. After you have established trust, ask for some recommendations for lawyers, counselors, and other professionals who can help you get out from under your mortgage.

What does Milligan tell those who come to him and explain their mortgages are under water and they are looking for a way out? He starts by asking them how much they want him to look into their finances. If they want him to act as an accountant, he says, "This would be my recommendation: I would take the money from here and pay off this, and then your payments will be this, and then you will be fine." Or, if they want to figure out their real estate finances on their own, they can go it alone.

Good real estate agents ask you the hard questions that help you find a way out from your underwater situation. Here are the kinds of financial questions Milligan asks his clients whose mortgages are under water:

- **Do you need to sell your car and buy a used car?** By putting that money into the bank, you can use it to continue to make your mortgage payments.

- **How long do you think you will be out of work?** Be realistic. Take steps to get back into some kind of regular employment, even if it is at a lower pay rate.

- **How long are you going to be in this kind of a situation?** Imagine a worst-case scenario and plan ahead for a prolonged duration of your current financial difficulties. Work to slash your budget wherever you can.

- **Can you find income elsewhere?** Perhaps your adult child who lives at home could start to pay some rent!

- **Can you rent a room out to a family member?** Other people in your family may be looking for a place to stay. If there is room in your home, this is a great option that can add income to your monthly budget.

- **Can you take money out of an IRA or a 401K?** People who have other assets can borrow against them so they can make their payments on their home. This strategy helps them prevent a foreclosure while they get their feet back on the ground.

THREE STEPS TO A REALISTIC BUDGET

Whatever your situation, dealing realistically with an underwater home means taking a good look at your personal finances so you can make an informed decision about your future. Whether you want to keep your underwater mortgage or seek a way to get out from under it, you must take a closer look at your personal finances. The numbers could mean the difference between one option and the next.

Where should you begin to review your personal finances? Here are three steps to take while getting them in shape:

Step 1: *Start with a realistic budget.* Start today to gather all your monthly expenses. Keep all your receipts for a month. Write down every single expense, including gas bills, clothing costs, trips to the grocery store, dining expenses, drinks, cable bills, magazine subscriptions, and so forth. Do not leave anything off your list.

Step 2: *Look at your quarterly bills.* Are there any bills that come around quarterly? Do you pay your taxes quarterly because you are self-employed? Does your garbage collection service charge by the quarter? Divide these bills by three and add them to your monthly expenses.

Step 3: *Look at your yearly bills.* Anything that you pay on a yearly basis, such as property taxes, magazine subscriptions, club dues, vacations, charitable giving, and so on, should be divided by 12 and added to your monthly expenses. After you have calculated these expenses, then you will have a better understanding about how much it costs for you to live, and how much you can afford to pay for your mortgage. Perhaps a mortgage and all the expenses that go along with a mortgage are simply too much for you at this time, considering your income. If so, perhaps renting is a better option. Maybe you need to reconsider where you live. Ask yourself the hard questions:

- Am I living somewhere that I cannot afford to live?

- Would another city, town, neighborhood, or street be more appropriate for my income level?

- Can I foresee a change in my income that will drastically affect how much I can afford to pay for my mortgage?

- Is renting a better option than owning a house at this time in my life?

- Am I spending money on things (like cable or club memberships) that I can do without until my income increases?

- What are the benefits of owning my house? Compare them with the benefits of renting a house or an apartment. Sometimes, the benefits and mobility offered by renting far exceed the long-term benefits of owning a home.

Trimming Expenses and Creating Income

"There are [always] other ways of trimming expenses," Milligan says. "There are other ways of creating income." Looking closely at your monthly budget will help you determine what you might be able to do to save or generate money. Also, if you have lost your job and have been out of work for a year, you may need to consider another career—any career that brings in money.

When the numbers no longer balance and homeowners can no longer afford their monthly payments, including their mortgage, Milligan says it is time to petition the mortgage holder and say, "This is the situation I'm in and I cannot afford it. I've looked at every possibility of saving money and earning more money—and I still cannot afford it. So, is there any way that I can get some kind of release from my mortgage for the time being?"

Loan Deferral Programs

Milligan explains that there are many programs available to homeowners that different lenders provide for people in these sorts of situations. "They will reduce their payment for 6 months, they'll defer part of the loan. It's kind of on a lender-by-lender case in order to find out what programs they have available. And then [the lenders] reevaluate [your situation] and see whether or not you fit into some of those programs they can put you in to get you through some short-period shortfalls."

■ **Tip** *Call your lender.* Each lender has specific programs that are unique to its organization. New programs for underwater homeowners sprout up all the time, so continue to stay in touch with your lender even after that initial call to find out if something else has come along that can help you through your situation. Talk to somebody in person. Do not be put off if you find yourself in an automated maze of rerouted phone calls. Keep trying. Eventually, you should be able to talk to somebody who can either help you or lead you in the right direction to someone else who can.

"Not every financial institution has these same tools," Milligan points out. "So it really comes down to, if your mortgage is with Wells Fargo, it's going to be very different than if it's with Citizen's Bank. By calling your lender, you'll be able to find out the options that it has for you and what it would take to qualify."

Have the Numbers Ready

Lenders are going to want numbers, all the numbers—your income and expenses. If you do your own taxes using Quicken or another type of accounting software, you are already a step ahead of the game because you have all your numbers at your fingertips. Make sure all your paperwork is entered and up to date. Get in the habit of keeping all your receipts so you can prove that all your expenses are real and justified. After you have accumulated all of your paperwork for the last 3 months and all of your tax information for the past few years, you should be prepared to discuss your underwater mortgage with your mortgage lender.

■ **Tip** *Be prepared.* Before you talk to your lender, get all of your paperwork together so you have the answers for the questions you are asked.

What can you expect when an investigator for your bank starts to look into your personal finances? "It gets pretty invasive," Milligan warns. "They want 2 years of tax returns. They want 2 months of bank statements. They want any kind of pay stubs you have for the past 2 or 3 months. Then they'll do the financial accounting to determine if you are spending money where you shouldn't be, and if so, they can suggest you cut it out. They'll do that type of investigation for you. [Then,] they'll say you do or you do not qualify."

Milligan says he sees clients who have made their way through this process successfully—and those who don't. "I talked to somebody who said, just recently, that she went through this process. She said that she petitioned the lender for a deferment or some sort of remortgaging of her house loan. She went through this for 9 months. One thing was not signed, some things were considered out of date, so she had to resend all of these papers to [the lender]. The borrower was extremely upset. It sounded like all they were doing was delaying, trying to ask for more and more stuff in order to tell her no, later. Eventually the bank told her, 'No, you don't qualify. There is no real reason; you just don't qualify.' [The whole process was] an exercise in paperwork."

Tip *Nothing is definite.* It is not unheard of for a borrower to petition a lender for a loan modification or even a short sale and get shot down after months, even years, of working with the lender. Sometimes the chips fall in a person's favor; other times, they don't. This is why it is always good to be ready with a plan B in case your first plan of action falls through.

Ignore Bad Advice

One bad piece of advice that the lender told the homeowner in Milligan's story was that she should stop making her mortgage payments while she was trying to get a loan modification so she would qualify for it. After she received notice that she did not qualify, she also received even worse news: The bank was demanding payment for $17,000 because she hadn't paid her mortgage for 10 months. Yet, the bank had told her *not* to pay the mortgage during that period because it would not accept any paperwork from anyone current on their mortgage. Says Milligan, "They told her not to pay and then penalized her for it when she was not approved." Not only did the homeowner have to pay the missed mortgage payments, she had to cough up all the late fees and interest, as well.

Tip *Keep making your mortgage payments.* No matter what some functionary at your lender tells you, stay up to date on your mortgage. Once you default on your mortgage, your credit suffers and your options begin to disappear.

Here is another word of advice: If you ever hear from your lender that you need to stop making your mortgage payments, talk to a real estate attorney first. That attorney will help you make the right decision. It might cost you some money, but it should not be as much as all those late fees you will owe if you follow the bad advice from your lender. Plus, it will not hurt your credit!

Milligan agrees, "I never tell people not to pay their mortgage." The final decision is up to the borrower. Just make sure that decision is well informed and all the repercussions of that decision are thoroughly considered.

Caveat Emptor

The bottom line is that buyers must beware because there are many parts of the real estate system that are ineffective. Although banks may claim they have never dealt with this kind of volume of short sales and foreclosures, or that these are all new processes for them, don't believe them. These billion-dollar, resource-laden corporations have had six years to fix the bugs in the system, yet they still cry poor when their flaws are recognized. For example, all the paperwork that gets filed with these organizations cannot be sent to the bank via e-mail! The Internet has been in full swing for more than two decades, yet these organizations, with some of the most sophisticated web sites online, cannot receive customer files as attachments to e-mail messages.

Milligan adds, "[Lenders] do not allow you, at all, to e-mail anyone. No one is allowed to communicate by e-mail, so all of the documents you have to send them have to be faxed. This is 2012 now, and they are asking for years of old tax returns, months' worth of bank statements, and other things." Sometimes these forms add up to 80 or 90 pages worth of documents. "They go to a centralized 800-number fax machine in the middle of nowhere. [The paperwork] doesn't go to the person you are speaking to. And I'm sure their multiple fax machines are running 24/7 because of the sheer volume of documents that are coming in. These documents get compiled, they get put into a folder, and, in some instances, they get scanned and put into their system that way. If just one page is missing, they start all over. They'll say, 'Well, it's been 30 days, so now we need all of your documents again that are most recent,' and you have to send them again."

■ **Tip** *Fight the frustration.* This whole process of getting your finances in order and your mortgage out from under water is not going to be easy. For some reason, major lenders do not allow customers to send PDF files when applying for loan modifications or short sales. They also don't allow borrowers to contact them by e-mail, preferring contacts by phone, mail, and facsimile. Why? Time is money. The longer the process takes for you to get your information to the bank, the more money they make on late fees. This is not conspiracy theory; this is modern banking in 2012.

Do Customers Trust Lenders? Maybe Not!

One indication that customers have lost faith in Bank of America to help them get out from under water can be found in a recent story that explained, "When Bank of America Corp. sent letters to 60,000 struggling homeowners offering to slice an average $150,000 off their loans, the lender got an unusual response from half of them: silence."

According to the report by Hugh Son, published July 11, 2012: "Homeowners who fell behind on their payments began receiving the mailings in May, part of the bank's effort to meet terms of the $25 billion industry settlement over foreclosure abuses."[9] More than half of those who received the mailing contacted the bank to get their share of the money.

This lackluster response to an offer of free money from a lender could be interpreted as an indication that consumers do not trust their lenders to help them get out from under water. They have seen programs come and go, so it is no wonder that they don't jump at the chance to take advantage of a legitimate program that can help them when they have been burned before by the same organization.

▦ **Tip** *Be patient.* The petitioning process takes longer than you think. All the extra time and effort it takes you to send and resend documents is taxing, but if you want to make a major change in your life and improve your financial situation by getting out from under an underwater mortgage, be prepared to face some daunting obstacles. The process is a waiting game that may become frustrating. Breathe deeply. Plow ahead. When it is all over, it will have been worth it.

Milligan's message to his clients is as follows: "It's going to be frustrating. I feel, personally, that they are trying to test you. And you're going to be tested, so you better be prepared. That's the only thing I can tell them to prepare them for the ridiculousness that is about to come, because some of the conversations that I have are very ridiculous—not getting documents that I know I sent, and things of that nature."

What are your odds of success for getting a loan modification from your lender? Milligan says, in the region where he works, "I would put your odds of actually being approved by your lender at less than 10 percent."

---

[9] www.bloomberg.com/news/2012-07-11/bofa-give-away-has-few-takers-among-homeowners-mortgages.html (Retrieved July 26, 2012).

■ **Tip** *Learn to love your home.* No matter what option you choose, you probably need to stay in your home for at least a few more years while you wait for approval from your lender for a modification, wait for the foreclosure to go through, or wait for the market to improve so you can sell your house at less of a loss.

Conclusion

Including such ethereal virtues as patience, trust, and love in a book about real estate is not an accident. Decisions with your finances must never overlook the big questions and the deeper emotions. Ignoring the emotional elements that guide your choices means forgetting a vital side of the real estate equation. Human beings are emotional creatures. When dealing with finances as personal as where you live, it is important not to forget what drives us to create a home in the first place.

Next, another mortgage broker presents additional input and advice on PMI, credit scores, reverse mortgages, LTV ratios, and HARP, among other things. In Chapter 10, Brett Stimpson moves us back from emotions to economics as he breaks down many of the complex forces that drive the real estate market behind the scenes.

Advice from a Mortgage Broker

Brett Stimpson

Smart advice about underwater mortgages can be found in a lot of places because the real estate market crashed all across the country.

Looking at the problem through the eyes of those in other regions of the country improves your insight into your personal living situation. More than 2,000 miles away from the East Coast sprawl, where many of the previous experts found in this book live and work, is the lovely town of Midvale, Utah. Even in this idyllic town near Salt Lake City, hundreds of foreclosures are currently on the market. Sadly, underwater mortgages can be found nearly everywhere.

Brett Stimpson is a loan officer at Innovative Mortgage Alliance in Midvale, Utah. He is a professional mortgage broker who is also one of the owners of Innovative Mortgage Alliance. Stimpson is a hands-on expert in mortgages. He has seen the rise and fall of the U.S. real estate industry from a Western vantage point. If there is a refinancing program for you, Stimpson will help you find it.

"Really, what I do for a living," Stimpson explained, "I do mortgages. So, I help people on the residential side, whether it's a refinance or a purchase."[1]

---

[1] All quotes from Stimpson were collected during a personal interview.

A good mortgage broker like Stimpson can be a great source of information and direction for people with underwater mortgages. The people Stimpson helps usually start by calling him or contacting him through e-mail and explaining their scenario to him.

"They are usually aware that they are under water, and they usually just want to know what their options are," he said. "I usually just tell them, 'We are a third-party originator. We don't have your loans. So what we have access to is really just what the government has provided for people like you to deal with your home.'"

Benefits of Refinancing Today

A top option for many underwater homeowners is a mortgage loan refinance. One of the reasons is that interest rates are at an all-time low. For example, a Fannie Mae or a Freddie Mac 30-year fixed loan can be found for an interest rate as low as 3.3 percent. To get a new loan, a homeowner will need to go through a third party, whether it is their current lender, another bank, or a mortgage broker. "Some licensed loan officer has to do their loan," Stimpson explained. For example, although Fannie Mae is at the center of the mortgage market, the organization does not offer loans directly. According to Fannie Mae's web site, "We ensure that mortgage lenders have funds they need to create loans in all economic cycles—good and bad."[2]

If you qualify, refinancing is a great way to lower your monthly mortgage payments and dramatically improve your financial situation. Although it will not change your loan-to-value (LTV) ratio, it will make it easier to get out from an underwater home because the interest rate will be reduced.

■ **Tip**   *Go for it.* If refinancing is a possible option for you, try it. You will never know if you qualify unless you pursue it. And most of the ways to find out if you qualify are free. As mortgage broker Brett Stimpson said, "There is no harm in trying."

HARP: For Fannie Mae- and Freddie Mac-Owned Loans

Stimpson works with people with underwater mortgages every single day, although he added that this work makes up only about three percent of his

---

[2] www.fanniemae.com/portal/index.html (Retrieved July 27, 2012).

business. He said this percentage is so low because "there are not that many programs available for people who are under water on their mortgage to be able to refinance or do something like that. There are some programs out there, because of the government's involvement, but they are few and far between and they don't always work."

Although some programs exist, such as the HARP 2.0[3] program—available until January 1, 2014—for the people whose home mortgages are owned by Fannie Mae and Freddie Mac, there aren't many. "It's almost a rare scenario where it is effective, where it does work. We are getting some of them done, but it's unfortunately not nearly as many as we would like to do," he explained.

For most mortgage brokers to be able to help underwater homeowners refinance their loan, they need to meet the following HARP criteria to qualify:

- Their loan needs to be owned through Fannie Mae or Freddie Mac.
- Their loan needs to be originated prior to June 1, 2009.

"There are other criteria, but those are really the two main ones," he added. "So, what I would do for a client is first just look up and see who owns their mortgage. Fannie Mae has their web site. I can go to Fannie Mae's site and plug in the person's address and they'll say yes or no, Fannie Mae does own or doesn't own the loan. I usually go there first because Fannie Mae owns more than Freddie Mac. If that doesn't work, I go to Freddie Mac's site and do the same thing."

- Here is Fannie Mae's site: www.fanniemae.com/loanlookup/
- Here is Freddie Mac's site: www.freddiemac.com/corporate/

Stimpson said that he finds Freddie Mac's program more difficult to work through than Fannie Mae: "It just has more stringent criteria than Fannie Mae does."

When Was the Loan Originated?

If Stimpson finds that either Freddie Mac or Fannie Mae owns the underwater homeowner's loan, he then investigates whether the loan was issued before or after June 1, 2009. Next, he finds out how much the homeowners owe.

---

[3] The Home Affordable Refinance Program (HARP) is a government program that is designed to help people with underwater loans backed by Fannie Mae and Freddie Mac to refinance their mortgages.

Then he asks how much they think their home is worth. "That's a factor as well," he added. "It affects loan-to-value."

To get ahead of the game, you can learn all of these criteria before you see a mortgage broker. Being proactive will not only save you time in the long run, but it will also help you ensure that you and your mortgage broker are on the same page. If your information does not match, find out why.

■ **Tip**   *Be aware.* Look at the facts and determine whether you owe more on your home than it is worth in today's market. Many people's homes are only slightly under water and simply have to wait a few years for the market to rise back up to bring enough value to their home to give them some equity. Many other people find that they are more than 20 percent under water; that's when it is time to take action by considering the options available to those mortgage holders.

An easy way to get a rough estimate on the value of your home is to look on zillow.com and find your house on the map. You can look at the estimated prices on your home and the homes around you.

LTV Ratio

Your LTV ratio is another important number to have on hand when dealing with lenders and mortgage brokers. It's a ratio that many lenders use to decide whether you qualify for a new mortgage or not.

How can you find your LTV? Go online. The following directs you to an online LTV calculator that can help you determine how much your loan is under water: www.bankrate.com/calculators/mortgages/ltv-loan-to-value-ratio-calculator. aspx

If you have a second mortgage or other lien on your property, you can calculate your cumulative loan-to-value (CLTV) on the calculator at bankrate. com as well.

Consider a home appraised for $160,000 with an outstanding loan of $200,000: That home has an LTV of 125 percent. This home is bordering on being severely under water.

■ **Tip**   *Get appraised.* How do you find out how much your home is worth? It's easy. Ask a real estate agent for an informal appraisal. If you want to get a more formal number, pay a specialist. Your real estate agent probably knows a good appraiser. Just ask.

LTVs and HARP 2.0

When HARP started, there was a cap of 125 percent LTV, which means anyone who had an LTV that was higher than 125 percent was ineligible for the program. In March 2012, that cap was removed from the program. HARP 2.0 can now help people who are severely under water on their mortgage.

Homeowners with severely underwater mortgages are still not getting relief from HARP 2.0. For example, according to the *San Francisco Chronicle* in June 2012, of the 180,185 loans that were refinanced under HARP 2.0 in the first quarter of 2012, which was nearly twice those done in the previous quarter, "The vast majority of Harp refis in the first quarter were loans with LTV ratios in the 80 to 105 percent range."[4]

According to the *Chronicle*, "Only 20 percent [of Harp refis] had LTVs between 105 and 125 percent and only 2 percent had LTVs greater than 125 percent." In other words, although the program has expanded to include mortgages that are more deeply under water than before, the program has not included homeowners who really need it.

▨ **Tip**   *Know your LTV.* Go to www.bankrate.com/calculators/mortgages/ltv-loan-to-value-ratio-calculator.aspx. Knowing your LTV will help you be better prepared for the answers when talking to your lender to find out whether you qualify for refinancing.

The HARP Process

Stimpson said the first thing he does is ensure homeowners meet all of the criteria for refinancing their home to get better terms on their loan, such as a lower interest rate or a lower monthly mortgage payment. They may also want to get out from under an adjustable-rate mortgage and switch to a fixed-rate mortgage.

So a mortgage broker will first find out if you qualify then quote currently available interest rates, closing costs, and the terms of the new mortgage. Stimpson added, "If they [the homeowners] agree to it and they like it, then we start all of the paperwork and get it into the lender. Then the lender does their part." Once your mortgage broker has determined that your refinanced loan is going to work, then the rest of the process simply involves completing the loan and closing the deal.

---

[4] www.sfgate.com/business/article/Harp-2-starts-to-help-the-severely-underwater-3626181.php (Retrieved July 26, 2012).

"Another thing that is interesting is that Fannie Mae and Freddie Mac have their own guidelines," Stimpson explained. "They have their own criteria, but lenders that we work with oftentimes have guidelines that are more stringent" than what Fannie or Freddie will give. So Fannie Mae may have an unlimited LTV—in other words, it doesn't matter how under water your home is. "But then I may have a lender who will say, 'Well, that might be the case, but if you want to do the loan through us, we're only going to allow 105 percent loan-to-value.'" In other words, you can be slightly under water, but not completely.

Fannie Mae and Freddie Mac sometimes offer a homeowner who is seeking to refinance a mortgage an "appraisal waiver." This is part of the HARP 2.0's revamped guidelines. When homeowners get an appraisal waiver, they no longer need an expensive and time-consuming appraisal before getting the loan modification.

When homeowners or brokers go online and enter their mortgage information into the system, they can find out whether or not Fannie Mae or Freddie Mac will do an appraisal waiver. If they get one, Fannie Mae or Freddie Mac will take the word of homeowners when they say how much the house is worth.

"Once we find out if there is an appraisal waiver or not, we are actually pretty far into the process at that point," Stimpson explained. The next steps are simply standard operating procedure.

> We'll gather all of the paperwork. We've submitted the loan to the lender who is going to underwrite it. And then, really, at that point it's just a matter of the normal due diligence, normal underwriting: checking income, assets, making sure that the property itself is adequate collateral—things like that. There is no issue with title. We'll go through the whole underwriting process, and when it's done we can close.

Refinancing Options from Fannie Mae

Fannie Mae currently provides two Refi Plus options to eligible borrowers:

- **Refi Plus** for manual underwriting. Refi Plus simplifies the process of refinancing loans that are already in a lender's servicing portfolio. This product has no limits on maximum LTV and provides mortgage insurance flexibilities for LTVs over 80 percent.

- **DU Refi Plus™** for loans underwritten through Desktop Underwriter (DU), an automated underwriting system that helps lenders make credit decisions on loans. DU Refi Plus makes it easier for lenders to originate and underwrite Fannie

Mae loans in DU with no maximum limits on LTV and provides mortgage insurance flexibilities for LTVs over 80 percent. Eligible loans identified in DU receive more flexible underwriting, such as expanded eligibility criteria and fewer documentation requirements.

Refinancing Options from Freddie Mac

The Freddie Mac Relief Refinance Mortgage program basically offers two options that can help you if you are making timely mortgage payments but have been unable to refinance due to declining property values in your area.

Both the Same Servicer and Open Access options under Freddie Mac's Relief Refinance Mortgage program allow unlimited LTV ratios for fixed-rate mortgages and relief from standard mortgage insurance requirements to provide qualified borrowers with more refinancing opportunities.

Part of Freddie Mac's Relief Refinance Mortgage program, which includes mortgages with LTV ratios greater than 80 percent, falls under HARP:

- **Relief Refinance Mortgage—Same Servicer.** This option offers simplified appraisal and borrower eligibility requirements. The mortgage loan being refinanced must be serviced by the seller, or an affiliate of the seller, and the Relief Refinance Mortgages must be originated by the seller/ servicer or an affiliate of the seller.

- **Relief Refinance Mortgage—Open Access.** This option requires full underwriting, offers simplified appraisal requirements, and the mortgage being refinanced may be originated and serviced by any Freddie Mac-approved seller/ servicer.

These refinancing options offer borrowers two more ways to refinance their mortgages through HARP.

How Lender Rules Trump Fannie Mae and Freddie Mac Guidelines

At the moment, thanks to HARP 2.0, Fannie Mae's guidelines state that "Our solutions provide mortgage refinances with no limits on LTV, and mortgage insurance flexibilities." On the other hand, most lenders have strict LTV restrictions that disqualify borrowers from refinancing. This adds another layer of security for the lender. Stimpson said this means the lender may say,

"Fannie Mae doesn't care how far under water you are, but we do. And you can only be under water by 105 percent."

How far under water can a home be before it no longer qualifies for refinancing under HARP? That answer really depends on the lender's criteria. While talking to a lender's representative, ask them the cutoff LTV the lender uses to disqualify a homeowner from refinancing. If you fall within the range of the lender, then you have jumped one hurdle. If your LTV is too high, then you may be disqualified from the running for refinancing.

One source of hope for a homeowner is the appraisal waiver. Stimpson said, "Sometimes we can get an appraisal waiver, so we won't need any appraisal to verify [home value], but in other cases we would. . . . The appraisal needs to be paid for. And [then] we need to find out what the home is actually worth to determine if it qualifies."

■ **Tip** *Wait before getting an appraisal.* Because your mortgage broker may be able to get you an appraisal waiver, do not pay for an appraisal before you are told you need one. This can save you hundreds of dollars. But if an appraisal is required before you can qualify for refinancing, then get one. There is no need to jump the gun on this. Wait until you are required to spend the money before you needlessly waste your cash.

However, in most cases appraisals are lender specific, Stimpson pointed out. "In other words, each lender wants to get their own appraisal." Lenders have their own criteria they need fulfilled, so even if you pay for your own appraisal, you may need to have your home reappraised to meet the requirements of a particular lender before it will approve your new refinanced loan.

Hiccups Along the Way

What problems can slow the process? Stimpson says, "Sometimes Fannie Mae says, 'No, we don't want to do it because they have mortgage insurance, and who they have mortgage insurance through is somebody that we don't work with anymore,' or just some variable. Small stuff like that derails the whole process. That does happen more often than we would like."

Who Owns Your Loan?

One hiccup can be figuring out who owns your loan. With loans changing hands so frequently these days, homeowners have gotten used to sending their monthly mortgage payments to several different companies over the years. Even if this is the case, it is still possible that Fannie Mae and Freddie Mac still own your mortgage. Many mortgage loans that are serviced by other companies are owned by Fannie Mae or Freddie Mac.

Stimpson explained.

> *For example, a credit union, let's say America First Credit Union, which is a pretty popular one here in Utah, they may service [your] loan, but Fannie Mae really owns it. A lot of times when I speak to people, I say, "We need to find out if Fannie Mae or Freddie Mac owns your loan." They say, "Oh no, they don't, because I make my payments to America First Credit Union." I say, "Well, that may be the case, that just means they service it, but they may not actually own it." So, it's hard to know who it is until you ask. You can either go to their web sites, or you can call your lender directly and say, "Who owns my loan? Do you own it? If you don't, then tell me who it is." That's the only way you can find out.*

■ **Tip** *Find out who owns your mortgage.* This small amount of information will allow you to make contact with your lender. Go online, find that lender's Web phone number, and talk to a real person. This contact will be crucial for determining your options. Your lender will tell you what is required to choose any of the options that are available. Take notes!

If you have trouble making this kind of contact, an attorney can serve as an intermediary. However, a cheaper route may be to find a mortgage counselor or even a mortgage broker who may do some of your initial legwork for free. A real estate agent may also offer you some free advice about the kinds of things you should ask your lender when discussing your options for getting out from an underwater mortgage. Making that initial contact with your lender is a solid step in the right direction. Mortgage broker Brett Stimpson said, "One thing I would do personally is I would always go directly to the lender who I'm making my payments to and find out what they could do. At the same time, for comparison purposes, I would talk to a third-party loan officer, like myself, just to see what they could do."

Stated Income Loans Disqualify Homeowners

Brett Stimpson said he personally went through a similar procedure:

> *For example, when I bought a house several years ago, I did a "stated income" loan [see Chapter 6], just because it was an easier loan to do, less paperwork. That was one criteria that prevents me from being able to refinance and get a better interest rate even if I'm upside down.*

Stated income loans were popular from 2002 to 2007. These loans simply required prospective homeowners with good credit scores to "state" how much they earned to the mortgage company before getting a loan. Although these types of loans helped home buyers to speed up the process when they were getting the loan, it worked against them when they would attempt to get refinancing from their lenders. Stimpson said, "You didn't have to verify your income. You qualified just basically off of credit, but Fannie Mae, one of their little guidelines is, 'If you did a stated income loan, ... we won't do it, because we just don't do refinances on stated income loans.'"

Private Mortgage Insurance (PMI)

Another problem some homeowners seeking to refinance run into is mortgage insurance. If you are still paying PMI on your mortgage, this could disqualify you.

Mortgage insurance is something that homeowners must purchase if they put down less than 20 percent of the cost of the house.

Fannie Mae and Freddie Mac once stayed away from refinancing loans to homeowners who were still paying for PMI. Today, thanks to HARP 2.0, many banks—including Wells Fargo, Chase, and Bank of America—offer HARP loans to homeowners with PMI.

In conclusion, Stimpson said, "Sometimes there are things that will get us off track, and there is nothing we can do about it. The bottom line, if Fannie Mae won't guarantee it, or the lender doesn't want to either, then the person just doesn't get a loan."

Modification: Start with Your Lender

A mortgage broker can usually help with a refinance of the loan. If you are looking for a loan modification, then you need to see your lender to see what is available. You can also talk to a loan modification specialist at a reputable company or advocacy group. Most mortgage brokers do not normally assist borrowers with loan modifications.

Stimpson explained:

> I'm not involved in any way in loan modifications. There are certainly companies out there who will do it. My understanding is that they have to be licensed as a loan officer, like I am, in order to be able to help people. Some outfits specialize in them.

Despite the rise of many specialized firms, Stimpson said he sees fewer mortgage modification companies today than there were at the beginning of the real estate market meltdown. "A lot of shops popped up, and in a lot of cases they would charge people money up front to help, and in a lot of cases [they] couldn't help. And people were out $2,500 or $3,000 or whatever their fee was."

Stimpson said that his company never got involved in the mortgage loan modification side of the real estate business. "It just wasn't our cup of tea," he explained. "All we do is mortgages."

■ **Tip** *Check credentials.* Make sure whoever you are dealing with, whether it is an attorney, a mortgage broker, or a loan modification specialist, is licensed to work in your state. Also, beware of brokers who ask for advance fees. For example, in California, any broker who asks for advanced fees must have an advance fee agreement that is signed by the California Department of Real Estate (DRE) commissioner. Advance fee agreements must be submitted by DRE-licensed brokers. There are also several rules for the agreement to be legal. Check your state requirements before you sign anyone's agreement or pay any broker an up-front cost. Similarly, before you work with any attorney, he or she should have you sign a well-written fee agreement that clearly spells out the exact terms of the attorney-client relationship.[5]

If you want to do a mortgage modification, then start with your lender. Call the company directly and learn exactly what it takes to get a loan modification. With so much money out there from recent court settlements with the big lenders over the robo-signing fiasco (signing a foreclosure document without reviewing it, like a robot), it is quite possible you may qualify. Even if you tried to get a loan modification in the past, try again. The rules are changing so frequently that it cannot hurt to talk directly to your lender. Plus, mortgages change hands so frequently these days, it is possible that yours is now owned by a lender with different criteria than the last company that owned your mortgage. Give them a call and find out where you stand!

BANK PAYS MILLIONS TO RESOLVE LAWSUIT OVER WRONGFUL FORECLOSURES

Some people defend lenders, claiming that borrowers who fail to pay their bills are simply not following agreements they signed with the banks. However, again and again, recent lawsuit settlements are pointing to problems with a lending system that has not followed the rules.

---

[5] www.dre.ca.gov/files/pdf/adv_fees_essential_elements.pdf (Retrieved July 26, 2012).

For example, on July 26, 2012, Capital One N.A. and Capital One Bank (USA) N.A. (together Capital One), agreed to pay approximately $12 million to resolve a lawsuit by the Department of Justice alleging the companies violated the Servicemembers Civil Relief Act (SCRA). The settlement covers a range of conduct that violated the protections guaranteed by the SCRA, including wrongful foreclosures; improper repossessions of motor vehicles; wrongful court judgments; improper denials of the six percent interest rate the SCRA guarantees to servicemembers on some credit card and car loans; and insufficient 6 percent benefits granted on credit cards, car loans, and other types of accounts. The proposed consent order, which was filed simultaneously with the complaint, is one of the most comprehensive SCRA settlements ever obtained by a government agency or any private party under the SCRA.

Commenting on the settlement, Attorney General Eric Holder said:

Today's action makes clear that the Justice Department will fight for our servicemembers, and use every available tool, resource and authority to hold accountable those who engage in discriminatory practices targeting those who serve. Every day, our brave men and women in uniform make tremendous sacrifices to protect the American people from a range of global threats—and my colleagues and I are determined to ensure that they receive our strongest support here at home.

The agreement requires Capital One to pay approximately $7 million in damages to servicemembers for SCRA violations, including at least $125,000 in compensation plus compensation for any lost equity (with interest) to each servicemember whose home was unlawfully foreclosed upon, and at least $10,000 in compensation plus compensation for any lost equity (with interest) to each servicemember whose motor vehicle was unlawfully repossessed.

In addition, the agreement requires Capital One to provide a $5 million fund to compensate servicemembers who did not receive the appropriate amount of SCRA benefits on their credit card accounts, motor vehicle finance loans, and consumer loans. Any portion of the $5 million that remains after payments to servicemembers are made will be donated by Capital One to one or more charitable organizations that assist servicemembers.

Full Cooperation

Servicemembers will be identified and compensated, with no action required on their part, on accounts dating back to July 15, 2006. As a result of the decree, Capital One has agreed to treat a servicemember's request for a 6 percent rate relief in one area of its lending, such as credit cards, as a request for a 6 percent rate relief for any other loan the servicemember may have with Capital One or its affiliates. This is the first time the Justice Department has obtained this type of enterprise-wide rate reduction relief from a lender under the SCRA. The settlement also requires Capital One to adopt policies and practices to prevent violations of the SCRA in the future.[6]

---

[6] www.justice.gov/opa/pr/2012/July/12-ag-933.html (Retrieved July 27, 2012).

MAKE YOUR PAYMENTS

While jumping through all of the hoops lenders set up for borrowers to qualify for a refinanced loan, never forget to make your monthly mortgage payments.

Once you stop making those payments, you become ineligible for most refinancing programs. The refinancing process (it should only take a few weeks) is usually much faster than the loan modification process, which could take several months. However, remember that every lender is different.

How Long Is It Going to Take?

"How long will this process take?" is a great question to ask your lender or your loan officer once you get started on refinancing your loan.

How can you speed up the process? According to Brett Stimpson, these are the requirements your loan officer needs to underwrite your refinanced loan:

- **Be a good credit risk.** Make sure all of your payments are on time. Bring down all of your credit card balances and other debts as low as possible. These will give you the credit score you need to get your new loan.

- **Be employed.** Lenders want to see a steady income. Continuous employment for the last 2 years looks very good to lenders.

- **Keep your pay stubs.** Having a few of these on hand will prove how much you earn.

- **Print out your tax returns.** Lenders typically want to see 2 years' worth of these.

- **Save your W2s.** You should have available 2 years of these as well.

- **Collect your bank statements.** At least 2 months' worth shows your lender how you spend and save.

Credit Risk

Having a good credit score is essential if you are going to refinance. To determine whether you are a good credit risk, your lender or your mortgage broker will look up your credit score by getting a credit report, which is a detailed summary of your financial accounts. Interest rates are often based on a person's credit score. The most common credit score is a FICO, which comes from the Fair Isaac Corp. Your FICO score will fall somewhere between 300 and 850: If you have a score of 850, you have excellent credit!

According to the Federal Trade Commission

> The Fair Credit Reporting Act (FCRA) requires each of the nationwide consumer reporting companies—Equifax, Experian, and TransUnion—to provide you with a free copy of your credit report, at your request, once every 12 months. The FCRA promotes the accuracy and privacy of information in the files of the nation's consumer reporting companies. The Federal Trade Commission (FTC), the nation's consumer protection agency, enforces the FCRA with respect to consumer reporting companies.

A credit report includes information on where you live, how you pay your bills, and whether you've been sued or arrested or have filed for bankruptcy. Nationwide consumer reporting companies sell the information in your report to creditors, insurers, employers, and other businesses that use it to evaluate your applications for credit, insurance, employment, or renting a home.

If you want to know whether you have good credit or not, you can find out for free. The three nationwide consumer reporting companies have set up a central web site, a toll-free telephone number, and a mailing address through which you can order your free annual report.

To order your free annual report, courtesy of the FTC, you can do one of the following: Visit annualcreditreport.com, call 1-877-322-8228, or complete the Annual Credit Report Request Form and mail it to Annual Credit Report Request Service, P.O. Box 105281, Atlanta, GA, 30348–5281.

The FTC allows you to order your reports from each of the three nationwide consumer reporting companies at the same time or one at a time every 12 months.

To get your free credit reports, you will need to provide your name, address, Social Security number, and date of birth.

■ **Tip** *Know your credit score.* If you have awful credit, refinancing may not be the option for you on an underwater mortgage. If you have great credit, you have already overcome one of the biggest obstacles to refinancing. Making all of your monthly payments on time is vital to keeping your credit score high. Currently, myFICO.com offers a free credit score if you sign up for a trial of their Score Watch service; alternatively, your mortgage broker may do it for you for free if you ask.

What Is a Good Credit Score?

When a mortgage broker is looking up your credit report, he or she is hoping to see a FICO credit score of 740 or above on each file from each of the credit reporting agencies. Stimpson states, however, that

> Typically, most people will know if they have good credit or not. Most people will know if they don't make their payments on time, for either their mortgage or their credit card or student loans or anything else. In most cases, they don't need to necessarily check their credit scores. As long as they know they are making on-time payments and keeping up-to-date on their bills, they're going to be OK.

But be aware that checking your credit score is one of the first things a mortgage broker will do at the beginning of the refinance process to ensure there are no challenges or issues that will prevent you from qualifying for a loan. Some mortgage brokers charge their clients to run their credit scores; others do not. Ask whether this is something for which you will be charged before you start working with a mortgage broker. If so, look around for a broker who waives this fee. Stimpson said he does not charge his clients for this service, which costs him about $20, because he sees it as being a cost of doing business.

■ **Tip** *Shop around.* Whether you are picking an attorney or a mortgage broker, ask for referrals and learn everything you can about the people with whom you are doing business. Ask up front about hidden costs. Try to get the best deal by comparing fees.

Conclusion

Although there are many options available for underwater homeowners, the best choice, when it can be attained, is a refinanced mortgage with a lower monthly payment and better terms. Mortgage brokers are the best place to start looking for a good deal.

If refinancing is not a consideration because your home is too far under water, then your search for answers should return to the options that are still within reach. In the age of the Internet, finding answers is easier than ever before. After you have talked to several people in your area who know your local real estate landscape, look to the variety of media sources that are now available to learn everything you can from people involved in the real estate business. There is much to be gained from broadcast and cable television outlets as well as radio, newspaper, magazine, and online sources.

One of the voices that often appears among those media outlets is Brendon DeSimone, a real estate expert. In the next chapter, DeSimone offers numerous tips for underwater homeowners about deficiency forgiveness, short-sale mistakes to avoid, and the value of protecting your credit score. He also sheds light into the importance of going to your lender first, avoiding fear, and looking at the big picture when making choices about your underwater home.

Advice from a Real Estate Expert

Brendon DeSimone

Brendon DeSimone is a real estate expert who has bought and sold houses from California to New York for more than 12 years. His ideas on the market have been heard on *Fox News*, *Good Morning America*, and over a dozen HGTV episodes of programs, including *Curb Appeal*, *Bang for Your Buck*, *My House is Worth What?*, and *National Open House*. He is also a regular contributor to the Zillow Blog, where his advice reaches more than 10 million readers each month. [1]

Every week, DeSimone advises many people all around the country who ask him what they should do with their underwater mortgages.

"They say, 'What should we do? We're under water?' I've heard this a lot over the last five years," he recalled:

> You never heard of it before 2007, and you can't stop hearing about it now. It's technically an individual situation. Like I say with every real estate question, it depends on the market, and their particular market, and their house, and their value, and what the story is, and how much they are under water by. If it takes them 10 or 15 years to get out from under water like a property in Phoenix or in Vegas or something, and they're just bleeding money every month and it's not helping them, it's probably best to just find an exit strategy from the property.

---

[1] All quotes from Brendon DeSimone were collected during personal interviews in July 2012.

On the other hand, DeSimone advised, some people should stick with their homes:

> If you plan on staying in the home for another 5 to 7 years and you have roots in the community and have reason to stay, then do what you can and see if you can get the mortgage modified by the lender. Try to reduce your principal balance. Do what you can to stay in the home, and don't focus so much on the mortgage amount and the value as long as your monthly payment is stable and fine.

Talk to Your Lender

The first place a homeowner should start to look for relief from an underwater mortgage is the lender. There are many options available to homeowners as long as they are current with their payments.

DeSimone pointed out that refinancing is the best place to begin: "If you already have a 30-year-fixed, you can get a [refinanced] fixed-rate mortgage. Or go back to the lender and ask them to modify it to maybe an interest only for 5 years loan. Or do a longer-term loan to keep you happy."

If at all possible, staying in the home is the best option for a homeowner, since other options can have devastating impacts on a person's credit score. This is why a short sale or foreclosure should be avoided if at all possible.

■ **Tip** *Protect your credit score.* Refinancing is the best option for a homeowner with an underwater mortgage. Short sales, deeds in lieu of foreclosure, and foreclosures have negative impacts on your credit score, which could prevent you from buying a new house in the near future.

"Be There for the Long Haul"

DeSimone said that he always advises underwater homeowners to avoid short-term thinking: "I tell people, 'Hey, you can't look at the value every single day like you look at the stock market. You have to be there for the long haul.'"

DeSimone said that he's seen people who have really wanted to move because the family grew or they had a great job offer. But many people ended up adjusting their lives and staying put.

> I've seen dozens of cases of people who didn't make the move, didn't upgrade their house, didn't take the job transfer, or either didn't downsize or upgrade

because they couldn't get a sale. I've seen a lot of them who just couldn't sell their house for what it was worth so they just didn't make [a] major life decision [then]. I think what's happened from 2008 is that people's life decisions have changed because of real estate. If you need to make the change, you've got to just do what's best given your particular situation, your particular market.

■ **Tip** *Be realistic about your situation.* Decide what is right for you and everyone who lives in your home. Look at all of your options. How much time do you realistically have? The real estate market is uncertain and moves slowly: If you are waiting to get equity out of an underwater home, your wait could be a long one. If you need to make a move and have the resources to get out from an underwater mortgage, balance the value of the move with the value that you may or may not be able to get out of your home in the near and distant future.

But if you really must move, do it. As DeSimone says, "If you have a crappy house [that's under water] on a busy intersection in front of a bus stop and you have an amazing opportunity to take a great job three states away, you're not going to turn that job down." Do not let the house rule your life:

Either throw cash at it and get out of it or do something. I've had sellers write checks for $100,000 at the closing just to cover the amount they owed because they had to move. They had two kids and had a third and couldn't stay in this one-bedroom-plus condo anymore. It really does depend on your particular situation.

■ **Tip** *Look beyond your investment in your house.* If you are sadly staring at the real estate market in your area, plotting the value of your house as it goes up and down every day, you will drive yourself crazy. Either decide that you are going to stay on for the long haul, when prices return and you rise out from under water slowly with the long-term market, or decide to get out. Sitting in the middle between these two decisions, forgetting about the intrinsic value of a home in which you love to live, will keep you from enjoying all of the other wonderful things in your life.

In the long run, a house is more than an investment. It's a lifestyle, DeSimone said:

That's what a home is. When I work with buyers and sellers from the day they start, [I ask,] "What kind of home do you want? What part of town do you want to live in?" Or sellers, "When do you want to sell?" It's all about your life, your lifestyle. "What are you going to buy? When do you want to sell? Have you considered how are you going to get out of your situation, or what your situation is?" It's not just a financial thing. I do realize of course [that finances are] important. There is a lot of money in it, yes, but also, a house is your home. A condo is your home. It's where you have roots set, it's where you have your memories, and you have to consider all that stuff.

DeSimone sees a real change in the market that is driving decisions to buy or sell. He tells people, "You know what? You can no longer just sit back and expect the market to pick up 5, 7, or 10 percent every year," so don't look at your house like a piggybank or a savings account: Look at it like the long-term investment it is. "If you are not in it for a minimum of 5 years, or more like 10 to 20 years, you shouldn't be buying real estate maybe."

■ **Tip:** *Think long term!* These days, you probably shouldn't buy a house unless you're planning to stay in it for at least 5 years and maybe even 10 or more.

DeSimone concluded, "If your house is under water by 10 percent or so, and you're already committed to the area, hang tight. Don't keep thinking about your house value. Stay in the home. Don't uproot your family and mess with your kids' schools and all that kind of stuff just to get out of your situation."

Examine Your Budget

If you are dedicated to the area where you live, and your house is less than 10 percent under water, perhaps you should be looking at other parts of your budget that you can cut to improve your lifestyle or even pay off more of the principal on your mortgage to help bail out your home. These may be easier ways to improve your situation than fretting about your mortgage or making a drastic move to end your experience with an underwater home.

"[As] another way to get value out of your home—it's not just equity— maybe you can work out of your house, have it be a home office. Then you're not going to spend money on rent for your small business. Or you get value out of your home by having kids there and raising your family."

Some benefits of being in a home, even if it is under water, cannot be measured by monetary value. DeSimone points out that there are many things of great value offered by staying in your home while you wait for its value to naturally rise as the real estate market grows. "You'll be able to watch your kids [on each] birthday. . . . Your home is about other things than just money," he explained.

How Long Until the Recovery?

How long will homeowners have to wait before the real estate market starts to grow again? Although he stated that he is not an economist, DeSimone said he has been seeing some bright signs of hope in the market lately.

> I don't look at the numbers. I look at the day-to-day stuff that I see, and all around the country, we're starting to see buyers. You're seeing buyers coming out. Open houses are busier. We're seeing some multiple offers in some situations. We're starting to see things pick up and make a turn.

One of the reasons why the real estate market is looking up is an influx of new buyers hoping to take advantage of the "buyer's market" and the low interest rates discussed daily by experts in the media. Great prices are bringing in purchasers who have sat on the sidelines waiting for prices to reach their lowest points.

DeSimone explained:

> I think we're seeing buyers stepping out for the first time in many, many years. They're putting their toes in the water and saying, "Gosh, you know what, if prices come down I'll buy." And they're seeing houses for sale that seem reasonable. They also realize that interest rates are so low right now, and they are saying, "This might be a good time."

Record changes in interest rates are fueling new speculation into the real estate market. For example, on October 4, 2012, *USA Today* announced the average rates on fixed mortgages fell to new record lows for the second straight week. Freddie Mac reported that the rate on the 30-year loan dropped to 3.36 percent, which was down from 3.4 percent the previous week, "which was the lowest since long-term mortgages began in the 1950s."[2]

Changing Attitudes

DeSimone said he has noticed a similar change in his clients' attitudes.

> Maybe all the fear and the doom and gloom of the last 10 years—maybe we're past that. And even though they have lots of friends and colleagues who got beat up or lost their homes or lost a lot of money or bought homes and are under water, they're realizing that there is potential. They can actually buy a home, and it would be a good solid investment. The rates are low and maybe they can be protected. They can get a 30-year-fixed mortgage and they don't

---

[2] www.usatoday.com/story/money/personalfinance/2012/10/04/30-year-mortgage-rate/1612845/ (Retrieved October 7, 2012).

have to worry like their friends did 3 or 5 years ago who had 5-year interest-only loans.

He pointed out that the real estate market of today is much different than it was 5 or 6 years ago. "They got [these loans] in 2005 and they got adjusted; and the rates were higher and the payments doubled or tripled. That's not going to happen anymore because the 30-year rates are just really good right now."

RENTING IS A GREAT SHORT-TERM OPTION

Many people who are under water are so worried about keeping their good credit that they decide to continue to pay on a house that is more than 20 percent under water to avoid taking the hit to their credit that comes with a short sale or a foreclosure. However, these people forget that their credit score will rebound in only a few years. Those who see a few years of transition ahead of them may not need a great credit score with which to buy a new house for several years, so that drop in their credit score is not as devastating as it might seem. If you are in transition, buying your next house right away might not be the best option.

People who are not planning to stick around a place for more than a couple of years may want to wait before buying a new home. Renting might be the best option. Many foreclosed houses have been bought and turned into rental units; thus, renters have more options than ever about where they can live.

New Market Rising

As the market changes, those who are ready to dip their toes back into the pool should not be deterred by their fear of the market from 5 or 6 years ago. Many things have been improved: Banks face tighter regulations, mortgage scams have been shut down. Consumers are more educated about the risks of subprime mortgages than ever before.

Homeowners who are rising up from their underwater mortgages have much to gain from keeping their credit scores high. Those who can keep their payments up and hold on to their homes long enough to watch them flip back over into positive equity territory have many benefits awaiting them in a real estate market that is far better than the one that burned them just a few years ago.

■ **Tip** *Be determined!* Your determination will help you get through the many barriers that have been erected in the system to stand between you and your goal of dry land. Do not see yourself as an underwater mortgage holder who is taking on more water; look at yourself as a solvent homeowner who is working his or her way out from a temporary setback. If you are told that you need to send all of your paperwork to the bank again because one page did not make it through the fax machine, be resolute. Gather your paperwork again and send it. These minor setbacks are just part of the process. It is a process that tests your determination. Stand strong and push ahead. The water only rises when you stop bailing.

The Keys to a Successful Short Sale

Short selling your home requires getting the best people on your side to help you get the most money, although you will not be getting everything that you owe for the house. Some people believe hiring an attorney is the way to go. Others say that it is cheaper to simply hire a good real estate agent who knows what he or she is doing. Now that many real estate agents have been performing short sales for several years since the crash of the real estate market, there should be a nice pool of qualified people from whom to choose at any of your local real estate agencies.

Real estate expert Brendon DeSimone explained:

> *If you are doing a short sale, you need to hire an agent to do it, a short sale professional. Don't hire somebody who has never done a short sale before because really, the key of doing a short sale is having that agent . . . negotiating with the bank. And the agent acts on behalf of the seller. You don't really need an attorney. But the last thing you need is some agent who . . . doesn't know how to deal with the right buyers or take the right offer, and then they go off to the bank and they don't know how to deal with the bank.*

Tip   *Hire a professional.* Don't go it alone. Hire somebody with a vast store of experience from which to draw when selling your home. Shop around. Because you don't have to pay a real estate agent until you sell your home, when the commission comes out of closing costs, you can look around for the best person. Ask several real estate agents how many short sales they have done. Get the number of a few clients you can call to ask them about their experiences with the agents. If you feel more comfortable getting an attorney's advice, and you don't mind paying for this person's opinion ahead of time, shop around for a good attorney as well. Then make a choice. Find somebody with whom you get along well, a person you trust to find you the best deal, because short sales generally take many months to complete. Due diligence will help you know you made the best decision.

Do I Need a Short Sale Facilitator?

Do you need to hire another third party? DeSimone said no.

> There are all kinds of companies that have come up in the last couple of years.
> I've seen them: "You can hire us as a short sale facilitator," They'll say. "The
> agent will sell in the market, but we'll help do the negotiations for you." I don't
> think you need that. A lot of times the banks won't pay for it, because don't
> forget, the bank's paying for the real estate agent's commission. I don't think
> you need that [short sale facilitator], but they're a new business that [has]
> boom[ed] for the last couple of years in places like Las Vegas and Phoenix. I
> don't think you need it if you have an agent who knows what the hell they're
> doing.

On its web site, Wells Fargo points its customers to the federal government's
Home Affordable Foreclosure Alternatives (HAFA) program. Depending on
your situation, you may be eligible for a short sale through this or another
federal program.

Your Credit Score

Keep in mind that doing a short sale has repercussions on your credit score.
However, because a short sale usually takes less time to wrap up than a
foreclosure, the delinquency reported by the bank is usually shorter than it
would be with a foreclosure. This means your credit score will likely improve
faster than it would if your house goes to foreclosure. Your bank is compelled
to continue to report the status of your account to the major credit reporting
agencies throughout the process. If the short sale is completed on your
property, the bank will report that your loan was "paid in full for less than the
full balance."[3]

In other words, a short sale does have a detrimental effect on your credit
score, although this affect may only last for a few years. DeSimone explained:

> If you've got good credit, and [especially if] you've got great credit in the high
> 700s, your credit score is going to be hit, . . . and it's not so much the short
> sale that nails it but your first missed payment. . . . Most banks will require you
> to miss at least one payment or two prior to approving your short sale. It
> sounds so backwards, but it's what they do. They just say, "We're not going to
> approve your short sale until you are behind. Call us back when you are two
> payments behind." Of course the short sale does [affect your credit], but . . .
> [it] doesn't show up on your credit report until three or four months after the

---

[3] http://homeloanhelp.bankofamerica.com/en/short-sale-process.html (Retrieved July 29,
2012).

sale, and by then you've already had a couple of missed payments. . . . I've seen people['s credit scores] go from 750 to 575 with one missed payment. If you have [bad] credit to begin with and you're in the low 600s, your credit's going down, but not so much, because the bureaus are sort of already seeing you as a credit risk. . . . For people who have really good credit, it will have the biggest affect. [See sidebar following.]

▓ **Tip** *Get legal advice!* Stopping payments on your home is a legal decision. When you stop making payments on your mortgage, you are breaking your signed agreement with your lender. This decision may come with legal ramifications, and could lead to your lender starting a foreclosure process on your home. Do not settle for advice from a real estate agent or anyone without a license to practice law before you stop making payments on your mortgage. Even if your lender says that you must do this before a short sale can be approved, ask an attorney if this is the right thing to do. Real estate agents are not authorized to give you legal advice.

HOW DOES A SHORT SALE OR FORECLOSURE AFFECT YOUR CREDIT?

Fair Isaac, the company that developed FICO scores, recently offered some estimates of point-score declines after short sales, deed in lieu of foreclosures, and foreclosures.

Here are some averages of the impacts these will have on your credit:

- **30 days late:** 40–110 points

- **90 days late:** 70–135 points

- **Foreclosure, short sale, or deed in lieu:** 85–160

- **Bankruptcy:** 130–240

According to a spokesperson for Experian, one of the country's main credit bureaus, credit bureaus generally slash scores equally for short sales, deed in lieu of foreclosures, and foreclosures. They are all considered serious delinquencies to credit bureaus.

It will usually take people about 7 years to bring up their credit to predistressed sale levels, but some people have been known to bring their credit up in only 2 or 3 years. It really depends on your individual record of spending, borrowing, and paying back your debts.[4]

---

[4] http://money.cnn.com/2010/04/22/real_estate/foreclosure_credit_score/ (Retrieved July 29, 2012).

To Foreclose or Not to Foreclose

Brendon DeSimone said he believes most people who are under water should not resort to the foreclosure option if possible. They should try in every way to pursue any one of the other options. As he explained:

> *You shouldn't do a foreclosure. . . . For all of the people who get foreclosed on, it's one of two things: They are just very irresponsible and don't even want to take the time to deal with the bank, [or] they don't realize [what they are doing], . . . and they don't go and figure out those other options. A bank does not want to foreclose. A bank does not want to be in the business of owning real estate. They will work with you to do short sales. . . . The other reason they get foreclosed is they tried to do a short sale and it didn't happen. They couldn't sell it, couldn't sell it, couldn't sell it, and the bank finally took the property back.*

Tip *Make foreclosure a last resort.* Try all of your other options (especially a short sale) first before considering a foreclosure.

DeSimone reiterated: "Foreclosure should only happen if you've exhausted all other efforts: You can't make your payments, and you've tried to work with the bank, you tried to do a loan modification, you tried to do a short sale. There is no reason why a short sale should not work. If you are not getting offers on your property, lower your price!"

He continued:

> *What I have seen a lot, and it's probably getting a little better nowadays because banks do not want to foreclose, is that you have the short sale departments, the loss mitigation at "Bank A," and then . . . you have a foreclosure department. They are not connected. They are not talking to one another. So you have—I've seen this—a seller who has it on the market as a short sale, they've missed their two payments. [Then] they miss their third payment.*

For example, the foreclosure department starts the process. Meanwhile, the homeowner gets an offer. The homeowner is moving through the short sale process, but the bank is behind in processing them. So, said DeSimone, the "department just has like 15,000 short sales, and it takes them a long time to approve. And your short sale is way behind. Meanwhile the foreclosure department is getting ready to foreclose on you. I've seen deals where sellers had offers ratified and were moving forward on the short sale process, and the bank still foreclosed."

He added that this practice is not as common as it once was in the early days after the real estate bubble burst, but it is still possible. "Now, you call the foreclosure department and say, 'Look, we have offers on this property and we're just going through the process.' I've seen it where people were trying the best they could, but the bank was saying, 'Look, we have to foreclose. You haven't made your payment in two months. We have to start the process.' It's actually getting a bit better. It's not as bad as it was 3 years ago."

Tip *Stay in contact with your lender.* If you are in the middle of a short sale, talk to somebody at the bank regularly. Make sure that you are not going to be surprised by a foreclosure.

Deficiency Forgiveness

How much money in deficiencies are banks forgiving these days? DeSimone explained that the amount can be very high. "They're getting a write-off from the government. It's a loss for them, so they want to push these through. You see it a lot. On my own, I have never seen a short sale denied." Although the bank will often return a short sale petition with some changes, or some additional conditions that need to be met by the seller, fulfilling these will usually lead to a short sale being approved by the lender.

DeSimone said, "In my mind, they do not want to foreclose. They don't want to be in the business of owning real estate." He pointed out that banks are anxious to avoid having to pay property taxes on the homes on which they foreclose. "They have to hire a real estate agent. They have to keep the lawn mowed. With an HOA [homeowners association] or a condo, they have to pay maintenance, homeowner's dues. They have to worry about people breaking in. They have to hire an agent to hold open houses. It costs them a lot of money, and they don't want to do that." At the same time, he added, "if somebody is not making their payments, they have nothing to do but take the property back. But it's a last choice. I think they wish a lot more people would come to them first . . . and say, 'Let's make a deal. Let's do a short sale.'"

Tip *Be proactive.* Call your lender immediately when you feel your home may be under water. Even if you have had a hard time dealing with your lender in the past, the situation at many banks is improving, and you may find that the bank is better prepared to help you sell your house and get you out from being under water.

People often slip into an underwater situation and pursue a short sale because of two primary reasons: You either can't afford the payment because the rate's gone up, or you need to sell because otherwise you have to make a life change. As DeSimone said, "And you have to be proactive. Call the bank from the get-go."

Relocation Short Sales

If your mortgage is under water and you find out that you have been transferred in your job and need to relocate, your list of options has suddenly become very short: You can either choose to short sale your home, rent it out from far away (which brings with it many additional headaches and responsibilities), or let it fall into foreclosure. Because you are a responsible homeowner who is going to do the right thing, and you do not want to be a landlord who lives in another city (and you don't want to pay a rental manager to oversee your property in your absence), you should try your hardest to short sale your house.

DeSimone agreed: "Look, if you have to take a job in Miami and you live in some other city, a loan modification is not going to help you. You need to do a short sale. You have no other choice. You need to sell the property."

"It's hard because you're moving and you have a new job and you can't afford to pay rent in a new city and keep paying your mortgage. Be proactive. There is no reason anybody should get foreclosed on."

BANK OF AMERICA OFFERS RELOCATION ASSISTANCE AFTER SHORT SALES

It seems nearly every day a new program pops up for helping homeowners avoid foreclosure. For example, in May 2012, Bank of America (BofA) announced a new nationwide program that offers people who are behind on their mortgage payments more assistance with relocation expenses—between $2,500 and $30,000—at the completion of a qualifying short sale.

Bob Hora, home transition services executive for Bank of America, commented: "This program can help customers make a planned transition from ownership when home retention options have been exhausted or they have made a decision not to keep the home."

Over the last 2 years (2010 and 2011), BofA completed 200,000 short sales, and another 30,000 in the first quarter of 2012.[5]

---

[5] http://newsroom.bankofamerica.com/press-release/residential-mortgage/bank-america-increases-relocation-assistance-payments-customers-c (Retrieved October 29, 2012).

To qualify for the enhanced relocation assistance payments under the new program, you must work proactively with the bank to obtain a preapproved sales price before submitting a purchase offer to the bank. The short sale must be initiated by the end of 2012 and close by Sept. 26, 2013, to be eligible for the payment. According to BofA, qualifying short sales that have already been started but have not closed may be eligible for the relocation assistance. BofA stated that the amount of assistance provided under the new program will be determined on a case-by-case basis using a calculation that includes the value of the home, amount owed, and other considerations.

Initially, the program will be offered on mortgages that are owned and serviced by BofA.

Customers who believe they may be eligible for BofA's short sale relocation assistance program should call (877) 459-2852.[6]

Short Sale Mistakes to Avoid

In addition, DeSimone said, when homeowners who are under water attempt to short sale their properties, they make mistakes that can lead directly to foreclosure. Here are four things homeowners should keep in mind when they short sell their houses:

1. Hire an agent who knows what he or she is doing. "If you think you need to sell because you are under water, or if it's hard to make your payments," DeSimone said, "you really should get an agent involved early on."

2. Have all your ducks in a row. DeSimone explained: "You need to have all your paperwork ready to go. When you are doing a short sale, it's much like doing a loan. To begin with, the bank wants to review all of your documents—your W2s, your savings, your income—and see what your story is. Should they grant you the short sale or not? They want to see a whole lot of paper."

3. Be proactive with the bank. "Know what they are going to want up front," DeSimone said. "I always tell the seller, . . . [to] call the bank right away and say, 'What's the short sale package you have, and what do I submit?'"

4. Be realistic about your assets. A bank wants to make sure that you deserve the short sale. "If they see that you have a $100,000 deficiency or difference, and you have $600,000 in the bank,"

[6] http://mediaroom.bankofamerica.com/phoenix.zhtml?c=234503&p=irol-newsArticle&ID=1696127&highlight (Retrieved July 29, 2012).

DeSimone pointed out, "they're going to be less likely to grant you the short sale."

■ **Tip** *Be thorough.* When doing a short sale or any kind of real estate transaction with the bank, make sure you ask many questions, make lists, check off those lists when you've satisfied requirements, and stay in regular touch with your real estate agent and your bank (and your attorney if you have hired one). Be truthful with yourself and your bank about your assets and your expenses. Check and double-check your paperwork. By making sure all of your paperwork is in order before you submit it, you can save yourself time and effort if the bank rejects your application and demands that you start the process all over again from scratch.

Improved Forgiveness

DeSimone said he has seen a lender forgive deficiencies as high as a million dollars.

In these cases, "the bank picks up all of the sales costs too," he added. "[With] my own client, . . . I sold his property [and] that [forgiveness] was probably a good half-million dollars." These sales costs can add up too. Here are some of the things a lender may include as a part of the deficiency that it forgives when a borrower sells a home in a short sale:

- Real estate commission.
- Transfer tax.
- Title and escrow fees.
- Any unpaid homeowner's dues.
- Back property taxes.

DeSimone added, "A lot of people who go under water who aren't making their payments aren't paying their property taxes and they owe back property taxes. Banks . . . add it to the money they're going to lose on the loan."

■ **Tip** *Add up the value.* There are hidden costs associated with a house that may also be paid if a bank allows you to do a short sale and forgives your deficiency. Find out all of the expenses that are part of your short sale. Then find out from your lender what will be covered in the deficiency that is forgiven. Looking at all of these extra expenses that are part of owning a home can also help you make the decision to pursue a short sale. If all of those additional expenses are weighing down on you, knowing that they may be off your shoulders after a short sale might be the incentive you need to move forward with your efforts to get out from under your underwater mortgage.

FIVE TIPS FOR PROTECTING YOUR HOME FROM FORECLOSURE

Here are five tips from the Board of Governors of the Federal Reserve System that can help you protect your home from foreclosure:[7]

1. **Do not ignore your mortgage problem.** If you are unable to pay—or have not paid—your mortgage, contact your lender or the company that collects your mortgage payment as soon as possible. Mortgage lenders want to work with you to resolve the problem, and you may have more options if you contact them early. Call the phone number on your monthly mortgage statement or payment coupon book. Explain your financial situation and offer to work with your lender to find the right payment solution for you. If your lender won't talk with you, contact a housing counseling agency. You can find a list of counseling resources at NeighborWorks (a national network of 235 community development and affordable housing organizations) and on the U.S. Department of Housing and Urban Development's (HUD) web site or by calling (800) 569-4287.

2. **Do your homework before you talk to your lender or housing counselor.** Find your original mortgage loan documents and review them. Review your income and budget. Gather information on your expenses, including food, utilities, car payment, insurance, cable, phone, and other bills. If you don't feel comfortable talking to your lender, contact a housing or credit counseling agency. Counselors can help you examine your budget and determine the options available to you. They may also advise you about ways to work with your lender or offer to negotiate with your lender on your behalf.

3. **Know your options.** Some options provide short-term solutions/help, while others provide long-term or permanent solutions. You may be able to work out a temporary plan for making up missed payments, or you may be able to modify the loan terms. Sometimes, the best option may be to sell the house. For information on different options, visit HUD's web site or the Foreclosure Resources for Consumers for links to local resources. This can be found at: www.federalreserve.gov/consumerinfo/foreclosure.htm

4. **Stick to your plan.** Protect your credit score by making timely payments. Prioritize bills and pay those that are most necessary, such as your new mortgage payment. Consider cutting optional expenses such as eating out and premium cable TV services. If your situation changes and you can no longer meet your new payment schedule, call your lender or housing counselor immediately.

5. **Beware of foreclosure rescue scams.** Con artists take advantage of people who have fallen behind on their mortgage payments and who face foreclosure. These con artists may even call themselves "counselors." Your mortgage lender or a legitimate housing counselor can best help you decide which option is best for you. Consumers should

---

[7] www.federalreserve.gov/consumerinfo/fivetips_protecthome.htm (Retrieved August 2012).

report suspicious schemes to their state and local consumer protection agencies, which can be found on the government's Consumer Action web site at: www.usa.gov/directory/stateconsumer/index.shtml

Conclusion

You are better off if you consider your options before diving directly into a foreclosure. Although it may seem like the only way out of a severely underwater housing situation, as you have heard from these experts, there are many continually changing options available if you know where to look. The government takes the issue so seriously that it is continually changing real estate rules, so it pays to check back with the programs regularly to find out what changes may apply to you.

At this point, now that you know about the ground rules guiding you and the options that are available, a wider macro view of the role real estate plays in the economy can be helpful. Once again, an economist's take on the real estate situation can help you see where your personal economics fit into the broader economic equation.

In the next chapter, economist John Mulville describes the big picture of the U.S. real estate market, and how the lending landscape has changed over time. He also describes what went wrong before the real estate market crashed, examines the role of the Community Reinvestment Act (CRA) in the problems we still face today, and where the signs of hope can be found on the near horizon. Statistics from his firm, Real Estate Economics, show homeowners how their mortgages fit into the whole picture of underwater housing in the United States today.

The Real Estate Market: An Overview from the Experts

Advice from a Real Estate Economist

John Mulville

John Mulville is senior vice president for the Consulting Group at Real Estate Economics, a leading provider of real estate consulting services and online research tools. Working with home builders, lenders, investors, developers, and others in the residential development industry, the team at Real Estate Economics has created some of the most comprehensive and insightful consulting services and online information tools available.[1]

Mulville directs all site-specific market analysis in California for Real Estate Economics in Irvine, California. "They hire us and we help them establish what types of homes to build, what prices of homes to build, the mix of homes to build. Quite often, a large master-planned community will have some apartments, some condos, detached homes of different sizes. We help with that."

To help land developers make better decisions about the homes they build, Mulville works to educate people about the macroeconomic conditions that are out there that will affect their projects. He explained that underwater homes play a big part of the work he does. "Obviously, a big part of that is the stressed part of the market, so we think we're pretty well versed in it, and probably have a somewhat different perspective than most just because we've followed the macroeconomics of it for so long," Mulville said. "We do quite a

---

[1] All quotes from John Mullville were collected during a personal interview in July 2012.

bit of work in terms of supply and demand and overvaluation and undervaluation, which would be helpful to the public, the builders, the stock market, [and] politicians."

Watching the Big Picture

As an economist, Mulville spends his time looking at the big picture. This means that he is a good person to describe what happened in the real estate market that led to the bubble bursting, and which in turn led to so many people with underwater mortgages today.

"For many, many years, the loan you could get was pretty closely tied to your income and your credit because they used to do loan underwriting," Mulville explained, referring to the process of verifying a potential homeowners' ability to pay back a loan. "And then we got into the subprime."

The trouble with subprime mortgages was that people had no personal stake in the process because they were able to purchase homes without down payments, which made it easy for them to walk away when the value of those homes dipped under water. Mulville explained:

> That really disconnected your income from your mortgage loan. You had "no-documentation loans," no employment [requirements], you didn't have to bring in any paperwork. Suddenly people could get whatever loan amount they wanted, and that really started to break the process down. Prices immediately skyrocketed because there's no place else for that excess demand to go except into prices.

But, he maintained, the real ownership cost of that home becomes apparent after the loan resets because most of them were adjustable loans. People couldn't afford the mortgage payment after the rate reset higher. They put homes on the market, homes were foreclosed on, and real estate values began to skid. "And now people are deeply under water in many, many cases."

One thing people do when their mortgages are under water is stop making payments on their homes. Figure 11-1 shows how the percentage of people with payments that were past due in the United States rose dramatically after the repercussions of the real estate market crash started to sink in:

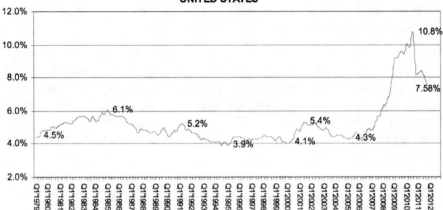

Figure 11-1. Percentage of mortgage payments past due. Graph courtesy of *Real Estate Economics*.

Valuation Problems

After the real estate market bubble burst, home values dropped and mortgages became under water. Mulville explained that today, housing is deeply undervalued on the basis of income. This is due to the market disruption associated with the subprime era, when loans were going to people who could not afford to repay them.

Despite the abundance of underwater homes currently in the market, Mulville said there is hope on the horizon. "As this undervaluation unwinds, prices will increase and underwater homeowners will benefit. Once the perception of housing market appreciation becomes widespread, more at-risk owners will stay in their homes."

How do we know this? One way to find out is by looking around your own local market for houses. In many places, homebuyers are finding few homes for sale. "The lack of listings in many markets is the result of improving expectations," Mulville said, "which incidentally deflects demand to the new home market."

Additional Lines of Credit

One of the difficulties that hit people with subprime mortgages was the fact that they also had additional lines of credit, such as home equity loans, stacked on top of their primary mortgage. This was something else that forced their loans to become under water so quickly when their adjustable-rate mortgages rose to their highest limits. Mulville said, "A lot of times we have 10-year liens and home credit lines on top of this. There's really no way to amortize your way out. You will not be able to pay that thing down."

Most people still under water have been bailing so long and are looking for relief soon. But Mulville said we still have a way to go before most homes in the United States regain their previous values. "It's already been—what, 5 or 6 years we're into this thing? We're a long way—we're back to maybe year-2000 values in some markets. . . . [You can only] hope that appreciation will [help] work your way out if you bought using a subprime loan at the top of the market."

A Farewell to ARMs? Not Likely!

One of the many tools that banks were using as the mortgage bubble was growing in the mid-2000s was the Adjustable-Rate Mortgage (ARM). These are loans offered by banks at a low interest rate that changes over time according to an index, such as the LIBOR (London Interbank Offered Rate). It starts at a base rate, but often moves from that rate to a much higher interest rate.

ARMs work great for borrowers when the rate is at its low base; however, ARMs become very problematic when the interest rate increases to its limit, or cap. This is what happened to most of the ARMs that were around when the real estate bubble burst.

Today, ARMs continue to be a way for borrowers to get a loan with a lower initial interest rate than a fixed-rate mortgage. The trade-off is more risk over the long run. Although many underwater homeowners remain stuck with high interest rates because they are unable to refinance adjustable-rate mortgages they took out before the real estate market crashed, ARMs remain a popular product today.

WHAT IS SUBPRIME LENDING?

In their 2006 report for the *Federal Reserve Bank of St. Louis Review*, economists Souphala Chomsisengphet and Anthony Pennington-Cross explained:

> Subprime lending is a relatively new and rapidly growing segment of the mortgage market that expands the pool of credit to borrowers who, for a variety of reasons, would otherwise be denied credit. For instance, those potential borrowers who would fail credit history requirements in the standard (prime) mortgage market have greater access to credit in the subprime

*market. Two of the major benefits of this type of lending, then, are the
increased numbers of homeowners and the opportunity for these homeowners
to create wealth.*[2]

After the bursting of the real estate bubble, the U.S. Department of Housing and Urban Development (HUD) offered the following synopsis of subprime lending: "Typically, subprime loans are for individuals with blemished or limited credit histories. The loans carry a higher rate of interest than prime loans to compensate for increased credit risk."[3]

Racial Disparities

According to statistics gathered over the last few years, minorities appeared to be overrepresented in the subprime lending market. Studies revealed that even in upper income African-American neighborhoods, people are 1.5 times as likely to have a subprime loan than those in low-income white neighborhoods. In neighborhoods where Hispanics comprise at least 80 percent of the population, they were 1.5 times as likely to have a subprime mortgage loan than the nation as a whole.

HUD pointed out that "some allege this disparity to be attributed to subprime lenders purposefully marketing to African-American communities—what some have called reverse redlining. They allege lenders will provide loans to these communities, but at a higher cost and with less favorable conditions."[4]

Here are some additional facts about subprime lenders:

- Home refinance loans account for higher shares of subprime lenders' total origination than prime lenders' originations.

- Subprime lenders have a larger percentage of their total originations in predominately black census tracts than prime lenders.

- Subprime lenders are more likely to have terms like "consumer," "finance," and "acceptance" in their lender names.[5]

---

[2] https://research.stlouisfed.org/publications/review/06/01/ChomPennCross.pdf (Retrieved July 21, 2012).

[3] http://portal.hud.gov/hudportal/HUD?src=/program_offices/fair_housing_equal_opp/ lending/subprime (Retrieved July 21, 2012).

[4] Ibid.

[5] http://portal.hud.gov/hudportal/HUD?src=/program_offices/fair_housing_equal_opp/ lending/subprime (Retrieved July 21, 2012).

Subprime Mortgages Return

Although subprime mortgages went out of style thanks to the bursting of the housing market and the financial market meltdown—both of which were linked back to the shoddy lending practices that preceded them—it seems that subprime mortgages are making a comeback in 2012.

On February 16, 2012, the *Huffington Post's* Jillian Berman wrote a story called "Subprime Mortgage Bonds Back in Fashion" that featured a time bomb as its graphic. "The home loans responsible for blowing up the housing market are regaining popularity," she wrote.[6]

Berman's article pointed to an article that appeared in the *Wall Street Journal* (*WSJ*) earlier that day titled "Toxic? Says Who? Taste For 'Subprime' Returns."

In that article, *WSJ* reporter Serena Ng wrote, "Prices of some distressed bonds backed by subprime home loans—those issued before the crisis to borrowers with sketchy credit histories—have chalked up double-digit percentage gains this year, with one prominent market index rising 14 percent."[7]

It seems that these gains are drawing investors back to the subprime credit market that nearly dropped off the face of the map from 2007 to 2009. Ng added, "The latest upswing has some money managers setting up investment funds dedicated to buying beaten-down mortgage bonds, hoping to reap fat yields while waiting for the housing market to turn."

ARMs Meet Subprime Lending

Mulville explained that the ARM is still part of the lending landscape. "It's still out there, and it's existed for many, many, many, many years. Some were good; some were bad."

What makes an ARM adjustable is that it is indexed to some other number such as the Cost of Funds index (COFI) or the prime rate. Mulville continued:

> Some of them are based on LIBOR, and some of them were based on bank deposit rates. Some of those were very, very good. There is nothing inherently wrong with [ARMs] if you are somewhat well educated about how they work and what the limitations and advantages are. I don't think there's any reason

---

[6] www.huffingtonpost.com/2012/02/16/subprime-mortgage-_n_1282157.html (Retrieved July 21, 2012).

[7] http://online.wsj.com/article/SB10001424052970204062704577223473258237102.html (Retrieved July 21, 2012).

why they had to default any more than any other type of loan except that they were the main product in the subprime mess.

Mulville said, "One of the reasons why so many adjustable-rate loans were made in that one time is just the fact that they would go up and down with interest rates." Theoretically, this would help a homeowner if rates went down, but many homeowners got stuck when interest rates went up. "If you were an investor in [a] mortgage and it was a 4 percent mortgage, and rates went to 7 [percent], then the value of your mortgage goes down. Nobody will pay you $100 for a 4 percent mortgage when rates are 7 percent."

One of the problems connected to the proliferation of adjustable-rate loans before the real estate crisis, according to Mulville, was a new product called an "option loan," which helped to push people into an underwater situation:

You could make a minimum payment. You could make no payment. You could make all these different payment options; none of those necessarily would amortize the principle. And you were doing it on a stated income that you couldn't support on a home that was grossly overvalued because everybody out there was doing the same thing.

■ **Tip** *Know your amortization schedule.* Amortization is the process of dividing a payment into the amount that applies to interest and the amount that applies to principal. Payments near the beginning of a loan contribute more interest, and less principal, than payments near the end of a loan.[8]

LIBOR SCANDAL ROCKS THE BANKING WORLD

On July 20, 2012, the *Christian Science Monitor* published the story, "LIBOR Scandal: What Is It and Why You Should Care," by Mark Trumbull. He pointed out, "With an estimated $300 trillion in loans or derivative contracts around the world pegged to the interest rate, the scandal is again shaking faith in major international banking centers like Wall Street and London City."[9]

LIBOR was created to measure the average interest rate that banks are charging when they lend to each other. The LIBOR rate is used as a foundation for other rates, such as ARMs. It was also used as a reference point for many of the complex financial derivatives that helped to

---

[8] http://h10025.www1.hp.com/ewfrf/wc/document?cc=us&lc=en&dlc=en&docname=bpia5036 (Retrieved July 21, 2012).
[9] www.csmonitor.com/World/Global-Issues/2012/0720/LIBOR-scandal-What-is-it-and-why-you-should-care (Retrieved July 21, 2012).

destabilize the financial markets in 2007 when the country teetered on the edge of a major depression before the bank bailout by the federal government.

Nearly $300 trillion in loans or derivative contracts are connected to LIBOR, according to the experts.

In the scandal that rocked the banking world in July 2012 and forced the resignation of Barclays chief executive Bob Diamond, the banks were charged with manipulating the LIBOR rate as far back as 2005, according to Trumbull. Barclays was ordered to pay $453 million in fines to settle the charges of moving the LIBOR levels up or down to benefit the bank's investments and underreporting LIBOR so the bank looked like it was doing better financially.

More Than a Dozen Banks Investigated

According to Reuters' reporters Katharina Bart and Diane Bartz, "More than a dozen banks are being investigated in the scandal, including Citigroup, HSBC, Deutsche Bank, and JPMorgan Chase."[10]

What does this have to do with underwater homes? When LIBOR was artificially manipulated upward, mortgage rates went up too, creating additional debt for homeowners with ARMs.

In response to the scandal, the U.S. House of Representatives overwhelmingly passed a bipartisan bill on July 26, 2012, to audit the Federal Reserve.[11]

Reporters noted that the bill came on the same day that the *Washington Post* reported that the New York Fed "did not communicate in key meetings with top regulators [and] that British bank Barclays had admitted to Fed staffers that it was rigging LIBOR," the index that sets interest rates worldwide.[12]

Why Did Things Go So Far Off Track?

Blame is often passed from one hand to the next when people try to explain the origins of the bursting of the real estate bubble. Democrats blame Republican lawmakers. Republicans blame Democratic lawmakers. Homeowners blame the U.S. Congress. Others blame the banks. Still other people

---

[10] www.reuters.com/article/2012/07/20/us-banking-libor-settlment-idUSBRE86J00H20120720 (Retrieved July 21, 2012).

[11] www.huffingtonpost.com/2012/07/25/federal-reserve-audit-bill_n_1702879.html?utm_hp_ref=mostpopular (Retrieved July 26, 2012).

[12] www.washingtonpost.com/business/economy/ny-fed-silent-on-barclays-admission-of-rigging-libor/2012/07/24/gJQA2eWg7W_story.html?hpid=z1 (Retrieved July 26, 2012).

blame the Federal Reserve and its leaders, and some blame regulators and economists for not sounding a louder alarm.

It is no wonder that the baton of blame continues to make its rounds: Blaming others for difficult problems is often easier than looking inward. But there are still a few solid reasons why so many people in the United States have underwater mortgages.

Economist John Mulville explained that a few specific actions preceded the downfall of the real estate market in the United States.

> This is more of a political issue than an economic issue, but a lot of people say the banks were forced by the [Housing and] Community Development Act to make more loans to people who essentially couldn't afford them. Some people say that was [George W.] Bush's fault. Some people say that was Barney Frank's fault. Some people say it was Congress. I mean, you can go on and on with it.

Meanwhile, to find a cause for so many underwater homes in the current market, economists look at the big picture data about the real estate industry as well as how the market has changed over long periods of time. As an economist, Mulville pointed out, "All we really see is that when underwriting wasn't part of the mortgage process anymore, that's when we had a problem, and there are tons of political actions that predate that."

Was the Community Reinvestment Act to Blame?

One act of Congress that may have ignited the slow burn that would eventually become the conflagration that burned many homeowners with undervalued homes and overvalued mortgages is the Community Reinvestment Act (CRA), which is also known as Title VIII of the Housing and Community Development Act of 1977. According to Mulville, "Many years ago, and this goes back quite some time, when the banks were all merging, to get approval for their mergers a lot of times they'd divest some banks and got rid of some branches, but they also agreed to do some community redevelopment lending."

In an effort to get more people into more homes, lenders started to really push subprime mortgages. "It essentially compelled them into this field," Mulville added.

So what started with the best of intentions on the part of the federal government went the other way. Banks took advantage of the mandate from lawmakers to make it easier for people to move into homes by loosening their restrictions on providing mortgages to homebuyers. But in the long run, banks did a disservice by selling houses to too many people who could not afford them. Initially, prices were driven up and up, but eventually, when the bubble burst, it undermined the entire industry.

Banks Were Not Alone

Did banks go too far? Mulville said he believes that banks may have gone too far, but ratings agencies, such as Moody's, Standard & Poor's, and Fitch, also played a part by overrating banks that were teetering on the edge of insolvency.

In July 2007, Ohio Attorney General Marc Dann was leading an investigation of all three credit-rating agencies to determine the role that they played in "the subprime-mortgage quagmire," wrote *Fortune* reporters Katie Benner and Adam Lashinsky.[13]

On July 7, 2012, *Bloomberg* reporters John Lippert, Zeke Faux, and Jef Feeley wrote, "Morgan Stanley successfully pushed Standard & Poor's and Moody's Investors Service Inc. to give unwarranted investment-grade ratings in 2006 to $23 billion worth of notes backed by subprime mortgages, investors claimed in a lawsuit, citing documents unsealed in federal court." They added that U.S. District Judge Shira Scheindlin was allowing investors to proceed with their case against the rating agencies on a claim of negligent misrepresentation.[14]

Rating Agency Mistakes

Mulville added, "The . . . agencies rated these mortgages . . . very high . . . when in fact they should have had terrible ratings. People thought they were buying AAA paper and really the underlying assets, people couldn't pay, and the homes were overpriced."

Some economists believe that the agencies overrated those mortgages so they could keep getting business from the people who were underwriting them. Mulville explained:

> It was really a stamp of approval and not a very good understanding of the
> creditworthiness of the people in some of these loan pools. Many, many years
> ago when loans were all fixed rate and loans were very well underwritten,
> foreclosure rates were only a couple of percent, and they could build a couple
> of percent of credit default into your mortgage-backed security and feel OK
> with it. But when they weren't underwritten anymore, and the people couldn't
> make all those payments, and they weren't fixed rate, and all of the other

---

[13] http://money.cnn.com/2007/07/05/news/economy/subprime.fortune/index.htm (Retrieved July 22, 2012).

[14] http://mobile.bloomberg.com/news/2012-07-02/morgan-stanley-pushed-s-p-to-boost-ratings-investors-say (Retrieved July 22, 2012).

things we've been talking about, then all of a sudden that mortgage-backed security [wasn't] worth what you paid for it.

Meanwhile, investors are trying to get banks to buy back foreclosures, which turns into a long process in and out of the courts. "That's very much in play right now," Mulville explained.

For example, in May 2012, *Bloomberg* reporter Jody Shenn wrote that "Bank of America, the second-biggest U.S. lender, will buy back $330 million of home loans from Freddie Mac, the mortgage company seized by the government, after flaws were found in how they were created."[15]

Turmoil Continues

While covering the same story, Rob Chrisman of *Mortgage Daily News* reported:

> *Freddie Mac and Bank of America announced a $1.28 billion settlement in January 2011 over bad loans sold through 2008 by Countrywide. Bank of America's backlog of pending demands for refunds on soured loans reached a record $16.1 billion in the first quarter as a dispute deepened between the bank and Fannie Mae. Fannie stopped accepting new loans from Bank of America in January.[16]*

In other words, the lending industry remains in turmoil even in 2012, several years after the housing market's bubble burst, making millions of homeowners under water on their loans.

Mulville explained that bad news for the banks often ends up being bad news for homeowners. "What all this subprime led to was a huge overstatement of prices. That's gradually collapsed and overcorrected. So, it got this huge run up, now the prices went back to what we would call a 'supportable home price.'"

A supportable home price is calculated in any given area by looking at the household incomes that are reported in the U.S. Census, along with the current interest rates, and the percentage of household income that people will put toward their mortgage payment. Although these numbers may vary from region to region, economists and housing industry experts can put together these amounts to determine what kinds of home prices work for a

---

[15] http://mobile.bloomberg.com/news/2012-05-23/bofa-will-buy-back-330-million-of-mortgages-from-freddie (Retrieved July 22, 2012).

[16] www.mortgagenewsdaily.com/channels/pipelinepress/05232012-foreclosures-delinquencies.aspx (Retrieved July 22, 2012).

specific area or even neighborhood. These are the "supportable home prices" for that area. Mulville added, "You can tell what a supportable home price is for almost anyplace. And the current median home prices are way below those."

Although this may be good news for those who are shopping for a new home, it is very bad news for those whose homes are under water.

Gross Overcorrection

Mulville is blunt:

> The market has grossly overcorrected. On a basis of income, houses are very, very affordable. You hear this all the time, but people take it with a grain of salt because a lot of time it's your realtor and the National Association of Realtors who are telling you this. And people say, "Gee, they told me it was a great buy a few years ago." You can prove mathematically that it is. Now, the only thing that's keeping people from running out and buying a bunch of homes is consumer sentiment is poor, and all kinds of taxes are coming, we think. But look at the foreclosure side. Rental investors are out paying all cash for these [homes] and buying them just as fast as they can.

The latest news reports show this to be true. For example, the *Wall Street Journal* in March 2012 reported, "Some of the biggest names on Wall Street are lining up to become landlords to cash-strapped Americans by bidding on pools of foreclosed properties being sold by Fannie Mae."[17]

It seems that the investors who are buying these homes are renting them out rather than looking to resell them. One thing this does is reduce the number of properties on the market, which could help the recovery of the housing industry.

In a recent issue of the *Wall Street Journal,* reporters Nick Timiraos, Robbie Whelan, and Matt Phillips wrote that bulk sales of homes can be a trade-off for real estate investors. In their March 20, 2012, story "Wall Street Keys on Landlord," they pointed out that the standard approach of selling homes one by one can be very expensive. Repairs, inspections, and closing costs can make investing in them inefficient. On the other hand, the reporters wrote, "selling properties in bulk to large investors could require Fannie Mae to sell at a big discount, leading to larger initial costs."[18] Still, nobody knows whether

---

[17] http://online.wsj.com/article/SB10001424052702303863404577285791317719200.html (Retrieved July 22, 2012).

[18] http://online.wsj.com/article/SB10001424052702303863404577285791317719200.html (Retrieved October 30, 2012).

one-by-one buying or bulk buying will cost taxpayers more in the long run because they're the ones footing the bill for any losses suffered by Fannie Mae.

Basically, how the real estate market looks right now as an investment depends on your perspective. Economist John Mulville explained, "If you are a knowledgeable local investor, you're buying these things just as quick as you can get them. If you are John Q. Public, and you are worried about your job and you don't know what's going on with Obamacare and all this sort of thing, then you're cautious, and you're not in the market."

Slow Growth Ahead

Most economists, including Mulville, predict that there are some years of slow growth ahead of us, but a recovery will eventually happen: sooner for some, later for others. It really depends on the area where you live since some places with many jobs will recover much faster than those outlying areas where jobs are few and many foreclosures still clog the real estate markets. "We're starting to get there," he said. "The areas of the country that have better economics, Silicon Valley and the high growth areas, are much closer to a recovery. The places that are very, very hard hit, Atlanta and some of these places, are much further from a recovery. Gradually, over time, people are recognizing that these homes are a bargain and are starting to buy them up, literally, across the nation."

Rental property sales are generally the first wave of a recovery. Mulville pointed out that nearly all markets are seeing an upturn in the activity of rental property investors. These buyers are the people who begin the gradual growth of the entire market. "That's actually a very dynamic process," Mulville pointed out:

> Those homes are usually the cheapest and most affordable in the market. A lot of times you can buy a home like this and immediately establish a huge positive cash flow. This is why these rental investors are buying these as quick as they can. But what happens is, soon they're all gone. In fact, the homes at the lowest, lowest price range just are completely gone in places like Phoenix and Vegas. In some of the very, very hardest hit, the lowest price rung on the price ladder, if you will, has been completely cleaned out.

This is just the first step of a rebalancing of the housing market. With each step, those who are under water are a little bit closer to seeing the value of their homes rise up to a better range. Once the lowest priced houses have all been bought, prices begin to rise on the next level of houses. These are the ones that people buy for themselves. Mulville explained:

> [A]ll of a sudden you're hearing about "median price appreciation." What's really happened is there are fewer and fewer sales at the lowest price ranges, so the median comes up. It's not that we're getting that great a list across all types of homes, but we're getting fewer and fewer distressed homes in the median figures month to month. Now, as that plays out . . . , pretty soon those rental investors are going to have to move up. All of the $100,000 homes are gone. They're going to have to pay $110,000, then $120,000, then $130,000. As long as they think they can [expect] a reasonable rate of return, they'll do that. So, that's really the beginning of the turn.

Eventually, the number of foreclosed homes will gradually decline in many areas, which will slowly drive up the prices of the homes around them. Mulville said, "The price of the typical distressed home will be much closer to the regular home, and that's the initial inning of the housing recovery. And that's well in place in some areas, and not in place at all, practically, in other areas."

Signs of Hope Are Out There

To learn whether your area is recovering, it helps if you have an in-depth knowledge of the market, which comes from constantly reading the reports that are generated regularly by real estate market professionals and government agencies. Mulville's firm, Real Estate Economics, offers many current reports and charts that show how the housing market is changing across the country. (See Figure 7-2 later.)

One example of a recovery that is currently in the works, which can be seen by the dramatic changes in market activity in the last year, is Phoenix, Arizona. It seems that low-priced homes in Phoenix are disappearing at an astounding rate. Houses in the under-$100,000 price range saw a dramatic turn from 25,000 sales in a year to 30,000 sales in a year. Mulville pointed out, "That's a huge difference. Five thousand cheap, foreclosed homes just disappeared from the market. That doesn't have to happen very long, and they're all gone."

The Phoenix area was one of the areas hardest hit by foreclosures. Now it is seeing its median list prices go up nearly 27 percent in the first quarter of 2012 compared to a year prior. According to Realtor.com, "The list of 25 Top Turnaround Towns, developed using year-over-year comparative data from the first quarters of 2012 and 2011, is led by Phoenix-Mesa, Ariz."[19]

Those with underwater homes can see this as a sign of hope. When the hardest-hit areas begin to see a recovery, it is likely that prices across the board will begin to stabilize and edge up as well.

---

[19] www.realtor.com/blogs/realtor-com-names-top-turnaround-towns-may-2012-data/ (Retrieved July 22, 2012).

How long will it be until people with underwater mortgages begin to see the value in their homes return to levels where they were before the bursting of the real estate bubble? Mulville said the answer to that question is completely relative:

> *The question you are asking is 100 percent dependent on where you are. . . . If you are close to jobs in a high-demand area, then that time frame is short. If you looked at Silicon Valley, California, or some of these markets that are performing quite well—Washington, DC, parts of New York—it's maybe 2 years, 3 years, 4 years? But in an outlying market with a long commute and not very good job prospects, we don't know when that is.*

Time Frames to Recovery Are Relative

In many places, the growth of home value appreciation will not only depend on the real estate markets in nearby areas but also on the price of gas and other energy costs. It will also depend on traffic patterns, the length of a commute to jobs and shopping, and employment prospects. Mulville added that the recovery of each local area will be very "demand dependent."

He pointed out that some areas of the country are already taking their first steps into recovery. "In fact, it's already in play in a lot of the close-in markets with good employment: The foreclosures are drying up very quickly and we can see a return to equilibrium in 2, 3, 4 years."

On the other hand, some places are not so lucky. "Other places, the time frame to get back to the subprime bubble prices could be more than 10 years."

▧ **Tip** *Don't despair, but be realistic.* Track your budget. Look at the macroeconomics of your area. If you see visible growth in areas such as jobs and population, then your time to recovery will be shorter than if you live in an outlying area where jobs are few and people are fleeing. If your home is deeply under water in one of these latter places, you may want to consider joining the flight and find an inexpensive home in another, more prosperous and job-saturated location.

Amortization Table

Mulville advises homeowners to look at an amortization table and see how quickly their loans are being paid off. This will give you a sense of how deeply under water you really are. If things don't look favorable, "you can't amortize your way out of it. This is where strategic default comes in." Even if you can continue to make the payments and continue to live in your home, you might still be unable to pay off your mortgage loan in a realistic time frame. Or the value of your home might never rise back to the amount of your mortgage cost. In other words, you are so deeply under water that bailing yourself out is not a realistic option.

Economically, your home, no matter how wonderful it is, has become a bottomless money pit. You may be better off taking a hit to your credit, which will go away in a few years while you rent another home, than sinking all of your hard-earned money into an investment that will never bring you any return. After the dust has cleared in 4 or 5 years, and your credit returns to normal, then you can buy another house that is a better value and a better investment.

But if you have decided that you are going to hang onto your underwater home and wait until it appreciates in value, there is hope on the horizon. Mulville explained: "Many, many markets will get some appreciation over the next few years. In fact, it's already started to appear in some markets. So, if you are 5 or 10 percent under water, you may be able to make your way out of it."

During the time when subprime mortgages were all the rage, overpriced new homes made up a much greater percentage of the share of homes on the market, so the average prices and the median prices went up much more than they would have if new home sales were the same percentage and sales were constant. "Now we're on the flipside of that." Mulville pointed out:

> The distressed sales and the foreclosure sales make up a much larger percentage than they ever would have historically. So that really led to the price at the top to be overstated, and it's also leading the price at the bottom to be grossly understated. So once these lowest cost homes are all sold and start to disappear, the median prices might rise fairly impressively without that big a fundamental change in the overall economic picture.

In other words, there is hope for your underwater home if you are only 5 or 10 percent under water, but if you are 15, 20, or 25 percent under water, it becomes much more difficult for you to bail yourself out any time soon.

■ **Tip** *Do the math.* Compare your home's value with what you owe on your mortgage. Contact your lender to learn how much you still owe on your principal and what you owe in interest. How deep are you under water? If you are more than 15 percent under water, Mulville says it may be many years before your home appreciates in value enough to lift your mortgage out of trouble.

Deeply Under Water

People with mortgages that are 50 percent and 60 percent under water should search for a way out as soon as possible. "There is no hope on it," Mulville said. "Cut your losses. Now. As soon as your lender calls you and gets ready to kick you out, it's time to go, because there is no point in holding on to this thing.

"There are still many, many people who haven't paid in years who haven't even gotten called by their bank," he continued. "It's amazing, but it's true."

When should a homeowner call it quits? Mulville pointed back to an old adage that still rings true. Legend has it that the late Lord Harold Samuel, a British real estate tycoon, once said, "There are three things that matter in property: *location, location, location.*" Although others, including *New York Times* columnist and former speechwriter William Safire, point out that people had been using those three words for many years before Samuel supposedly coined the phrase, it still carries much weight. Look at where you live before you decide how deep an underwater mortgage can go before you decide too much is too much. "If we're close to employment and my area's coming back really well, then it might be worth [holding on to] it," Mulville added, "but if I bought in some sort of outlying suburb without that great of employment and a longtime travel into employment, it's not going to work out very well."

■ **Tip**   *Face reality.* There is no magic number to arrive at that indicates it is time for homeowners who are under water to sell their homes and cut losses. Even in the greatest markets, Mulville adds, a house that is 60 percent under water is probably not worth saving. By facing reality now, you will have more options from which to choose than if you wait too long and your options are chosen for you (probably by your lender), especially if you have to pay taxes on a deficiency that only grew while you waited.

It gets worse for those in outlying areas. Mulville stated, "The same thing will happen on the flipside. Let's just say hypothetically that the market flipped around tomorrow and the economy turned around, the close-in areas are going to appreciate twice as fast as the far-away areas," he pointed out. "So you're losing out under almost any circumstance. Your house might not be appreciating as fast as the median. So you could be five or 10 years out and diligently paying, and now have [less] equity. That's no good. It's better off to just face it."

Secondary Loans

One thing that can push an underwater mortgage even deeper is a secondary loan on that mortgage, whether a junior lien loan or a home equity credit line. Although some experts say it is fairly easy to get a lender to subordinate these to your primary loan, making you eligible for mortgage modifications or refinancing, Mulville said these are difficult to push aside. "It's very hard to get them to release you on your junior liens. Also, there are many states where they can sue you for that."

In California, for example, they call it "non-recourse." This means your lender can only get back your house as collateral (and cannot take other further legal actions against you such as garnishing wages) if you default on your mortgage. "If you default on your first loan, and you don't pay it, they can't sue you for it. You could get a 1099 for it, but they can't come after you legally. On the junior liens and home equity credit lines and all that sort of thing, typically they can come after you, and if you have the assets, they can sue you for it," he pointed out.

■ **Tip** *Take care of your second mortgages and other lines of credit.* While working with your lender to avoid foreclosure, don't forget to make provisions for paying off your other loans while you're at it. Each state has its own laws regarding what lenders can do about unpaid secondary loans. Talk to an attorney or mediator who is familiar with the laws of your state to find out where you stand.

Mulville said that lenders may modify your first loan, but he said that he has been told by realtors and brokers that it is rare for a lender to modify a second loan. "The lenders have just not been that flexible on the junior liens," he said. "That's been a big, big problem in doing loan modifications."

Finally, as an economist who understands that a level of "irrational exuberance" pervades the marketplace, and the bursting of the real estate bubble in 2007–2008 will not be the last time a bubble will burst for the consumer, Mulville has these parting words of advice for underwater mortgage holders:

> If you've got a stable employment history, you're not too far under water, you like your house, you want to stay there, all the stars align, and you're 5 percent, you're 10 percent [under water], that number could disappear pretty quickly. If you don't like the house, you never really wanted to move there in the first place, it was just a place you could live for two years before you flipped into something else, and your wife left you, you lost your job, and you're 40 percent under water, I'd make a move and get out of it before the Mortgage Forgiveness Act expires, so you can save that additional hurdle.

How Fast Are Houses Appreciating?

One way underwater homeowners return to an equity positive position is when their houses become more valuable from the gradual appreciation of their local real estate market. Economist John Mulville's firm Real Estate Economics has run the numbers, and their forecasts for the future are promising. If their predictions come true, homes will slowly, but surely, gain back their lost equity over the next few years.

Figure 11-2 is an annual appreciation forecast. Notice the middle column that shows how much homes are expected to appreciate over the coming years:

RESIDENTIAL MARKET OPPORTUNITY/RISK INDEX
UNITED STATES
JULY 2012

Year	Housing Demand	Housing Supply	Market is Over/(Under) Built		Median Home Price	Ann. Price Change	Equilibrium Home Price	30-Yr. Mtg. Rate	Median HH Income	Market is Under/(Over) Valued		O/R Index (100=Equil.)	Mkt. Health in 24-36 Mos.
1990	101,307,148	102,891,854	(1,584,706)	(1.5%) Overbuilt	$97,017	-	$95,174	10.13%	$33,817	($1,842)	(1.8%) Overvalued	98.4	Stable
1991	100,488,124	104,299,984	(3,800,860)	(3.6%) Overbuilt	$102,500	5.7%	$103,714	9.25%	$34,227	$1,214	1.2% Undervalued	97.8	Weak
1992	101,026,743	105,414,401	(4,387,658)	(4.2%) Overbuilt	$105,017	2.5%	$113,411	8.40%	$34,965	$8,394	8.0% Undervalued	99.8	Stable
1993	103,211,494	106,647,094	(3,435,601)	(3.2%) Overbuilt	$108,742	3.5%	$127,436	7.33%	$35,761	$18,695	17.2% Undervalued	102.9	Stable
1994	106,645,746	108,003,697	(1,357,950)	(1.3%) Overbuilt	$112,808	3.7%	$117,401	8.36%	$36,563	$4,592	4.1% Undervalued	100.3	Stable
1995	109,662,780	109,536,806	145,974	0.1% Underbuilt	$116,492	3.3%	$122,591	7.96%	$37,129	$6,100	5.2% Undervalued	101.7	Stable
1996	112,174,379	111,078,393	1,095,987	1.0% Underbuilt	$122,257	5.0%	$126,733	7.81%	$38,228	$4,486	3.7% Undervalued	101.6	Stable
1997	115,294,078	112,688,373	2,605,705	2.3% Underbuilt	$128,650	5.2%	$133,062	7.60%	$39,687	$4,412	3.4% Undervalued	102.6	Stable
1998	118,506,813	114,331,460	4,175,353	3.7% Underbuilt	$135,467	5.0%	$144,909	6.94%	$40,924	$9,322	7.0% Undervalued	104.7	Strong
1999	121,646,153	116,150,157	5,497,995	4.7% Underbuilt	$142,657	3.8%	$140,741	7.43%	$42,032	$74	0.1% Undervalued	103.3	Stable
2000	124,545,954	117,957,938	6,579,010	5.6% Underbuilt	$146,517	4.2%	$134,515	8.03%	$43,118	($12,002)	(9.2%) Overvalued	101.4	Stable
2001	124,851,782	119,498,602	5,353,179	4.5% Underbuilt	$155,483	6.1%	$150,533	6.97%	$43,788	($4,950)	(3.2%) Overvalued	100.2	Stable
2002	123,711,042	121,043,921	2,667,121	2.2% Underbuilt	$167,042	7.4%	$158,008	6.57%	$44,458	($9,033)	(5.4%) Overvalued	99.8	Stable
2003	123,651,591	122,677,864	973,707	0.8% Underbuilt	$179,325	7.4%	$170,293	5.85%	$44,842	($9,032)	(5.0%) Overvalued	99.0	Stable
2004	125,287,914	124,476,831	811,083	0.7% Underbuilt	$194,208	8.3%	$170,771	5.84%	$45,376	($23,437)	(12.1%) Overvalued	96.6	Weak
2005	127,725,202	126,458,111	1,267,092	1.0% Underbuilt	$219,017	12.8%	$171,724	5.87%	$46,189	($47,293)	(21.6%) Overvalued	94.2	Weak
2006	130,283,269	128,466,564	1,816,705	1.4% Underbuilt	$221,583	1.2%	$165,493	6.41%	$47,827	($56,090)	(25.3%) Overvalued	93.4	Weak
2007	132,015,360	130,180,305	1,836,055	1.4% Underbuilt	$214,190	(3.4%)	$169,495	6.34%	$49,503	($44,694)	(20.9%) Overvalued	94.7	Weak
2008	131,526,055	131,454,019	72,036	0.1% Underbuilt	$193,375	(9.7%)	$176,674	6.04%	$49,837	($16,701)	(8.6%) Overvalued	97.4	Weak
2009	128,046,927	132,317,595	(6,270,668)	(4.7%) Overbuilt	$172,425	(10.8%)	$195,998	5.04%	$50,038	$23,543	13.7% Undervalued	99.9	Stable
2010	125,422,527	132,914,244	(7,491,717)	(5.6%) Overbuilt	$172,258	(0.1%)	$206,104	4.89%	$51,015	$33,845	19.6% Undervalued	100.7	Stable
2011	127,134,055	133,445,366	(6,311,302)	(4.7%) Overbuilt	$169,594	(1.1%)	$213,572	4.45%	$51,878	$46,978	28.0% Undervalued	103.4	Stable
2012est	129,191,633	133,904,780	(4,813,148)	(3.6%) Overbuilt	$170,444	2.1%	$220,561	3.80%	$52,488	$58,116	34.1% Undervalued	105.6	Strong
2013prj	131,246,484	134,510,160	(3,261,675)	(2.4%) Overbuilt	$174,783	2.5%	$223,590	4.13%	$53,198	$48,806	27.9% Undervalued	105.2	Strong
2014prj	133,503,293	135,227,721	(1,884,428)	(1.2%) Overbuilt	$180,800	3.4%	$215,063	4.59%	$54,001	$34,263	19.0% Undervalued	103.6	Strong
2015prj	136,182,541	136,116,937	85,604	0.0% Underbuilt	$187,858	3.9%	$200,976	5.33%	$54,504	$13,117	7.0% Undervalued	101.8	Stable
2016prj	138,610,756	137,189,639	1,421,117	1.0% Underbuilt	$195,375	3.4%	$188,776	6.07%	$55,914	($6,599)	(3.4%) Overvalued	99.5	Stable
2017prj	140,772,308	138,437,886	2,334,422	1.7% Underbuilt	$202,751	3.8%	$185,529	6.42%	$57,033	($17,122)	(8.4%) Overvalued	99.2	Stable

Figure 11-2. Residential Market Opportunity/Risk Index. Graphic courtesy of *Real Estate Economics*.

Who Should Consider a Short Sale

How quickly can homeowners rebound from a short sale? Just ask those who have already returned to the market for another mortgage. Mulville said: "We are already seeing the 2008 short sellers coming back into the market for loans and getting approved. Underwater owners can get rid of the current overleveraged home—that may not be close to employment and/or fit their current needs—and buy something cheaper, possibly larger and better located."

He added, "Better hurry though. I'm not hearing much about extending the Mortgage Forgiveness Act."

▨ **Tip** *Do your financial analysis.* Every person's story is different. Get a seasoned expert in on the conversation. Find a good attorney. Mediation services are available for low-income people. Don't fall for any scams because you are in dire straits. Look at all the numbers, decide what is best for you, then "make a move." Your decision should be based on your life and your finances and not solely what your lender is telling you.

ADVICE FROM A CONSUMER ADVOCATE

In July 2012, the AARP held a public forum titled "The Foreclosure Crisis: Ending the Nightmare for Older Americans." One topic covered by the panelists was the inefficiency of many federal programs designed to help underwater homeowners avoid foreclosure.

One panelist was Janis Bowdler, the director of the Wealth-Building Policy Project at the National Council of La Raza. She is also a regular blogger for the *Huffington Post*. Her expertise is in home ownership and housing discrimination, predatory lending, and other financial abuses.[20]

Bowdler is concerned about protecting homeowners from abuses. During the forum, she pointed out that many states are dealing with lender financial abuses by passing new rules and regulations designed to protect homeowners. Bowdler explained that California's Homeowners Bill of Rights is a recent law that "gets servicers to play by the rules [and] you can sue if they don't." The problem in most states, she said, is that many lenders do not follow the regulations that lawmakers have created for their industry. "We have protections, but they are not being followed. . . .

It's a behavior changer," said Bowdler. "It's carrots and sticks."

One federal program that has recently been beefed up to make it easier for homeowners to avoid foreclosure is the Home Affordable Modification Program (HAMP). HAMP is for people who are employed but are still struggling to make their mortgage payments. In June 2012, HAMP expanded to include more homeowners who previously could not take advantage of the program. Bowdler pointed out that other changes to HAMP make it harder for lenders to break their rules. California's Homeowner Bill of Rights is an extension of those changes. She explained:

> The HAMP program tripled its incentives for playing by the rules. California said, "You can sue if they don't play by the rules," so there's now this tradeoff here that's available in California. I certainly think it's something we're going to see other states take a look at because they are desperate to find a way for these rules to be enforceable. Again, we have a certain amount of protections [and] they're not being followed.

---

[20] www.huffingtonpost.com/janis-bowdler/ (Retrieved August 6, 2012).

She continued: "We talk about who's going to pay investors versus taxpayers . . . but when it comes to Fannie Mae and Freddie [Mac], the investors are the taxpayers, so either way, what's going on there, every time Fannie or Freddie takes a loss from a foreclosure, that is a loss to the taxpayers."

Today, lenders and lawmakers are working to simultaneously minimize losses and reduce foreclosures. Bowdler pointed out that one way to do it is through principal reduction. "I'm not saying that's the only way to do it—but one important example is Ocwen, which is a subprime servicer which has been doing principal reduction within its legal bounds and having to comply with servicers. It does not service very many Fannie and Freddie loans, if any, and the way they do it is by equity sharing." In other words, when the home's value goes up, some of the principal that was forgiven would go back to the investor. This is just one option lenders and lawmakers could pursue to help underwater homeowners.[21]

What You Should Know About the Mortgage Forgiveness Debt Relief Act

If you owe a debt to someone else and they cancel or forgive that debt, the canceled amount may be taxable.

But the Mortgage Forgiveness Debt Relief Act of 2007 generally allows taxpayers to exclude income from the discharge of debt on their principal residence. Debt reduced through mortgage restructuring, as well as mortgage debt forgiven in connection with a foreclosure, qualifies for the relief.

The Debt Relief Act applies to debt forgiven in calendar years 2007 through 2012. Up to $2 million of forgiven debt is eligible for this exclusion ($1 million if you are married and filing separately). The exclusion does not apply if the discharge is due to services performed for the lender or any other reason not directly related to a decline in the home's value or the taxpayer's financial condition.

With an impending end of the Mortgage Debt Relief Act at the end of 2012, the pressure is on. If you are still on the fence whether you should short sale your underwater home, take a look at the amount of money you may have to pay in taxes on your deficiency. Even though the bank may forgive the deficiency, after Jan. 1, 2012, you will still have to pay taxes on that deficiency.

According to John Mulville:

> If you're deeply under water, it's a great time to approach your lender and say,
> 'I want to short sale this house, and I want it to close before December 31,

---

[21] http://capitolconnection.net/capcon/aarp/072312a/main.htm# (Retrieved August 6, 2012).

2012.' Congress could extend this, and your lender could conceptually forgive you and not issue you a 1099 for that, but if they don't, we're going back to where we were 5 or 6 years ago, where the IRS might treat that as income. What a nightmare!

■ **Tip** *The Debt Relief Act is set to expire on December 31, 2012!* Because short sales can take several months, now is the time to take action if you are trying to use the Mortgage Relief Act to save tax money on your debt. Also, the U.S. Congress still has time to extend this tax break—and the Obama administration has proposed extending the act into 2015—so watch the news!

Answers to Common Questions About the Mortgage Forgiveness Debt Relief Act

The following are the most commonly asked questions and answers from the Internal Revenue Service about the Mortgage Forgiveness Debt Relief Act and debt cancellation:

Question: *What is "cancellation of debt"?*

Answer: If you borrow money from a commercial lender and the lender later cancels or forgives the debt, you may have to include the cancelled amount in income for tax purposes, depending on the circumstances. When you borrowed the money you were not required to include the loan proceeds in income because you had an obligation to repay the lender. When that obligation is subsequently forgiven, the amount you received as loan proceeds is normally reportable as income because you no longer have an obligation to repay the lender. The lender is usually required to report the amount of the canceled debt to you and the IRS on a Form 1099-C, Cancellation of Debt. Here's a very simplified example. You borrow $10,000 and default on the loan after paying back $2,000. If the lender is unable to collect the remaining debt from you, there is a cancellation of debt of $8,000, which generally is taxable income to you.

Question: *Is cancellation of debt income always taxable?*

Answer: Not always. There are some exceptions, the most common of which are the following:

- **Qualified principal residence indebtedness:** This is the exception created by the Mortgage Debt Relief Act of 2007 and applies to most homeowners.

- **Bankruptcy:** Debts discharged through bankruptcy are not considered taxable income.

- **Insolvency:** If you are insolvent when the debt is cancelled, some or all of the cancelled debt may not be taxable to you. You are insolvent when your total debts are more than the fair market value of your total assets.

- **Certain farm debts:** If you incurred the debt directly in operation of a farm, more than half your income from the prior 3 years was from farming, and the loan was owed to a person or agency regularly engaged in lending, your cancelled debt is generally not considered taxable income.

- **Non-recourse loans:** A non-recourse loan is a loan for which the lender's only remedy in case of default is to repossess the property being financed or used as collateral. That is, the lender cannot pursue you personally in case of default. Forgiveness of a non-recourse loan resulting from a foreclosure does not result in cancellation of debt income. However, it may result in other tax consequences.

Question: *What is the Mortgage Forgiveness Debt Relief Act of 2007?*

Answer: The Mortgage Forgiveness Debt Relief Act of 2007 was enacted on December 20, 2007. Generally, the Act allows exclusion of income realized as a result of modification of the terms of the mortgage or foreclosure on your principal residence.

Question: *What does "exclusion of income" mean?*

Answer: Normally, debt that is forgiven or cancelled by a lender must be included as income on your tax return and is taxable. But the Mortgage Forgiveness Debt Relief Act allows you to exclude certain cancelled debt on your principal residence from income. Debt reduced through mortgage restructuring, as well as mortgage debt forgiven in connection with a foreclosure, qualifies for the relief.

Question: *Does the Mortgage Forgiveness Debt Relief Act apply to all forgiven or cancelled debts?*

Answer: No. The Act applies only to forgiven or cancelled debt used to buy, build, or substantially improve your principal residence or to refinance debt incurred for those purposes. In addition, the debt must be secured by the home. This is known as qualified principal residence indebtedness. The maximum amount you can treat as qualified principal residence indebtedness is $2 million or $1 million if married filing separately.

Question: *Does the Mortgage Forgiveness Debt Relief Act apply to debt incurred to refinance a home?*

Answer: Debt used to refinance your home qualifies for this exclusion, but only to the extent that the principal balance of the old mortgage, immediately before the refinancing, would have qualified.

Question: *If the forgiven debt is excluded from income, do I still have to report it on my tax return?*

Answer: Yes. The amount of debt forgiven must be reported on Form 982 and this form must be attached to your tax return.

Question: *Do I have to complete the entire Form 982?*

Answer: No. Form 982, Reduction of Tax Attributes Due to Discharge of Indebtedness, is used for other purposes in addition to reporting the exclusion of forgiveness of qualified principal residence indebtedness. If you are using the form only for this purpose as the result of foreclosure on your principal residence, you only need to complete lines 1e and 2. If you kept ownership of your home, and modification of the terms of your mortgage resulted in the forgiveness of qualified principal residence indebtedness, complete lines 1e, 2, and 10b.

Question: *Where can I get this form?*

Answer: If you use a computer to fill out your return, check your tax-preparation software. You can also download the form at IRS.gov, or call 1-800-829-3676.

Question: *How do I know or find out how much debt was forgiven?*

Answer: Your lender should send Form 1099-C, Cancellation of Debt, by Feb. 2, 2013. The amount of debt forgiven or cancelled will be shown in box 2. If this debt is all qualified principal residence indebtedness, the amount shown in box 2 will generally be the amount that you enter on lines 2 and 10b, if applicable, on Form 982.

Question: *Can I exclude debt forgiven on my second home, credit card, or car loans?*

Answer: Not under this provision. Only cancelled debt used to buy, build, or improve your principal residence or refinance debt incurred for those purposes qualifies for this exclusion.

Question: *If part of the forgiven debt doesn't qualify for exclusion from income under this provision, is it possible that it may qualify for exclusion under a different provision?*

Answer: Yes. The forgiven debt may qualify under the insolvency exclusion. Normally, you are not required to include forgiven debts in income to the extent that you are insolvent. You are insolvent when your total liabilities exceed your total assets. The forgiven debt may also qualify for exclusion if the debt was discharged in a Title 11 bankruptcy proceeding or if the debt is qualified farm indebtedness or qualified real property business indebtedness.

Question: *I lost money on the foreclosure of my home. Can I claim a loss on my tax return?*

Answer: No. Losses from the sale or foreclosure of personal property are not deductible.

Question: *If I sold my home at a loss and the remaining loan is forgiven, does this constitute a cancellation of debt?*

Answer: Yes. To the extent that a loan from a lender is not fully satisfied and a lender cancels the unsatisfied debt, you have cancellation of indebtedness income. If the amount forgiven or canceled is $600 or more, the lender must generally issue Form 1099-C. An exclusion is also available for the cancellation of certain non-business debts of a qualified individual as a result of a disaster in a Midwestern disaster area.

Question: *If the remaining balance owed on my mortgage loan that I was personally liable for was canceled after my foreclosure, may I still exclude the canceled debt from income under the qualified principal residence exclusion, even though I no longer own my residence?*

Answer: Yes, as long as the canceled debt was qualified principal residence indebtedness.

Loan Forgiveness May Not Be the End of Your Debt

In other words, if you thought your loan forgiveness from the bank was the last time you had to worry about your deficiency, think again. Starting in 2013, barring any last-minute reconsideration by the U.S. Congress and an extension of the Mortgage Forgiveness Act, you will have to pay income tax on loan money forgiven, which could be quite a bit of money if your debt forgiveness was in the five or six figures. "If you owed $200,000 and sold it for $160,000, they could consider that [$40,000] as income, and give you a 1099 to that effect," Mulville added.

Will Congress step up and protect their constituents from these taxes? Will the banks protect their customers? Mulville said it's anyone's guess. "Congress looks like they've got a full plate," he said, "and nobody knows if the lenders would really stand the public uproar over this whole thing. But, on the other side, people have had 5 or 6 years to deal with it. If you can't deal with it in that much time, who knows where your head is at?"

▨ **Tip** *Act now.* Don't count on Congress or the banks to save you from this giant tax burden. If you can close your short sale before Jan. 1, 2013, you may be able to save yourself thousands of dollars in taxes.

WILL SEIZING UNDERWATER MORTGAGES THROUGH EMINENT DOMAIN SLOW FORECLOSURES?

While many homeowners in the United States struggle with underwater mortgages, some localities are suffering from a massive drop in their real estate markets. Several cities and regions are looking into the possibilities of setting up programs to prevent the foreclosures that depress nearby home values.

In California's San Bernardino County, lawmakers are pursuing a plan to seize and restructure underwater mortgages using eminent domain. Other cities in the state are also considering similar plans. According to the *Los Angeles Times*, the Chicago City Council recently held a hearing on the idea.[22] City officials in each of those areas are currently deciding whether these plans will work to prevent foreclosures in their regions.

Many experts and critics claim the program is unnecessary. For example, according to a recent report from the Royal Bank of Scotland (RBS), underwater mortgages in areas such as San Bernardino County, California; Suffolk County, New York; Chicago; and Berkeley, California, will hold steady and not slip into foreclosure without eminent domain.

"A majority of underwater borrowers who would qualify for proposed government programs using eminent domain to seize the loans and write down principal, are still current on their mortgage, according to research from the . . . RBS," wrote reporter Jon Prior in *HousingWire* in early August 2012.

"As of June," he added, "slightly more than 14,000 underwater mortgages in San Bernardino County could qualify for the program, but if home values continue to improve and borrowers remain steady on their mortgages as they've displayed, there may be no need for such a controversial program, according to RBS."[23]

Meanwhile, as San Bernardino moves closer to adopting the program, government leaders from other areas are watching closely to see how well the program works to prevent foreclosures.

---

[22] http://articles.latimes.com/2012/aug/16/business/la-fi-mo-eminent-domain-20120816 (Retrieved October 6, 2012).

[23] www.housingwire.com/news/rbs-underwater-loans-hold-steady-without-eminent-domain (Retrieved August 2, 2012).

Conclusion

While lawmakers across the country seek better solutions to their real estate market problems, homeowners everywhere are watching the values of their homes slowly creep up, but the pace of the progress often looks slower than it really is to an underwater homeowner. Recovery cannot come too fast for homeowners whose homes are worth less than they are paying for them.

An economist's broader view on the real estate market puzzle can provide you with a better look at your own personal housing situation. One economist's ideas can be a valuable part of any strategy for dealing with an underwater home. Two economists' opinions would be even better to help you support your decision. Three are even better than that.

The next chapter introduces another economist with thoughtful insight into the real estate market and underwater mortgages: Dr. Rob Wassmer from California State University. In Chapter 12, Wassmer describes the questions underwater homeowners should ask themselves, urges them to talk to housing counselors, and delves into the ethical questions involved in walking away from an underwater home.

After that, in Chapter 13, a third economist, CoreLogic's Chief Economist Mark Fleming rounds out the conversation by tracking the trends beneath the numbers about underwater mortgages, and revealing where homeowners may find even deeper value hidden in their underwater homes.

12

Advice from an Economist

Rob Wassmer

Dr. Rob Wassmer is chairperson and professor in the Department of Public Policy and Administration at California State University, Sacramento (Sacramento State). Professor Wassmer is also the Director of Sacramento State's Master's Program in Urban Land Development. In addition, he teaches courses in applied microeconomics and public policy, urban economics and public policy; benefit/cost analysis; regression analysis; and state and local public finance.[1]

As an economist, Wassmer said that there are many things that people with underwater mortgages should consider when they look at the state of their finances. For example, if you are you are looking at a mortgage that is $50,000 under water, try to stay focused on the big picture. One way to do that is to stop worrying so much about your "sunk costs" as you try to get a grip on your real estate situation.

Ignore Sunk Costs

What is a sunk cost? This is a cost that has already been incurred by a homeowner and can no longer be recovered. This is something for which has been paid in the past. It will never come back. Said Wassmer:

> You paid a quarter-million dollars for this home, and now it's only worth $200,000. And now you are lamenting that $50,000 that you paid. That's a sunk cost. Economists and businesspeople say you need to ignore those. You're looking to the future. . . . Some people will say, 'Well, I've got this quarter-

---

[1] All quotes from Rob Wassmer were collected during a personal interview in July 2012.

million-dollar asset, and I'm going to have to stay here, and if I just wait long enough, I think it's going to come back.' I think that's not the attitude to have. You have to take the realistic expectation in regard to what the property is worth now and what the appreciation is going to be over time.

Here are three questions Wassmer said homeowners should ask to get an economist's perspective of their underwater home:

1. How many years do you have to stay to get back to that quarter-million dollars?

2. Are you going to be there that long?

3. What are your other options?

I think . . . you have to explore some of these federal or state programs that are available that a lot that people still don't know about. . . . I think before you talk to your bank about renegotiating your mortgage, explore those [programs] and see what's available and see what your legal options are. And then I think you've really got to go and talk to your bank. Talk to a real person about what the options are and do not be afraid to talk about maybe renegotiating the terms of your mortgage.

■ **Tip** *Don't be afraid.* Fear can force people to make irrational decisions. Think clearly and calmly about your next steps. Talk to people you can trust who have experience in this area. You are not the first person to go through this process. Get some professional people on your side and explore your options rationally and calmly. Take time, but work to make steady progress.

HOUSING COUNSELING PROGRAMS

Many urban areas have organizations that offer homeowners who are facing mortgage delinquency free default counseling and foreclosure prevention and intervention counseling. They can also help homeowners identify and avoid predatory lending practices and mortgage refinancing scams. Professionally trained housing counselors at these agencies often conduct free group or individual counseling sessions on many of the concerns faced by homeowners including mortgage foreclosure prevention, rights and responsibilities of homeowners, and financial assistance programs.

For example, in Philadelphia, the city's Office of Housing and Community Development offers a page on its web site that lists more than 25 housing counseling agencies that are available to homeowners. Some of these agencies have eligibility requirements.[2]

---

[2] www.phila.gov/ohcd/cslgagencies.htm (Retrieved July 30, 2012).

The best way to find an agency in your area is to do an online search for free housing counseling agencies in or near your closest city. Another place to start is your local office of community development.

You can also get advice on housing issues by calling U.S. Department of Housing and Urban Development's interactive voice system at (800) 569-4287 and asking about housing counseling agencies in your region.[3]

These programs are usually free and services are often available in a number of language options.

Ethical Considerations Will Arise

A decision to abandon a property or pursue a short sale will not be based on financial considerations alone.

Economist Rob Wassmer reminded homeowners that there are some deeper implications to abandoning a mortgage. "There's kind of an ethical issue here," he said. "You've made a commitment to this property: Do you walk away from it?" Looking at the issue from an ethical perspective, many homeowners will want to balance their own actions with the allegedly unethical practices of predatory lenders and other agents who sold people homes they could not afford. If these issues bog you down, a good lawyer can tell you whether there are legal implications that ride along with your ethical decisions.

"A lot of people are walking away from their homes even if they can afford to make their mortgage payments," Wassmer said. "They stop making them because it would cut back too much on the rest of their lifestyle." There's a trade-off, of course. Your credit score will often become too low to purchase another home for 5 to 7 years. When you think like an economist, however, you can look into the future and see the light at the end of the credit score tunnel. "After the 5 or 7 years, it [the score] comes back," Wassmer pointed out.

The real ethical issues that can have deeper legal ramifications arise when the owner of an underwater home continues to live in the house after it has been foreclosed and does not take care of the home. "They take appliances out or take fixtures out and destroy the house. That's really a double whammy" and is unethical behavior.

Some people might say that a person who lives in a house for years while it is going through the foreclosure process is unethical, but this choice may be

---

[3] http://portal.hud.gov/hudportal/HUD?src=/i_want_to/talk_to_a_housing_counselor (Retrieved July 30, 2012).

mitigated by the homes' occupants remaining responsible stewards of that property. This might be seen as an ethical decision that actually benefits the lender who will eventually take ownership of the property.

■ **Tip** *Be a good homeowner.* Even if you continue to live in a foreclosed home, keeping the house in good shape for the next owner will be seen as a better sign of "good faith" than creating thousands of dollars of repairs for the next owner.

Rob Wassmer said he believes states should create policies that promote more responsible home stewardship. Why? "Because you [are] really taking care of it for the bank so they can find another owner for it."

He added:

> That's kind of what a short sale does at the same time too, right? Both parties realize that the mortgage is too high for what it's worth now, and we're going to try to sell it at a lower rate. It's advantageous to both sides if you let the person live in there until the short sale can occur. Banks have to become realistic about what it's worth, too.

Do Not Cheat the System

Wassmer said he also believes that homeowners should not be able to cheat the system when they get a break from their mortgage debts from government programs that help people with underwater mortgages.

He explained:

> When a homeowner who owes $250,000 on a mortgage for a house that is currently appraised to be worth only $200,000, what you really need to do is renegotiate the terms of the loan and bring it down to $200,000 or $225,000. If the bank does that, or the government has some program that subsidizes the doing of that, I don't think the homeowner then should be able to take advantage of that, say if the property goes up to $275,000 while the homeowner is still living there. If they only had it for $225,000, that $50,000 should go back to the government or go back to the bank who negotiated that lower mortgage.

Why is it often so difficult for many homeowners to get loan modifications? Wassmer said it's probably because lenders are not making these kinds of arrangements—getting more money back from the borrower if the value of the home goes up when it is sold. "The banks are taking the hit of cutting back on the payments they are receiving, but then the homeowner's going to get the equity back," Wassmer said. More loan modifications might get done if the banks reduced the principal but regained some of it if the property is ultimately sold for more than it was worth at the renegotiation.

WHY DO HOMEOWNERS CHOOSE STRATEGIC DEFAULT?

Many borrowers are skipping their mortgage payments even though they're able to pay the bills. This is a phenomenon commonly known as "strategic default." So said a July 2009 study titled "Moral and Social Constraints to Strategic Default on Mortgages" by Luigi Guiso from the European University Institute, Paola Sapienza from Northwestern University, and Luigi Zingales from the University of Chicago.[4]

According to their report, 26 percent of the defaults at that time were strategic. The researchers also found that homeowners did not choose the option of strategic default if their equity shortfall was less than 10 percent of the value of the house.

On the other hand, the researchers reported that 17 percent of the households they studied said they would default, even if they could afford to make their mortgage payments, when the equity shortfall reached 50 percent of the value of their house. (In other words, if their LTV was 150 percent or higher.)

Why would they do this? Many homeowners cited relocation costs as the primary reason they would choose to default strategically. The next most popular reasons were "moral and social considerations." The researchers explained that "people who consider it immoral to default are 77 percent less likely to declare their intention to do so, while people who know someone who defaulted are 82 percent more likely to declare their intention to do so."

The researchers concluded:

> That moral attitudes toward default do not change with the percentage of foreclosures in the area suggests that the correlation between willingness to default and percentage of foreclosures is likely to derive from a contagion effect that reduces the social stigma associated with default as defaults become more common.

Ask: How Much Am I Under Water?

The real question that many people need to answer to decide their next step is, How much am I under water? Again, going online to determine your LTV can easily provide you with that answer:

---

[4] http://financialtrustindex.org/images/Guiso_Sapienza_Zingales_StrategicDefault.pdf (Retrieved July 20, 2012).

www.bankrate.com/calculators/mortgages/ltv-loan-to-value-ratio-calculator.
aspx

Then, look around and see how much your area is rising out of the real estate doldrums, if at all. If it is recovering, figure out how fast it is rising: 1 percent each year? 5 percent each year? 10 percent? Talk to real estate agents in your area. How much are home prices rebounding in your neighborhood? Are they going up or staying flat? Knowing the numbers can help you figure out how long you will need to wait before seeing some real equity in your home.

■ **Tip** *Hold tight.* Although your largest financial investment is under water, hang on! If you are 10 percent or less under water, hanging on through these tough economic times for the real estate market may pay off in the long run. Take a long-term perspective and start enjoying your investment for what it really offers you: a place to live happily and comfortably. When the real estate market rises back up, "all boats rise with the tide," and you will see your equity rise with it. Spend more time enjoying your investment than fretting over the money it entails. Help is on the way, although it may still be a few years away from gathering the strength to rebound completely.

"It's just a matter of magnitude—how much are they under water?" Wassmer asked. Much of the economy is slowly recovering from the recent deep economic downturn. "Actually, the recession is over," he pointed out, "so we just have to plan economic growth after that—it's different over different metropolitan areas. So I think if you are in a $250,000 home, if you are $50,000 under water in California as compared to North Carolina, you have to look and see where the projections are for home values. I think in California it is more flat than in a place like North Carolina, where they are coming back."

There are several crucial questions that Wassmer said homeowners should ask themselves once they have looked at their local market and the speed at which home prices will likely rise:

- How long will it take to recoup the value until it goes back to where I am above water on my home?

- How long do I plan on staying here?

He added, "And then you just work out some type of rational calculation in regard to whether you should [sell] it or not." This calculation should also include the following questions:

- How will a short sale, deed in lieu of foreclosure, foreclosure, strategic default, or bankruptcy affect my credit score? Strategic default means choosing not to pay your mortgage even if you could, perhaps choosing to continue to live in the home for several years before foreclosure or eviction. Deed in lieu is making a nicer exchange with the bank instead of foreclosing. This will also help you avoid an auction or public sale, and hopefully soften the impact on your credit score.

- Do I want to take that risk? This is an important personal choice. This answer will depend on what you can rationally, ethically, emotionally, and financially handle. Once again, research will help you learn which way the wind is blowing in your area when figuring out how much risk is involved. Searching values of local homes is a great place to start looking for real numbers.

One place you can go online to determine the state of the real estate market in your area is the commercial web site for RealtyTrac: www.realtytrac.com/trendcenter/

Other organizations regularly offer their projections for the next year for the nation or specific areas. An online search, and some free help from a local realtor or stockbroker, can help you get a better grip on your market's outlook.

Projecting Future Home Values

What kinds of projections should you seek? As Wassmer said:

> How much have property values, median home values changed from 2007, 2008, 2009, 2010? Then, just look for a trend and where it's going. There are people out there who are even prognosticating, using those numbers and looking at basic economic fundamentals in that area. Is that going to continue or not? I think you can just do a linear trend yourself, and go back and look over the last 5 years, what's been happening. Then you can try to find some experts who are making some predictions. I think Google searches can give you that stuff pretty easily.

■ **Tip** *Google search your future.* Although nobody can perfectly predict the future of the housing market, a solid Internet search can reveal many facts, figures, and expert opinions that can tell you if your local real estate market is on a solid rebound, is flattening, or is even going downward. Try entering "Real Estate Market Trends + [your zip code]." Use this information to learn whether you have time to wait for your underwater property to recover, or if the waiting game will simply take too long for you to see any equity in your home in the time you plan to live there. Chart the trends yourself, or look for the work of others. These simple graphs can tell you approximately where your equity may be several years down the road.

Why Did Economists Fail to Sound the Alarm Before the Real Estate Bubble Burst?

Economist Rob Wassmer said he saw the bubble growing in Sacramento as home prices grew steadily for years. "I remember Sacramento was a real boom metropolitan area where the median home value had risen close to $300,000, close to $400,000, and the median income was only $70,000 or $80,000." People were wondering how that could continue.

"In hindsight people recognize it, but I think it's 20/20 [hindsight], as they say," Wassmer explained. He added that many people who should have noticed the impending crisis did not recognize it for the catastrophe it would become. "There were a few people out there, they were saying this wasn't sustainable, but others were not, including Greenspan, the chairman of the Federal Reserve. He's been quoted as saying that he didn't see this coming at all."

A Perfect Storm

Nonetheless, most experts missed the convergence of economic forces that forced the real estate market into crisis mode in record time. Wassmer added, "It was kind of the perfect storm in many ways, with things coming together."

On the brighter side, one positive thing that came out of the collapse of the real estate market is that it opened the eyes of individual investors about the risks involved in real estate investing. Banking on your home is not a sure thing. Wassmer agreed: "I think people are more aware of this reality now, and perhaps they even erred more on the other side, thinking that this is the new norm, where there is going to be flat housing growth."

Where does the real estate market stand now? Wassmer said it is not simply a wildly growing bubble, nor is it a flat line with no growth potential. He explained, "I think it's probably somewhere in between the two."

What should an individual homeowner do? He added, "I don't think it's good advice to never buy a home, but depending upon your situation and where you live, it might be wise to sit it out for a while."

■ **Tip** *Seriously consider whether to buy.* Things to consider include the stability of the local job market, whether house prices are going up or down, and whether renting may be a better option. Get as much advice as possible from professionals in your area before jumping into any real estate market.

Irrational Exuberance Vs. Irrational Pessimism

Before the bubble burst, irrational exuberance clouded the judgment of many professionals, including economists and real estate experts around the country. Today, Wassmer said there is another problem that has a detrimental effect on the market:

> *Irrational pessimism [is a problem], at this point. That is what's keeping the economy back. Businesses have a lot of money that they are sitting on. Individuals have a lot of money they are sitting on. In fact, a lot of private investors are putting money back into homes, and buying these foreclosed or short sale homes, which isn't really doing a lot for the economy, in regard to building new ones.*

One thing to remember when listening to any expert in any market is that they often simplify concepts to make them easier for the average person to understand. Wassmer said that economists make errors of judgment just like everyone else, so it was not surprising that most of them missed predicting the collapse of the real estate market in 2006 and 2007. "Nobody really has a crystal ball and can gaze into the future, but economists always err on the side of being too pessimistic or too optimistic." Wassmer explained. He added that it is easy to make firm statements about the past, but very difficult to guess what is coming next, especially when it involves the real estate market, which is influenced by so many variables. "You never can really predict where it turns," he added.

▓ **Tip**   *Don't believe the hype.* Scrutinize expert opinions. People like to get excited, even when very little is happening. Use your own power of reason to decide what is the truth and what is hyperbole. And if it sounds too good, it probably is.

Today, the real estate market is in the middle of a fundamental rebalancing act. Some will say it is going better than predicted, others will say it is stagnating worse:

> *Many people have been hit pretty hard. The home is the typical American major source of wealth. If the equity in your home is being preserved or it's growing, you're going to feel more confident to go out and buy a car or to buy appliances or even to buy a second home and take vacations. Americans can borrow against their equity to do those types of things. And with the housing market flat, I think that people aren't doing that anymore.*

Wassmer said that this was the cause of the Great Recession and continues to be the reason people continue to be afraid of spending their money in the same ways they did in the past. "There's kind of a doom that sits over us from the severe downturn," he added, and this continues to influence what people choose to do with their homes.

A cost–benefit analysis can help anyone make a better decision. Wassmer said the way he does this goes back to an idea he attributes to Benjamin Franklin: "You take a piece of paper and you draw a line down the middle of it. On one side you write down the costs of staying in this home. And then on the other side of the piece of paper you write down the benefits." Some of the items are tangible costs and benefits in regard to mortgages, for example, how long it would take for the house to get above water. Some are intangible, for example, how you feel about having this bankruptcy on your record forever. I think people just have to do that kind of mental calculation . . . and then make a decision."

A simple diagram like this is a great place to start. If your informal calculations leave you with two perfectly balanced sides that do not help you make your decision, move on to more formal mathematical calculations to really flesh out the finer points of your decision. In addition, an accountant's opinion will also add some weight and realism to your calculations. A real estate agent can also help you look at your options more realistically by describing your local housing market.

▓ **Tip** *Weigh the pros and cons.* Look at both sides carefully before you choose the option that is right for you. Sleep on your decision before you act on it. Be sure of your decision because you will have to live with it for the rest of your life. Once you have made your choice, take action. Move on to the next phase of your life.

Ethical Dilemmas: Part Two

One thing that will also play into your decision about whether to stay or go will include the ethics of the choice. This is the most personal part of the decision and will require you to take a look at your own moral compass, especially if you decide to walk away from the home to which you made a commitment.

While looking for direction, many underwater homeowners sense they are at a disadvantage to their lenders: and they are. Economists and other experts point out that markets favor the most knowledgeable. Banks have vast experience from years of daily transactions. A homeowner often has only one or two experiences from which to learn about selling or buying a home. This "information asymmetry" is naturally advantageous to lenders. Many people were sold homes they really could not afford by lenders who capitalized on that imbalance. It is the same imbalance that people feel when they must decide whether to fall behind on payments, live in a home while making no payments, or abandon a cherished home. Wassmer said:

> Some people maybe shouldn't feel so bad about [what they do] because of information asymmetry. They were kind of hoodwinked. They weren't given all the information. And we've moved into a different state of the world too. Even if they were given all the information, people still expected homes to appreciate 2 or 5 percent each year instead of all of a sudden dropping the 10 or 20 percent they did in a couple of years.

WHERE IS THE MARKET HEADING?

At the end of July 2012, Reuters reported that the latest numbers showed that there have been about 3.7 million foreclosures in the United States since the financial crisis started in September 2008.

CoreLogic's latest numbers showed that about 1.4 million homes, or 3.4 percent of homes with mortgages, were involved in the foreclosure process in June 2012. That number was lower than the 1.5 million homes, or 3.5 percent of the U.S. market, in June 2011. The number was about the same as the number of foreclosures in May 2012.[5]

Are we there yet? Has the real estate market completely tanked? That would probably depend on housing prices more than the latest foreclosure report.

According to a recent report on *CNNMoney*, "Zillow estimates that home values nationwide will fall another 3.7 percent by the end of 2012, and that price will likely bottom out by early 2013."[6]

Moral Obligations and Ethical Decisions

In other words, before your guilt pushes you into making a bad decision because you feel it is unethical to default on your mortgage, seriously consider the actions of others that led to your current situation. The playing field was changed mid-game, and promises made on the part of lawmakers (from both parties), lenders, real estate agents, ratings agencies, home appraisers, and many others were not kept. In addition, sometimes the rules of the market were changed without homeowners knowing it until it was too late to recoup

[5] http://in.reuters.com/article/2012/07/31/usa-housing-corelogic-idINL2E8IV1PK20120731 (Retrieved August 1, 2012).

[6] http://money.cnn.com/2012/04/13/real_estate/foreclosures/index.htm (Retrieved August 1, 2012).

their lost equity. Yes, there are ethical questions to ask yourself regarding your decisions to get out of your underwater home, but there are many factors to consider beyond the simplicity of a broken mortgage contract. Is there a moral problem when a homeowner seeks to get out of a contract that was signed while being deceived by predatory organizations? That is something you'll need to decide for yourself.

■ **Tip**   *Make your own decision.* Ethics are personal. Only you know what is right or wrong for yourself. If there is an ethical choice, it is up to you to decide. If there are legal decisions to make, hire an attorney to help you get through it.

Are More Regulations the Answer?

Wassmer said he believes that the lesson for the future that should be learned from the real estate market crisis is to work to equalize the information asymmetry by providing borrowers with more information with which to make real estate decisions: "Let's try to get away from as much of that deception as possible—and that's where you get much greater regulation in regard to mortgages."

Disappointingly, Wassmer explained, most of the regulations that were proposed to protect consumers from the lending practices that led to the real estate bubble bursting several years ago have been "watered down." As a result, communities continue to lose the local connections that once made them strong. He added that:

> We're going back to the same type of situation we had before, because there's money to be made in granting those mortgages and then selling them off someplace else. The bank itself doesn't even hold onto it anymore. That was part of the issue in the past: A community would lend mortgages, would lend them money for homeownership, but then hold on to those mortgages, and they were much more careful in the mortgages that they gave.

Today, mortgages are often bundled up into a portfolio shortly after they are signed and sold to "some foreign investor," Wassmer said. "And if things go bad, don't even worry about it." Anyone who has taken out a loan recently should expect that mortgage to change hands almost immediately once it is signed. Banks usually make this clear from the beginning, as the practice is now commonplace.

How should lawmakers fix the system so another real estate bubble does not expand too far and burst? Wassmer said regulators should help to level the playing field by giving consumers the information they need to make rational choices. He explained:

> As an economist and a strong believer in the market, markets can fail, especially when you have this information asymmetry. . . . I think that's where we need to move in terms of reform—getting it all out there, and even having mandatory counseling sessions for somebody who's right on the margin. Even if they say, "I want to do this," lay it out to them very carefully, and get them to sign a piece of paper that [says], "I've heard all this and I understand it."

He explained that this kind of policy change would indicate people could then be held responsible for the decisions they make when choosing to default on their mortgages.

Tip (for lenders) *Create greater transparency.* This would help borrowers make more informed decisions about their real estate investments. Mandatory mortgage counseling is an idea with many advocates.

U.S. DEPARTMENT OF HOUSING PROVIDES $42 MILLION FOR HOUSING COUNSELING

As part of its continuing effort to help families find decent housing and to prevent future foreclosures, in March 2012 HUD announced more than $42 million in housing counseling grants to 468 national, regional, and local organizations. As a result of this funding, HUD reported, "hundreds of thousands of households will have a greater opportunity to find housing or keep their current homes."

More than $36 million in grant funds have directly supported the housing counseling services provided by 27 national and regional organizations, 6 multistate organizations, 16 State Housing Finance Agencies (SHFAs), and 419 local housing counseling agencies.

In addition, HUD awarded $2 million to 3 national organizations to train counselors and receive the certification necessary to effectively assist families with their housing needs. Counseling agencies will also receive $4 million to help seniors who seek reverse mortgages.[7]
A list of the organizations that received the funding can be found at: portal.hud.gov/hudportal/documents/huddoc?id=2012HCAwardslist.pdf

---

[7] www.hud.gov/offices/adm/hudclips/handbooks/hsgh/7610.1/76101HSGH.pdf (Retrieved August 1, 2012).

Are Homeowners Better Citizens?

Some people believe that home ownership is overrated in the United States. Wassmer pointed out, "I think there is a wakeup call now that home ownership is not all that great financially. And I don't think that the evidence is all that strong that it really transforms a person either. That's really kind of shaky evidence."

Denise DiPasquale of the University of Chicago and Edward L. Glaeser of Harvard University wrote a paper on that very topic: "Incentives and Social Capital: Are Homeowners Better Citizens?" After studying information they found in the U.S. General Social Survey, they attempted to measure the effects of home ownership on citizenship and community. In their conclusion, they wrote, "In the U.S., it appears that a significant fraction of the effect of homeownership occurs because homeownership is associated with longer community tenure." But, they added, "While it is likely that homeownership generates positive externalities, we have no measure of the size of these externalities. . . . Promoting homeownership also limits mobility, which may impose costs that far exceed any benefits from better citizenship."[8]

"A Spurious Correlation"

Wassmer added that simply owning a home does not necessarily equate with being a better person. "It's kind of a spurious correlation."

Likewise, offering home ownership to people who cannot afford it can have some very serious consequences. "You can really destroy their lives in many ways," Wassmer said, "and even destroy the lives of their children." For example, many children may feel terrible shame when facing friends and neighbors after they are forced to move out of a home their parents could not afford.

Although it seems that everyone on television and the Internet makes it a point to connect home ownership with all of the great things that are part of the American dream, it is important to look beneath the surface when searching for the truth behind the façade. When comparing the benefits of home ownership to the benefits of renting, don't forget where all of the propaganda about the joys of home ownership originated. Ask yourself who is paying the bill for all of those advertisements and reports. Wassmer explained, "There is a huge effort to show this correlation between home ownership and all these good things, and most of the research is supported, directly or indirectly, by the real estate industry."

---

[8] www.law.uchicago.edu/files/files/54.Glaeser.Home_.pdf (Retrieved August 1, 2012).

■ **Tip**   *Follow the money.* When you worry that renting is going to be a blow to your dreams of homeownership, remember who paid to keep those dreams at the forefront of your mind throughout your life. Before you take any advice from anyone, ask yourself, "Will this person benefit financially from my choice?" If so, keep that bias in mind if you follow that advice.

Likewise, when making any lifelong decision, look at the connections that are not apparent at first glance. Ask yourself:

- What is the truth?
- What is just advertising?
- What are the long-term repercussions of this decision?
- Why am I choosing this option over another?
- What will make me happy and secure?
- Who do I trust?
- What is the best option for me and my family?
- Have I completely thought out this decision?

Answering such questions will not just help you make a decision; it can give you peace of mind. It may also help you realize that renting a home often makes much more sense than owning one.

Put Aside Cynicism of the Government

The Pew Research Center for the People & the Press's 2011 Political Typology study recently found that a majority (55 percent) of Americans say that government is almost always wasteful and inefficient (compared with 39 percent who think that government often does a better job than people give it credit for).[9] Although the majority of people are somewhat cynical about the role of government in their lives, when a person is under water, it might be time to put away that negative attitude, use some of those tax dollars in action, and seek some help from the agencies that are available. Some are government sponsored, others are community based. Either way, get some help.

"I think people are cynical about government," Wassmer said, but he said that if a homeowner is looking for real estate advice, federal or state programs can be very helpful for people who are under water. "Their vested interests really

---

[9] http://pewresearch.org/databank/dailynumber/?NumberID=1337 (Retrieved August 2, 2012).

are not with the real estate industry. Talk to [government agencies] and get some advice beginning there. Even before you go to your bank, look at your options there."

Like many federal and state programs, those intended to help underwater homeowners are often underutilized. Wassmer added, "Feds have put a bunch of money into those and made options available for a certain number of homeowners, and [the programs] weren't even being taken advantage of." States also have underutilized programs, so make contact with them and learn what services are available.

▓ **Tip**   *Search out free resources.* Too many programs go unused when they could offer many people some help when they need it most. Go online and search for a program near you. If you don't qualify for the one you find, ask if there would be a better program for you and your situation. Stay online or on the phone until you find somebody who can truly help you. Remember that a Google search is free.

Finally, if you feel that there are not enough people out there to help people like you who are under water, use your power as a citizen and a taxpayer and demand a change in the system. Call your local congressperson or senator. Demand that more of your tax dollars go out to help people in your type of situation.

Wassmer agreed: "If you can't get in touch with those federal people or there are not enough free programs, you may even use the political process to call for more of that."

Conclusion

Whereas Dr. Rob Wassmer teaches his students at California State University how to prepare for the future of public policy and urban land development, others are gathering the numbers economists can use when analyzing the current and future real estate situation. One of those economists is Mark Fleming.

Fleming works for an organization that specializes in helping people in the real estate business understand the latest numbers from the market. CoreLogic is world famous for getting to the bottom of the real estate trends that are shaping the nation and the world. In the next chapter, Fleming helps underwater homeowners analyze the latest numbers to learn where they stand now so they can make decisions about the future.

Advice from CoreLogic Chief Economist Mark Fleming

The one place where the top organizations go to learn more about the state of the real estate industry is the firm CoreLogic. Why do they go there? CoreLogic is a well-respected company that has provided data and analytical solutions to mortgage, finance, real estate, and other industries around the world for more than two decades.[1] The company aggregates and collects data and uses that to build products that help its clients handle the market with more efficiency, understand risk better, and evaluate the real estate market more accurately.

CoreLogic's chief economist, Mark Fleming, has worked at CoreLogic for nearly a decade. As chief economist, his job entails using all of the data and assets of the company to evaluate, analyze, and understand the real estate

---

[1] http://articles.latimes.com/1991-09-04/business/fi-1687_1_estate-information (Retrieved August 9, 2012).

market, as well as to provide the company's clients with insight into what is going on in the world of real estate. [2]

In July 2012, CoreLogic released numbers that described how the real estate market was doing at the end of the first quarter of 2012. The data looked very promising. Fleming explained: "The headline numbers are that 23.7 percent of all mortgaged homes are under water or in negative equity conditions at the end of the first quarter [a decrease from the end of the last quarter of 2011], and that's 11.4 million households."

Three months later, in September 2012, the second quarter numbers for the year were in: Residential properties in negative equity decreased again. CoreLogic reported 600,000 more borrowers were "above water" for a total of 1.3 million in the first half of the year. The new data showed 22.3 percent of residential properties with a mortgage were in negative equity at the end of the second quarter of 2012. That is 10.8 million people who are under water.

Fleming explained: "Surging home prices this spring and summer, lower levels of inventory, and declining REO sale shares are all contributing to the nascent housing recovery and declining negative equity." In other words, underwater houses are rising above the surface and staying there. The slogging real estate market was moving forward for the first time in a while, and everyone involved is hoping it builds steam. Whereas Nevada, Florida, Arizona, Georgia, and Michigan continued to represent a sizable portion (34.1 percent) of the total amount of negative equity in the country (see Figures 13-1 and 13-2), other states—such as North Dakota, Arkansas, West Virginia, and New York— have the fewest underwater mortgage holders.[3]

Strong Step in the Right Direction

In an interview for this book in July 2012, Fleming said he believes the numbers from the first quarter were a very strong step in the right direction. "The good news, which is *really* good news, is it [negative equity conditions] is down from 12.1 million or 25 percent at the end of 2011. There's been a big improvement on the order of about 600,000 borrowers are no longer under water that were at the end of the quarter."

---

[2] All quotes from Mark Fleming were collected during a personal interview in July 2012.

[3] www.corelogic.com/about-us/news/asset_upload_file516_16435.pdf (Retrieved October 10, 2012).

Q2 2012 Equity Share

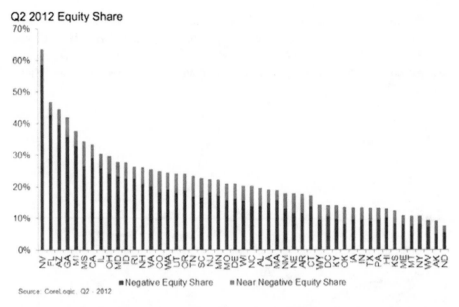

Source: CoreLogic, Q2 - 2012

Figure 13-1. Negative Equity Concentrated Mostly in Sand States. Graphic courtesy of CoreLogic.

Q2 2012 Equity Distribution

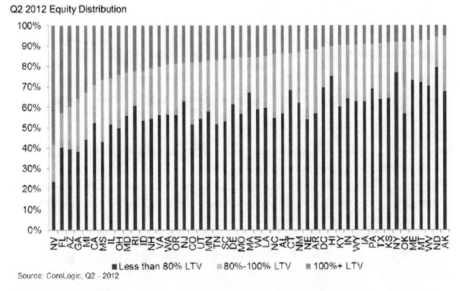

Source: CoreLogic, Q2 - 2012

Figure 13-2. Distribution of Equity Widely Varies by State. Graphic courtesy of CoreLogic.

Fleming explained that he believes that the main reason why this number is going down—why fewer people are under water today than just a few months ago—is because home prices are appreciating. "We've seen in the first quarter, into the second quarter of 2012, the housing markets have sort of come off their bottom and house prices are slowly improving right now." He explained that there are a variety of factors that are currently balancing out, which also has helped to reduce the number of underwater homeowners. (See Figure 13-3.)

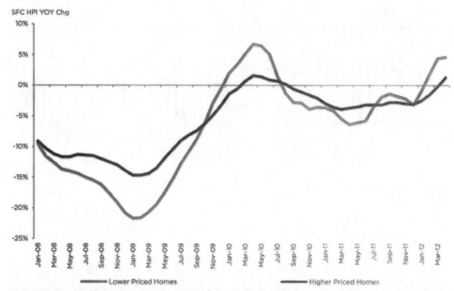

Note: Lower priced homes are less than 75% of the median and higher priced homes are >125% of the median price.
Source: CoreLogic April 2012

Figure 13-3. Lower Priced Homes Appreciating Rapidly. Graphic courtesy of CoreLogic.

Surprisingly, housing markets where price appreciations are improving are also the same ones that have the most negative equity. Why? Fleming explained: "The reason is because negative equity presses the supply of homes for sale, so demand is improving a little bit." Here are some of the reasons demand for homes in these areas are going up:

- People are coming off the sidelines and buying homes.
- Houses are really affordable.
- Interest rates are very low.
- People have more economic certainty in their lives.
- People believe more strongly in their future job prospects.
- The economy has slowly improved.

"Demand just kicks up a little bit," Fleming added, "but we can't get the supply out there because a lot of the homes that would be supplied to us through the real estate market are existing homes that are under water." In other words, existing homes make up the largest share of the market, and a lot of those homes are under water. These homeowners cannot put their homes on the market because the sale price still won't cover the mortgage. Fleming continued: "So, it's created this depression of supply that is [recently] coming into alignment with the low and slowly improving demand." This creates some tight markets—especially those that suffered the most from the burst of the real estate bubble.

Rising Fortunes in Phoenix

For example, Phoenix, one place that suffered the most, is currently watching its home prices rise faster than anywhere else. Fleming said, "Phoenix has a very short supply relative to the demand. [It] is very tight so house prices are responding by rising and improving." This house price appreciation in Phoenix has helped to improve the fortunes of everyone there with negative equity.

Today, CoreLogic's numbers show a virtuous cycle happening in places like Phoenix. Their area's high levels of negative equity are helping them see more growth than any other places in the country. Fleming said, "In other words, the markets with the largest price appreciation are exactly the ones with the largest share of negative equity." These are the markets that were rising fastest out of negative equity during the first quarter of 2012. Why a virtuous cycle? In this case, because as prices rise, fewer homes are under water and homeowners are more willing to put their homes on the market. Slowly but surely, the market is becoming unstuck.

This is also a good example of why certain areas in the United States are faring better than others regarding home valuation. There is a wide variation in how fast localities are recovering. Some are watching their home values increase, others are seeing them stay the same, and others are still declining. Overall, though, the prices in the U.S. housing market are rising.

Fleming said, "Of course real estate is very local, so there's wide variation. Many markets are improving. House prices are rising. There are still markets where house prices are falling . . . [and] more people are falling into negative equity and not less."

While Phoenix has seen the largest house price appreciation, other markets that had serious underwater problems have also improved. For example, in 2012, Nevada had the highest percentage of underwater mortgages at 59 percent. Florida, Arizona, and Georgia followed. The top five combined had an average negative equity share of 34.1 percent. Even though this is a big improvement compared to the previous quarter's 44.5 percent, it is still pretty high. This means about one in three houses with a mortgage is under water in those states. On the bright side, many of the markets that were hardest hit with negative equity have seen the largest improvement in their home values. Fleming calls this a "virtuous cycle."

This is the virtuous cycle CoreLogic called "The Paradox of Negative Equity" in its *MarketPulse* newsletter in June 2012. Fleming explained: "We all think of negative equity as a very bad thing, right? And it certainly is bad for the individual homeowner. If your home is under water, that creates a lot of problems, just like you are talking about in your [this] book."

Negatives Lead to Positives

For example, if homeowners are delinquent on their loans because of a lost job or some sort of income shock, they cannot make a mortgage payment. If a homeowner has equity, viable options for solving this problem are selling the house or refinancing potentially into a lower mortgage payment.

Fleming continued:

> When you don't have equity, then we're in a much more difficult set of situations: Can't make my mortgage payment, can't do a basic sale, or a basic refinance. Now we need to look at options like dealing with the lender and negotiating a short sale or modification, or the worst-case scenario, foreclosure. So, clearly being under water is a bad thing for the homeowner. The paradox we have here is that there is a beneficial outcome, if you will, at the market level, in that we're finding the markets that have more borrowers under water are actually the ones that are improving in house prices more quickly.

He pointed out that this improvement is bound to fade over time:

> because what happens is, as house prices rise and borrowers are shifted into positive equity, it unlocks them from being stuck. So, as they become unlocked or regain positive equity, and because house prices have risen, a lot of borrowers in Phoenix now all of a sudden have equity and much of them may choose to go and put their homes for sale. Then they increase the supply to go with demand.

Adding more homes to the market helps to stabilize the supply-and-demand imbalance. Fleming added, "So, the cycle as this process happens, in a dynamic sense, relieves the pressure, which is causing these price increases. It also puts people less at risk for foreclosure because now they have equity, they have more options if they can't make their mortgage payment."

Rebounding Prices

In other words, the places that were once hit the hardest by the burst of the real estate bubble are the first ones to see their home prices rebound. Although this upward trend is beneficial to many, it is not a straight line to recovery because markets never work that way. As prices in these areas go up, more houses hit the market, which slows the recovery as they continue to trend upward.

"In the real world nothing ever goes in a nice straight line," Fleming explained. "We have these effects, but we get an improvement. People will then react to that information. Things will change. In all likelihood, in a market such as Phoenix, you would see that upward price pressure begin to fade. As more people buy homes, negative equity shares trend down. But then they start to trend down more slowly, and house prices rise more slowly." Meanwhile, the transition to a better real estate market in these areas fluctuates as it tries to find a healthier equilibrium.

The point is that the market will not simply recover in a year or 2 and return to pre-2006 home values. Fleming said, "This doesn't go away quickly. [It is] fundamentally going to be with us in the market for many years."

No Jobs Slows Equity Growth

Although places like Phoenix are seeing substantially improved housing markets, other places will take much longer to recover from deep levels of negative equity. These are the places that are not seeing improvements in one of the most important factors that creates home equity: jobs. Without jobs, places such as Detroit will take much longer to recover from the real estate market crash.

Fleming explained that, in these areas, "there's not a lot of upward price pressures. So, like in Detroit for example, or some of these other places, you're not getting this virtuous cycle because fundamentally there's less demand." The supply of houses on the market is still abundant, which keeps the prices for the houses that are on sale lower than they ever were. Without an influx of jobs to the area, those home prices will stay flat, or worse.

"So, you can't necessarily say that all the markets that have negative equity will necessarily have a price improvement," Fleming reflected. "It never works that way in the real world. That is one of many factors that contribute to the situation right now. These deep negative equity shares will have a positive influence, but there might be other more negative influences that outweigh this."

A lack of job growth in many areas contributes to the extreme variations in home prices from market to market in the United States. This means that how fast underwater homeowners can expect to see equity in their homes depends greatly on the location of the homes.

Home as an Investment?

How can an individual take advantage of the latest CoreLogic numbers? People with underwater homes should be able to find some hope in the latest statistics that show there are fewer people facing foreclosure now than there were before. If this trend continues, equity will soon return to many major markets in the United States. But Fleming said there is something else that people should take away from the latest real estate research: Homeowners should fundamentally reexamine the way they see their homes as an asset.

He commented:

> We all need to live somewhere, so whether it's the home that's rented or a home that's lived in directly by the owner: People need housing. And in the long run, looking at it less as an investment and more as a source of shelter helps you understand. If you like to live where you're living, is there reason to be concerned about your house being under water? Not really. Like it not for its investment return, but for the shelter that it provides and the pool of amenities that it provides. You want to live and work in that community.

Of course, when people have trouble making their mortgage payments, the value of a house becomes a relevant issue. But, if you love your home, you can make your payments, and you plan to stay there for a long time, its underwater status is almost irrelevant. It's only when you have problems in your ability to pay your mortgage, whether or not you're under water, that it becomes a relevant issue. Although this might be difficult to swallow, looking at a home as a lifestyle and not an investment can help underwater homeowners improve their daily satisfaction.

■ **Tip** *Reexamine your home as an asset.* Consider everything else that you get out of your home before viewing it as a burden. If you can make your payments, and you love your house, ignoring its underwater status can help you enjoy all of the other things that make it wonderful while its value returns over time.

Fleming continued:

> It's very hard as human beings to completely divorce ourselves from the investment concept of this asset. We bought this home. We've paid a lot for it.

We have a big mortgage on it. And now this thing is worth less than the mortgage itself. Right? So it's hard from a personal perspective to pay the mortgage payment on it after an asset is worth less, particularly if it's significantly worth less. By the same token, you have to say, well, talking in financial terms, "What is my holding period? I like where I live. I can make that mortgage payment and there's some value in that. You can stay where you are, and even though the asset is worth less than the mortgage, over time this thing will begin to appreciate again. It may take many, many years for it to become above water but I like owning and having this asset.

Negative equity can be solved by two things:

- **Asset appreciation.** As the real estate market improves and house prices go up, your asset gains value and your equity rises from negative to positive.

- **Debt reduction.** As you pay down the mortgage, your equity improves.

Fleming explained:

In either scenario, ultimately you end up owning that asset. I think it's tricky but it's an issue of separating housing as an investment asset to it being a shelter, using the economic terms, "providing the utility of shelter." If you have an investment asset, [for example,] you own stock in Google, it has no utility other than its pure investment return capability. Housing is a different story— [with] housing, there's potentially the investment return possibility, but you also gain a lot from using it for your shelter. That should not be discounted.

Investing in a Home Is Different Than Buying Stocks

You might think of your home as one of your most important investments. You might tabulate the value of your home, or lack of it, by watching the daily movements of the market. Even if you like to check Zillow regularly hoping for a boost to your number, you must still remember that buying stocks and buying a home are two very different things. Investing in a home is not like putting money in the stock market. A home is much longer term and utilitarian. A stock or bond does not keep you warm at night, but your home does. It is not a short-term investment. If it were, you would be renting.

If you want to improve your underwater mortgage situation, stop waiting for instant gratification. It is not like a stock in your portfolio that you notice going down one day and say, "Oh, I just lost a little money. I need to get rid of it." It is a home, not simply a financial investment.

▣ **Tip**   *Don't treat your home like a stock.* Stop watching your home's value go down every day. Look at it like the long-term investment it was when you took out a 30-year mortgage. You will drive yourself crazy waiting for that watched pot to boil. People faced with underwater homes tend to look at this tangible, personal, and emotional place as simply a stock. Rethink your fundamental, psychological perspective.

Look for Deeper Value

Fleming agreed:

> *How would you value, in certain dollars, for example, the utility that you gain from being able to go home and have a roof over your head every day, in a house that you like or occasionally like? That has significant value and doing something about the fact that you're under water means that you would lose that utility from that house, if you short sold it or went through a strategic default or something like that.*

According to the latest CoreLogic data, the vast majority of underwater borrowers are paying their mortgages. Fleming pointed out, "Every month they could choose not to make their mortgage payment, but we do for a variety of reasons. The vast majority of underwater borrowers continue to pay. I think that's largely because they do recognize that there's this great utility that I have living in a house that I want to live in. It's my home."

▣ **Tip**   *Look deeper at the value of your house.* You loved this house when you bought it. You cherished it when you moved in. Do not let familiarity breed contempt. Learn to appreciate the wonderful things about it that go beyond its value in dollars and cents. Your investment is worth more than the price listed for your home on the popular real estate web site Zillow.

Every family not only lives in a house, but it decorates that house and customizes it to the tastes of each individual member of that family. This is one reason to overlook the underwater status of a home with negative equity. Another thing to remember is that it is not cheap to switch living arrangements. Even if a homeowner gets out from an underwater home, there are many more costs involved in setting up a new home. Sometimes it may be worth sticking around and enjoying some of the inherent value that comes out of a house that has grown into a comfortable home. And, as Fleming pointed out, that value extends beyond the limitations of the home's property line: "A lot of times it has to do with the community that you're in," he explained. "You're part of that community. Your kids go to school in that community, if you have children. There are ties to that community—all part of your utility of living in that secure location separated from the pure financial calculation."

Fleming explained that it is interesting how personally people take their investment in their homes. They often act more pragmatically with their investment in their home than any other investment in their lives. For example, some people will say. "'I own an asset that's worth less than I what borrowed for it. We're out!' People don't even act that rationally with stock!" Fleming pointed out.

> I think it goes back to people are considering their homes in more complex ways than purely financial. You can see differences in those investor homes, [which] have a much higher default rate than owner occupied. It's not the home that I live in, it's usually a rental home, which is more of a pure financial asset right? And they're acting more financially with it. So, I think a lot of it is being driven by people recognizing this is where I live. It's a much more complex decision then purely financial.

Benefits of Real Estate Market Improvements

As a top real estate economist, what does Fleming see overall when he looks at the latest statistics showing the number of underwater homes going down? What does that mean for the country? He explained that having equity creates many benefits for homeowners. For example, "More homeowners having equity in their homes reduces risk to the mortgage industry," he pointed out. "The risk of foreclosure is reduced. People who have equity have more choices." When fewer people have negative equity, he added, the amount of risk that is in the market also goes down, which helps to improve the stability of the country's entire economy.

"Having equity in your house in the long run allows individuals to do things like—I believe it's referred to as mortgage equity withdrawal (MEW)," Fleming continued.

> It is one of the things that a lot of people did. They withdrew equity out of their house and home when values were rising and they used that money to do things like improve their homes, send their children to college, maybe less than efficiently buy cars and boats and vacations, etc. All of which is consumer demand. The buying of goods and things in the economy helps the economy to grow.

One of the biggest problems with having no equity in a home is that it cannot be extracted, which means that consumers buy less. That, naturally, has a negative effect on the economy. On the flipside, Fleming explained, "As people regain equity they'll be able to again withdraw that equity and use it for consumption. Now, there are different forms of consumption of household equity that are better than others," he continued. "It's not such a good idea to withdraw it for the purposes of buying the fancier cars and boats and vacation. To take a home equity loan to redo your kitchen, you're basically putting that money back into your home. That seems reasonable while generating economic activity and helping the economy."

"Good Use of Wealth"

Fleming said that using a home's equity to pay for a better college education for a homeowner's children is an example of "a good use of wealth" that can lead to much bigger returns for a family than simply spending home equity on a bigger car. It is a way to broadly increase wealth over the long run, because sending children to college often means that they have better jobs, are able to earn more income, and have better lives. It is not just a way to improve the child's life, but it is a great way to improve the wealth of future generations of the family.

"Removing negative equity will help to stimulate the economy a little bit as people begin to use that equity for consumption," Fleming continued. This is more important today since the economy is ripe for a boost.

Did Government Action Help?

Was there a single action on the part of the U.S. government that has led directly to the improved real estate market numbers seen by CoreLogic? Fleming said that he does not think any specific government action had a direct major impact over the last six months. He said, "I think it's more the fundamental balance of return of these markets and them responding to those things. A lot of regulatory stuff is more in the finance side than it is directly on the real estate side."

On the other hand, Fleming credited one program with helping the current underwater mortgage situation: "Maybe the HARP program has had some benefit in that they're allowing underwater borrowers to refinance their mortgage and take advantage of the low rates. It's not benefiting the real estate market directly but it is benefiting those consumers in that they can lessen their monthly [mortgage payment] and they might do something else with that new income, with that freed up cash."

If it's not the government's intervention, with what does he attribute recent improvements in the nation's economy? "Fundamentally, many of these markets balance again; supply has come down to a level that meets the low but improving demand," he said. "That's a healthy market."

Natural Fluctuations

Remember, there is a natural flux in the real estate markets. Today, the nation is beginning to see those markets slowly balance themselves out after the real estate bubble burst and blew the bottom out of the industry, creating a deep, black hole with no bottom in sight. Many experts say that the worst is now behind us and the market is beginning to get a tenuous foothold on a firmer foundation. Although many government programs have played into this new situation, and some increased consumer confidence has played a role, as have new regulations and policies, the one thing that CoreLogic Chief Economist Mark Fleming said he believes has played an integral part in improving the real estate market has been with us all along: time.

He explained:

> Maybe the policy is time. That's what's helped, time. The markets have sorted it all out, well maybe not every market but these things have begun to get themselves sorted out of their own accord. The markets themselves, there have been some influences like first time homebuyer tax credits and things like that. They certainly have temporary positive influence. We had a lot of demand in 2010 from that tax credit, people buying homes, but when it faded the housing market still wasn't in balance and we still had to go through correction. These markets have done a lot of correcting that they need to do at this point. Therefore, we're seeing the benefits of time and the markets themselves having worked through a lot of these issues.

▥ Tip *Be patient!* Time may not cure all ills, but it will help an underwater homeowner slowly rise out of the equity hole eventually.

Fleming said time is an essential element that all those with underwater homes should use to their advantage. He concluded, "Time is in a way a good housing policy in that it's free and it's unlikely to have unintended consequences. Time will heal, if that's the only thing that happens, time will eventually heal a lot of this as house prices will grow with incomes and wages and inflation. Over time, which might be measured in the long term in terms of decades, these things will fix themselves."

This is why patience is such a powerful virtue for the underwater homeowner.

Conclusion

Short-term thinking is the wrong way to size up your underwater status. Economists like Mark Fleming understand that long-haul, big-picture thinking is the best way to look at any smart investment, especially when it involves the home where you live. As his early 2012 predictions for a better future housing picture begin to come true—as the numbers for the second quarter of 2012 are confirming—Fleming's advice offers enough hope and reason to help you get through the tough times as we all move toward what is beginning to shape up as a brighter future.

What is next? Before your patience runs thin, it is time to take a closer look at the organizations that offer the most options to underwater homeowners: Fannie Mae and Freddie Mac. A better understanding of the role both of these big players in the mortgage market play can help you get a handle on your underwater home and find relief for your personal finances. By looking closely at these two organizations, you can improve your chances of picking the option that is right for you and your situation today.

Housing: Fannie, Freddie, Legal Issues, and Government Programs

What You Should Know About Fannie Mae and Freddie Mac

According to the Congressional Budget Office (CBO):

> Four decades ago, Congressional charters set up Fannie Mae and Freddie Mac as government-sponsored enterprises (GSEs)—privately owned financial institutions established by the government to fulfill a public mission. The two GSEs were created to provide a stable source of funding for residential mortgages across the country, including loans on housing for low- and moderate-income families.

> Fannie Mae and Freddie Mac carry out that mission through their operations in the secondary mortgage market. They purchase mortgages that meet certain standards from banks and other originators, pool those loans into mortgage-backed securities [MBSs] that they guarantee against losses from defaults on the underlying mortgages, and sell the securities to investors—a process referred to as securitization. In addition, they buy mortgages and MBSs (both

each other's and those issued by private companies) to hold in their portfolios. They fund those portfolio holdings by issuing debt obligations, known as agency securities, which are sold to investors.[1]

Let's take a deeper look at each one.

Who Is Freddie Mac?

Freddie Mac is short for the Federal Home Loan Mortgage Corporation. Like Fannie Mae, Freddie Mac buys mortgages from banks. According to freddiemac. com, foreclosure prevention was also a top priority for Freddie Mac in June 2012. Freddie Mac reported it helped more than 656,000 struggling borrowers avoid foreclosure since the housing bubble burst through its own programs and the federal Making Home Affordable program. Of the borrowers the organization has helped, more than 8 out of 10 were able to stay in their homes, according to Freddie Mac officials.

Freddie Mac stated that its recent efforts to help homeowners include the following:

- The firm participated in hundreds of foreclosure prevention workshops nationwide.

- Freddie Mac opened borrower help centers to provide free counseling for distressed borrowers in cities especially hard hit by the foreclosure crisis, including Chicago, Phoenix, and Washington, DC.

- The firm partnered with nonprofits to hold direct-to-homeowner auctions of Freddie Mac-owned properties in cities across the country.

- Freddie Mac introduced a balanced servicer scorecard in an effort to intervene early and find solutions for underwater homeowners.

- It also implemented a Servicing Alignment Initiative—including a new standard loan modification—to improve how it serviced delinquent loans.

---

[1] www.cbo.gov/taxonomy/term/161/all (Retrieved June 18, 2012).

Who Is Fannie Mae?

Fannie Mae is short for Federal National Mortgage Association. According to www.fanniemae.com, Fannie Mae has served America's housing market for more than 70 years. The firm states that its mission is to ensure that working families have access to mortgage credit to buy homes they can afford over the long term or that they can secure quality rental housing.

As the CBO pointed out above, Fannie Mae is a government-sponsored enterprise chartered by the U.S. Congress to keep money flowing to mortgage lenders, to help strengthen the U.S. housing and mortgage markets, and to support affordable home ownership. It is a national mortgage finance company, but it doesn't offer home loans. It supports mortgage lenders—local and national banks, thrifts, credit unions, and other financial institutions in all 50 states—by securitizing or buying the mortgage loans they originate, enabling them to replenish their funds so they can lend to other homeowners. Similarly, Fannie Mae works to keep funds flowing to support rental housing.

Basically, the firm tries to help homeowners prevent foreclosure and keep their homes whenever possible. When foreclosure is unavoidable, Fannie Mae says it strives to sell homes for the highest price possible and to people who will live in those homes. This strategy is part of Fannie Mae's efforts to help stabilize neighborhoods and home values, and build a strong, sustainable housing market for the future.

How Fannie Mae and Freddie Mac Differ

On the surface, there really is not much difference between Freddie Mac and Fannie Mae. Both mortgage servicers have similar criteria for buying and guaranteeing mortgage loans.

On the other hand, the two firms have very different origins: Fannie Mae was created under President Franklin D. Roosevelt in 1938 to ensure there were enough funds available in the housing market during tough economic times. The federal agency was turned into a publicly traded company in 1968. Today, it is a government-sponsored enterprise (GSE) chartered by the U.S. Congress to "provide liquidity, stability and affordability to the U.S. housing and mortgage markets."[2] Freddie Mac was created in 1970 so that Fannie Mae would not have a monopoly on government-backed mortgages.[3]

---

[2] www.knowyouroptions.com/about-fannie-mae (Retrieved October 14, 2012).

[3] www.cbo.gov/sites/default/files/cbofiles/ftpdocs/120xx/doc12032/12-23-fanniefreddie.pdf (Retrieved July 8, 2012).

According to the *New York Times*, "The Federal National Mortgage Association (Fannie Mae) is the nation's largest mortgage buyer and a financial juggernaut that affects the lives of tens of millions of home buyers."[4] In September 2008, the federal government took over Fannie Mae and Freddie Mac when both mortgage buyers faced an imploding real estate market.[5] In 2011, the two federally chartered institutions together guaranteed three quarters of new residential mortgages originated in the United States.[6]

Fannie Mae's Role in the Market

Today, Fannie Mae plays an even greater role in the housing market as the nation recovers from the worst housing crisis since the Great Depression. Fannie Mae officials state that the organization is committed to serving in all communities across the United States in good and bad economic times.

Fannie Mae works to keep money flowing to mortgage lenders and to make sure people can buy or rent housing. The firm has one of the largest foreclosure prevention operations to help struggling homeowners keep making their mortgage payments and avoid losing their homes.

For example, here are five Fannie Mae programs:

1. KnowYourOptions.com is the online portal where homeowners seek help from Fannie Mae.

2. Fannie Mae recently opened 12 Mortgage Help Centers in areas hit hardest by the real estate market crash.

3. The firm implemented the Servicing Alignment Initiative with the Federal Housing Administration (FHA) and Freddie Mac to require loan services to reach out to struggling homeowners.

4. Fannie Mae required servicers to shorten their short sale timelines.

5. The firm also developed and implemented the Servicing Total Achievement and Rewards (STAR) program to push lenders to help homeowners.[7]

---

[4] http://articles.latimes.com/2008/sep/08/business/fi-qanda8 (Retrieved July 8, 2012).

[5] http://topics.nytimes.com/top/news/business/companies/fannie_mae/index.html (Retrieved October 14, 2012).

[6] http://articles.latimes.com/2008/sep/08/business/fi-qanda8 (Retrieved July 8, 2012).

[7] www.fanniemae.com/portal/about-us/media/corporate-news/2012/5779.html (Retrieved October 14, 2012).

Fannie Mae works with mortgage servicers, housing counselors, and other partners to help distressed homeowners understand their options and find the best solution to meet their needs. It says its goal is to help as many families as possible stay in their homes, protect property values in communities across the country, and build a stronger foundation for the U.S. housing market.

Here are three ways Fannie Mae says it focuses on building a sustainable foundation for the future of America's housing:

- **It keeps funds flowing to the mortgage market.** Fannie Mae says it is committed to its fundamental mission—providing mortgage liquidity.

- **The firm helps distressed homeowners.** Fannie Mae established one of the largest foreclosure prevention operations in the country in less than 2 years. The firm's efforts help to stabilize communities and limit losses on its legacy book of business (pre-2009), which benefits taxpayers.

- **It encourages sustainable lending.** Fannie Mae has strengthened lending standards to help ensure that working Americans who buy homes can afford them over the long term. The firm emphasizes long-term, fixed-rate mortgages—loans that protect homeowners from interest rate swings.

Fannie Mae works with its regulator, the Federal Housing Finance Agency (FHFA), and others to develop a better model for servicing mortgages to help reduce risk, increase flexibility, and improve service for borrowers.

Uncertain Future for Fannie and Freddie

Fannie Mae and Freddie Mac may not be around much longer. According to the *New York Times*, the Obama administration was making plans in 2011 to "slowly dissolve" the two mortgage giants in hopes of reducing federal involvement in the mortgage system.[8]

Meanwhile, the two firms continue to serve as major players in the mortgage industry. Recent reports show the financial portfolios of the two organizations are worth about $1.5 trillion. Along with the FHA, the *New York Times*

---

[8] http://topics.nytimes.com/top/news/business/companies/fannie_mae/index.html (Retrieved October 14, 2012)

reported, Fannie and Freddie guarantee about 90 percent of all new mortgages in the United States.

ADVICE FOR SENIORS CONSIDERING A REVERSE MORTGAGE

According to the Consumer Financial Protection Bureau (CFPB), a reverse mortgage is a specific type of home equity loan sold to homeowners who are 62 years old and older. This kind of loan allows older people to turn a portion of their home equity into cash. In a reverse mortgage, interest is added to the loan balance each month, and the balance grows.

The loan for a reverse mortgage must be repaid to the lender when the borrower sells the home, moves out of the home, or dies, the CFPB explains. Most reverse mortgages today are called Home equity Conversion Mortgages (HeCMs). HeCMs are federally insured.

How a Reverse Mortgage Works

After paying off a mortgage for many years, a homeowner has built up value in the home in the form of equity. With a reverse mortgage, the homeowner borrows against the equity that has built up over the years.

In a reverse mortgage, the balance of the new loan grows over time. This means that the homeowner does not have to pay the loan while he or she lives in the home. Instead, the homeowner receives cash for the home's equity while continuing to live in the home.

When the homeowner moves out, sells the home, or dies, the loan must be paid off. Usually the loan is paid off when the home is sold.

When Is It Too Early to Consider a Reverse Mortgage?

If you are under 60 years old, a reverse mortgage is not for you. If you are too young when you take out a reverse mortgage, you could run out of money when you are older and need it the most. The older a borrower is, the more money he or she can borrow in a reverse mortgage.

Before you take out a reverse mortgage, you should always consider other options first. A home equity loan or a home equity line of credit might be a cheaper and more sensible way to borrow cash against your home's equity. However, these loans also carry risks and usually have monthly payments. Whether you are eligible for any of these loans will depend on your income and credit.

Alternative Option

One smart alternative is to simply work to lower your expenses before taking the drastic measure of taking out a reverse mortgage. According to the Consumer Financial Protection Bureau, homeowners should first look into state and local programs that may help them defer property taxes, lower their heating costs, or save on other bills, in effect lowering their living expenses. Another thing to consider is simply selling your current home and moving to a more affordable home. Also, by simply refinancing your current mortgage, you may be able to lower your monthly expenses.

Free Help for Older Americans with Reverse Mortgages

Before taking out a reverse mortgage, get some free advice from an expert. Homeowners who are 62 years old or older may be eligible for some free real estate counseling from the National Foundation for Credit Counseling (NFCC). Struggling older homeowners with reverse mortgages can get free help from the NFCC thanks to a recent grant from the U.S HUD Department. The free program is aimed at older Americans who signed up for an HeCM.

To find out more about this program and to ask about other mortgage issues, homeowners can call the NFCC's toll-free number (1-866-363-2227) to work with counselors.[9]

■ **Tip** *Think twice.* There are many other programs available for seniors beyond reverse mortgages. Talk to an attorney, call a consumer advocate, and/or contact the AARP. Make a reverse mortgage your last alternative. If you have tried all other avenues and determined that a reverse mortgage is your best bet, then start shopping for the best deal with a seasoned professional counselor in your corner.

---

[9] http://realtytimes.com/rtpages/20110428_free.htm (Retrieved July 27, 2012).

Lenders Settle with Homeowners for $25 Billion for Abuses

While homeowners struggle with mortgage lenders, they sometimes fight back over abuses that they see in the actions taken by banks. And sometimes they win!

Banks around the country faced a lawsuit from the country's attorneys general for alleged abuses of borrowers when the housing bubble first burst. When that case was settled, many people with underwater mortgages stood to benefit from the settlement.

On February 9, 2012, the U.S. Justice Department announced that the federal government and 49 state attorneys general reached a landmark $25 billion agreement with the nation's five largest mortgage servicers to address mortgage loan servicing and foreclosure abuses. These abuses included the infamous practice of pushing many foreclosures forward without bank personnel following the required review process. This practice became known as "robo-signing."[1]

The settlement agreement provided financial relief to homeowners and established new homeowner protections for the future.

"Largest Joint Federal-State Settlement Ever"

The unprecedented joint agreement was the largest federal-state civil settlement ever obtained and was the result of extensive investigations by federal agencies—including the Department of Justice, HUD, and the HUD Office of the Inspector General (HUD-OIG)—and state attorneys general and state banking regulators across the country.

The joint federal-state group entered into the agreement with the nation's five largest mortgage servicers: Bank of America Corp., JPMorgan Chase & Co., Wells Fargo & Company, Citigroup Inc., and Ally Financial Inc. (formerly GMAC).

Attorney General Eric Holder commented:

> This agreement—the largest joint federal-state settlement ever obtained—is the result of unprecedented coordination among enforcement agencies throughout the government. It holds mortgage servicers accountable for abusive practices and requires them to commit more than $20 billion towards financial relief for consumers. As a result, struggling homeowners throughout the country will benefit from reduced principals and refinancing of their loans. The agreement also requires substantial changes in how servicers do business, which will help to ensure the abuses of the past are not repeated.

HUD Secretary Donovan added:

> This historic settlement will provide immediate relief to homeowners—forcing banks to reduce the principal balance on many loans, refinance loans for underwater borrowers, and pay billions of dollars to states and consumers. Banks must follow the laws. Any bank that hasn't done so should be held accountable and should take prompt action to correct its mistakes. And it will not end with this settlement. One of the most important ways this settlement helps homeowners is that it forces the banks to clean up their acts and fix the problems uncovered during our investigations. And it does that by committing them to major reforms in how they service mortgage loans. These new customer service standards are in keeping with the Homeowners Bill of Rights

---

[1] www.justice.gov/opa/pr/2012/February/12-ag-186.html (Retrieved July 8, 2012).

recently announced by President Obama—a single, straightforward set of commonsense rules that families can count on.

Banks Held Accountable

State attorneys general also weighed in:

- "This monitored agreement holds the banks accountable, it provides badly needed relief to homeowners, and it transforms the mortgage servicing industry so now homeowners will be protected and treated fairly," said Iowa Attorney General Miller.

- "This settlement has broad bipartisan support from the states because the attorneys general realize that the partnership with the federal agencies made it possible to achieve favorable terms and conditions that would have been difficult for the states or the federal government to achieve on their own," said Colorado Attorney General Suthers.

On February 9, 2012, the Associated Press posted the story "National Mortgage Settlement Finally Reached," in which it reported that the settlement was the largest ever involving a single industry since 1998, when the tobacco industry had to pay up in a similar deal over abuses.[2]

According to the Associated Press story, the five major banks mentioned previously "will reduce loans for nearly 1 million households. They will also send checks of $2,000 to about 750,000 Americans who were improperly foreclosed upon. The banks will have three years to fulfill the terms of the deal."

The settlement was reached because many banks during the initial burst of the real estate bubble processed foreclosures without properly verifying documents. This scandal involved some bank employees signing papers that they later revealed they had not read, and robo-signing.

The Associated Press reported that funds from the settlement would be divided this way:

- About $1.5 billion will go to direct payouts to nearly 750,000 homeowners who could prove they were unfairly or improperly foreclosed on.

---

[2] http://realestate.aol.com/blog/2012/02/09/national-mortgage-settlement-finally-reached/ (Retrieved July 8, 2012).

- About $3.5 billion of the settlement will go directly to states. Only Oklahoma will not receive funds because it did not sign on to the deal.

- At least $10 billion will go toward reducing mortgage amounts for homeowners.

- Up to $7 billion will go toward other state homeowner programs.

- At least $3 billion will go toward refinancing loans for homeowners who are currently under water but continue to make their house payments.[3]

■ **Tip** *Find out if you are eligible for your cut.* If you believe that you were unfairly foreclosed on during the early days when the housing bubble burst, you may be able to receive part of this settlement. Talk to a consumer advocate to find out more information or go to www. NationalMortageSettlement.com.

Who Is Eligible for Compensation?

If your primary residence was involved in a foreclosure process between January 1, 2009, and December 31, 2010, you may qualify for a free Independent Foreclosure Review.

The Independent Foreclosure Review will determine whether individual homeowners suffered financial injury and should receive compensation or other remedy because of errors or other problems during their home foreclosure process.

■ **Tip** *Submit a Request!* If you believe you are eligible to participate in the program, complete and submit a Request for Review Form. It is important that you complete the form to the best of your ability; all information you provide can be useful. Go to independentforeclosurereview.com to learn more.[4]

---

[3] http://realestate.aol.com/blog/2012/02/09/national-mortgage-settlement-finally-reached/ (Retrieved July 8, 2012).

[4] https://independentforeclosurereview.com/ (Retrieved July 8, 2012).

New Mortgage Loan Servicing Standards

The joint federal-state agreement requires servicers to implement comprehensive new mortgage loan servicing standards and to commit $25 billion to resolve violations of state and federal law. These violations include servicers' deceptive practices in the offering of loan modifications, failures to offer nonforeclosure alternatives before foreclosing on borrowers with federally insured mortgages, and filing improper documentation in federal bankruptcy court.

Under the terms of the agreement, the servicers are required to collectively dedicate at least $10 billion toward reducing the principal on loans for borrowers who, as of the date of the settlement, are either delinquent or at imminent risk of default and owe more on their mortgages than their homes are worth. At least $3 billion will go toward refinancing loans for borrowers who are current on their mortgages but who owe more on their mortgage than their homes are worth. Borrowers who meet basic criteria will be eligible for the refinancing, which will reduce interest rates for borrowers who are currently paying much higher rates or whose adjustable-rate mortgages are due to soon rise to much higher rates. Up to $7 billion will go toward other forms of relief, including forbearance of principal for unemployed borrowers, antiblight programs, short sales and transitional assistance, benefits for service members who are forced to sell their home at a loss as a result of a Permanent Change in Station order, and other programs. Because servicers will receive only partial credit for every dollar spent on some of the required activities, the settlement will provide direct benefits to borrowers in excess of $20 billion.

The new servicing standards make foreclosure a last resort by requiring servicers to evaluate homeowners for other loss mitigation options first. In addition, banks will be restricted from foreclosing while the homeowner is being considered for a loan modification. The new standards also include procedures and timelines for reviewing loan modification applications and give homeowners the right to appeal denials. Servicers will also be required to create a single point of contact for borrowers seeking information about their loans and maintain adequate staff to handle calls.

Banks Have 3 Years to Comply

The settlement requires mortgage servicers to act quickly to pay back borrowers who suffered because of abuses or misconduct: They have 3 years to do it. To encourage them to provide quick relief to borrowers, the settlement includes incentives for servicers who provide relief to borrowers within the first 12 months. They must also reach 75 percent of their targets within the first 2 years. Servicers that miss settlement targets and deadlines must pay substantial cash penalties.

In addition to the $20 billion in financial relief for borrowers, the agreement requires the servicers to pay $5 billion in cash to federal and state governments. Another $1.5 billion of the payment will be used to establish a Borrower Payment Fund to provide cash payments to borrowers whose homes were sold or taken in foreclosure between January 1, 2008, and December 31, 2011, and who meet other criteria. This program is different from the restitution program currently being administered by federal banking regulators as a result of wrongful servicer conduct. Borrowers will not release any claims in exchange for a payment. The remaining $3.5 billion of the $5 billion payment will go to state and federal governments. That money must be used to repay any public funds lost as a result of servicer misconduct and to fund housing counselors, legal aid, and other similar public programs determined by the state attorneys general.

"Fraudulent and Wrongful Conduct"

The $5 billion includes a $1 billion resolution of a separate investigation into fraudulent and wrongful conduct by Bank of America and the mortgage servicing company Countrywide Financial Corp.'s entities related to the origination and underwriting of FHA-insured mortgage loans, and systematic inflation of appraisal values concerning these loans, from January 1, 2003, through April 30, 2009. Payment of $500 million of this $1 billion will be deferred to partially fund a loan modification program for Countrywide borrowers throughout the nation who are under water on their mortgages. The investigation was conducted by the U.S. Attorney's Office for the Eastern District of New York, with the Civil Division's Commercial Litigation Branch of the Department of Justice, HUD, and HUD-OIG. The settlement also resolves an investigation by the Eastern District of New York, the Special Inspector General for the Troubled Asset Relief Program (SIGTARP), and the Federal Housing Finance Agency-Office of the Inspector General (FHFA-OIG) into allegations that Bank of America defrauded the HAMP.

The joint federal-state agreement requires the mortgage servicers to implement unprecedented changes in how they service mortgage loans, handle foreclosures, and ensure the accuracy of information provided in federal bankruptcy court. The agreement requires new servicing standards that will prevent foreclosure abuses of the past and create dozens of new consumer protections. The new standards provide for strict oversight of foreclosure processing, including third-party vendors, and new requirements to undertake pre-filing reviews of certain documents filed in bankruptcy court.

New Servicemember Standards

The new servicing standards agreement will also provide enhanced protections for servicemembers that go beyond those required by the SCRA (discussed in Chapter 9). In addition, the four servicers that had not previously resolved certain portions of potential SCRA liability have agreed to conduct a full review, overseen by the Justice Department's Civil Rights Division, to determine whether any servicemembers were foreclosed on in violation of the SCRA since January 1, 2006. The servicers have also agreed to conduct a thorough review, overseen by the Civil Rights Division, to determine whether any servicemember, from January 1, 2008, to the present, was charged interest in excess of six percent on their mortgage, after a valid request to lower the interest rate, in violation of the SCRA. Servicers will be required to make payments to any servicemember who was a victim of a wrongful foreclosure or who was wrongfully charged a higher interest rate. This compensation for servicemembers is in addition to the $25 billion settlement amount.

A Step in the Right Direction but Not an End to the Crisis

Homeowners with underwater homes are beginning to see some relief after the banks were found guilty of foreclosure abuse and forced to pay back $25 billion.

According to CNNMoney, some banks were offering homeowners with underwater mortgages up to $35,000 to move quickly into a short sale to avoid foreclosure entirely. In other words, lenders were forgiving all or a portion of the difference between the sale price and the mortgage amount.

According to MoneyNews.com in February 2012, Chase Mortgage sent letters to borrowers with a cash offer to move quickly. "The first choice is a modification but if that's impossible then a short sale is a faster, more efficient solution," explained Chase Mortgage spokesman Tom Kelly to CNNMoney.[5]

The issue went beyond the well-publicized problem of "robo-signing." The government's investigation into bank abuses identified other servicer-related

---

[5] www.moneynews.com/StreetTalk/Underwater-Banks-pay-Homes/2012/02/10/id/429098 (Retrieved July 8, 2012).

problems including deceptive practices in the offering of loan modifications (such as telling consumers that a loan modification was imminent while simultaneously foreclosing). The performance failures resulted in more than just poor customer service. Unnecessary foreclosures occurred due to failure to process homeowners' requests for modified payments and shoddy documentation leading to protracted delays.[6]

Many people thought that the $25 billion settlement was too low a cost for the banks to pay for such a serious mistake. Many lawmakers and regulators agreed with them.

For example, when talking to CNNMoney about the $25 billion settlement in February 2012, Delaware Attorney General Beau Biden said

> This is a very good beginning first step. It's a belated first step, from my perspective. You're going to get to see, homeowners are going to get some real relief. You're going to get underwater borrowers who are on time be able to refinance, and as you know that's a good thing for the economy and the housing market and the citizens and for the borrower.[7]

Biden pointed out that many people who were hurt by lenders were finally going to get some compensation, but that would not be the end of the states' focus on the issue. He predicted that many more attorneys general across the country would continue to investigate and prosecute mortgage lenders and services for abuses and misconduct.

Is an End to the Crisis in Sight?

When asked by interviewer Ali Velshi whether the settlement money would affect the housing crisis in the United States, or move the needle on the crisis meter any closer to indicating an end, Biden explained that it would not end the problem, although it was a step in the right direction:

> From what I hear, from what I've seen reported, and from the experts I've talked to, it doesn't move the needle that much. It is significant in terms of the people it's going to effect and the relief it's going to bring to certain borrowers and certain underwater borrowers, that's meaningful to me here in the State of Delaware. We're going to have $45 million we're going to be able to put towards people, the hardships they've been through. But look, there's a lot more that needs to be done. The thing that we can do from my perspective, Ali, to move the housing market, is to stop foreclosures.

---

[6] www.riag.ri.gov/mortgagesettlement/ (Retrieved July 8, 2012).

[7] www.youtube.com/watch?v=1hDULVPs188 (Retrieved July 30, 2012).

Biden (who is the son of Vice President Joe Biden), said he sees a solution to the problem beyond simply persecuting the banks for abuses:

> We have to find a way to align the interests of the borrowers and the investors, because when a property is foreclosed upon, it hurts the investor, not quite as much, but it hurts the investor because they now have a property that is 25 cents on the dollar, and the borrower doesn't have a roof over their head. If you get to a place where you have meaningful modifications, meaningful measures short of foreclosures, the investors may hold more than they otherwise would [hold] and the borrower gets to have a roof over their heads. And also, by the way, for the neighbor of the borrower, who is the diligent on-time payer of their mortgage, they have an interest in that too because they don't want their neighbor to be foreclosed upon because it hurts the value of their home.

Ali pointed out that banks only settled up with borrowers after abuses were investigated and prosecuted by government regulators. Biden agreed that there was indeed something wrong with the fact that banks had to be forced to admit mistakes: "It should not have taken the attorneys general, 50 of us, to get together with HUD and the United States Department of Justice to force the banks to do what they should do and what they might have to ultimately do anyway," including taking a loss when selling underwater homes.[8]

How Was Settlement Money Spent?

Months after the $25 billion nationwide mortgage settlement, other states, such as Florida, were deciding how to spend the money they received. According to *Legal Newsline*, Florida Attorney General Pam Bondi asked her state's residents how they wanted to best spend $300 million that was recovered on behalf of consumers as part of the settlement.[9]

Florida's share of the total monetary benefits under the settlement was an estimated $8.4 billion. Of that, Florida borrowers will receive an estimated $7.6 billion in benefits from loan modifications, including principal reduction and other direct relief.

About $170 million was made available for cash payments to Florida borrowers who lost their home to foreclosure from January 1, 2008, through December 31, 2011, and suffered servicing abuse. The value of refinanced loans to Florida's underwater borrowers was an estimated $309 million.

In addition, Florida received a direct payment of $350 million.

---

[8] www.youtube.com/watch?v=1hDULVPs188 (Retrieved July 30, 2012).

[9] www.legalnewsline.com/news/236018-fla.-ag-asks-for-public-input-on-how-to-spend-settlement-funds (Retrieved July 8, 2012).

HOW SOME STATES SPENT THEIR SHARE OF $25 BILLION ROBO-SIGNING SETTLEMENT

Several states have begun to put their share of the $25 billion in settlement money from the big banks' robo-signing debacle into their state coffers to balance their budgets rather than return that money to homeowners who were burned by unfair foreclosure practices. Instead, the money went to make up for budget shortfalls. Many people are not happy about this development.

In an interview for this book, economist John Mulville commented: "[It was] unconscionable. Has there ever been a greater bait-and-switch? It was legalized thievery. I don't understand why there wasn't a huge uproar about that." He pointed out that California's Governor Jerry Brown announced in May 2012 that he would be using $411 million of the settlement money to help shrink the state's general deficit.[10] Mulville added, "It went straight to the black hole of state government. I just can't imagine, and it just seemed like it didn't draw any reaction at all. Completely amazing."

Military Protections

Delaware's Attorney General Biden pointed out that military personnel who were hurt by unfair foreclosure practices would also benefit from the settlement money. On June 27, 2012, Biden commended the military protections that were part of the $25 billion foreclosure settlement, according to LegalNewsline.com.[11]

While he testified before the Senate Committee on Banking, Housing and Urban Affairs during a hearing called "Empowering and Protecting Servicemembers, Veterans and Their Families in the Consumer Financial Marketplace: A Status Update," Biden praised the provisions that protect servicemembers and their family members.

Biden, who spent a tour of duty in Iraq with the Delaware Army National Guard, said he would not have joined the settlement if not for provisions relating to the Servicemembers Civil Relief Act:

> I know that the need to expand the SCRA as well as strongly enforce its current provisions is well understood by the members of this committee. You have heard the stories about countless servicemembers who have had to contend

---

[10] www.inman.com/news/2012/06/18/states-using-robo-signing-funds-plug-budget-gaps (Retrieved August 13, 2012).

[11] www.legalnewsline.com/news/236571-del.-ag-commends-military-protections-in-25b-foreclosure-settlement (Retrieved July 8, 2012).

with the frustration and uncertainty of mishandled mortgages and other SCRA infractions while also carrying out the duties of service. Servicemembers should not have to worry about these issues while deployed. They must be able to focus on the mission without distraction.

■ **Tip** *Get your fair share.* If you served in the military and your mortgage was mishandled by your lender, find out more about the settlement. Contact your local attorney general's office. There may be money waiting for you.

Twelve Valuable Government Programs

As you can see by the size of the recent $25 billion settlement state attorneys general reached with the five biggest lenders in the country (described in the last chapter), or new laws that aim to improve lending options for borrowers, many government agencies are working for underwater homeowners. These organizations protect people with upside-down mortgages from the dangers of robo-signing lenders, mortgage industry scams, and other real estate abuses. Along with their watchdog role, federal agencies also offer many types of resources that are working to smooth the path for underwater homeowners seeking relief from an untenable circumstance.

If you are under water, you owe it to yourself to familiarize yourself with the many types of programs that have been developed over the years since the real estate bubble burst. This chapter offers an overview of 12 programs you should know about and consider when choosing options for dealing with your underwater mortgage. Before you settle for a foreclosure, voluntary foreclosure, or even a short sale, make sure you have exhausted all of the possibilities for taking advantage of one of the many programs that have been designed for people in exactly the same situation as you.

There are many resources from the federal government that can help you get mortgage relief and avoid foreclosure. Many of them fall under the Making Home Affordable Program (MHA—www.makinghomeaffordable.gov). This program is a part of the Obama administration's comprehensive plan to stabilize the U.S. housing market by helping homeowners get mortgage relief and avoid foreclosure. To meet the various needs of homeowners across the country, MHA programs offer a range of solutions that may be able to help you take action before it's too late. These include options that allow you to:

- Refinance and take advantage of today's low mortgage interest rates.

- Reduce your monthly mortgage payments.

- Get mortgage relief while searching for re-employment.

- Get help when you owe more than your home is worth.

- Avoid foreclosure when homeownership is no longer affordable or desirable.

In an effort to enable more struggling homeowners to take advantage of the MHA program, the federal government extended the application deadline of the program to December 31, 2013. Officials also expanded the eligibility criteria for MHA to be able to offer assistance to more struggling homeowners.

Before you speak to a HUD-approved counseling agency, which will be either free or low cost, gather your financial information. The more prepared you are, the faster you can get help. You'll need documentation detailing your mortgage, your current and past financial situation, and the reasons you are having financial difficulty. Your housing counselor will help you understand the law and your options, organize your finances, and represent you in negotiations with your lender. To find a HUD-approved counselor in your area, call (800) 569-4287.[1]

How to Prepare for a Call to a Housing Expert

To assist you, a housing expert from the MHA program will need to gather some information from you. Have as many of the following documents on hand as possible:

- Monthly mortgage statement

- Information about other mortgages on your home, if applicable

---

[1] http://portal.hud.gov/hudportal/HUD?src=/topics/avoiding_foreclosure/foreclosuretips (Retrieved October 15, 2012).

- Two of your most recent pay stubs for all household members contributing toward mortgage payment

- Last 2 years of tax returns

- If self-employed, the most recent quarterly or year-to-date profit and loss statement

- Documentation of income you receive from other sources (alimony, child support, social security, etc.)

- Two most recent bank statements

- A utility bill showing homeowner name and property address

- Unemployment insurance letter, if applicable

- Account balances and minimum monthly payments due on all of your credit cards

- Information about your savings and other assets

It may also be helpful to have a letter describing any circumstances that caused your income to be reduced or expenses to be increased (job loss, divorce, illness, etc.) if this applies to your situation.

With that information in hand, you can call the federal help line at 1-888-995-HOPE (4673), or your mortgage provider, to find out if you are eligible for a MHA program. Spending time up front gathering these documents pays off in a smoother, more efficient process.

▧ **Tip** *Take action immediately.* MHA has help to offer, but you must contact your mortgage company or a housing expert to take action. The sooner you do, the sooner you can get on the road to financial recovery. Not doing so can only make things worse. Remember, many Americans have taken the first step toward modifying or refinancing their mortgages and so should you if you are having trouble making your mortgage payments.

Twelve Programs That Can Save You

Here are a dozen specific programs offered under the MHA. Note that these eligibility criteria are for guidance only. Only your mortgage company can qualify you for these solutions:

1. HAMP (see Chapter 11): If you are employed, but you're still struggling to make your mortgage payments, you may be eligible for HAMP. This program may lower your monthly mortgage payments to make them more affordable and sustainable for the long term. The goal of this program is to help borrowers avoid foreclosure whenever possible.

If you currently occupy your home as your primary residence, contact your mortgage servicer to begin the HAMP evaluation process.

In an effort to continue to provide meaningful solutions to the housing crisis, effective June 1, 2012, the Obama Administration expanded the population of homeowners that may be eligible for HAMP to include:

- Homeowners who are applying for a modification on a home that is not their primary residence, but the property is currently rented or the homeowner intends to rent it.

- Homeowners who previously received a HAMP permanent modification, but defaulted in their payments, therefore losing good standing.

- Homeowners who previously did not qualify for HAMP because their debt-to-income ratio was 31 percent or lower.

- Homeowners who previously received a HAMP trial period plan, but defaulted in their trial payments.

If you fall into any of these criteria, you may be eligible for a modification under the expanded criteria. Check with your mortgage servicer to see if you are eligible to begin the HAMP evaluation process.

You may be eligible for HAMP if you meet all of the following criteria:

- You obtained your mortgage on or before January 1, 2009.

- You owe up to $729,750 on your primary residence or single-unit rental property.

- You owe up to $934,200 on a two-unit rental property, $1,129,250 on a three-unit rental property, or $1,403,400 on a four-unit rental property.

- The property has not been condemned.

- You have a financial hardship and are either delinquent or in danger of falling behind on your mortgage payments. (Nonowner occupants must be delinquent to qualify.) You have sufficient, documented income to support a modified payment.

- You must not have been convicted within the last 10 years of felony larceny, theft, fraud or forgery, money laundering, or tax evasion in connection with a mortgage or real estate transaction.

- The HAMP program aims to create a new mortgage payment that is as close as possible, but no less than, 31 percent of your gross monthly household income.

2. Principal Reduction Alternative (PRA): If your home is currently worth significantly less than you owe on it, the MHA's PRA was designed to help you by encouraging mortgage servicers and investors to reduce the amount you owe on your home. You may be eligible for PRA if:

- Your mortgage is *not* owned or guaranteed by Fannie Mae or Freddie Mac.

- You owe more than your home is worth.

- You occupy the house as your primary residence.

- You obtained your mortgage on or before January 1, 2009.

- Your mortgage payment is more than 31 percent of your gross (pre-tax) monthly income.

- You owe up to $729,750 on your first mortgage.

- You have a financial hardship and are either delinquent or in danger of falling behind.

- You have sufficient, documented income to support the modified payment.

- You must not have been convicted within the last 10 years of felony larceny, theft, fraud or forgery, money laundering, or tax evasion in connection with a mortgage or real estate transaction.

3. Second Lien Modification Program (2MP): If your first mortgage was permanently modified under HAMP and you have a second mortgage on the same property, you may be eligible for a modification or principal reduction on your second mortgage as well through MHA's 2MP. 2MP works together with HAMP to provide comprehensive solutions for homeowners with second mortgages to increase long-term affordability and sustainability. If the servicer of your second mortgage is participating, the servicer can evaluate you for a second lien modification. You may be eligible for 2MP if you meet all of the following criteria:

- Your first mortgage was modified under HAMP.

- You must not have been convicted within the last 10 years of felony larceny, theft, fraud or forgery, money laundering, or tax evasion in connection with a mortgage or real estate transaction.

- You have not missed three consecutive monthly payments on your HAMP modification.

4. FHA-HAMP: The FHA, the Veteran's Administration (VA), and the U.S. Department of Agriculture (USDA) all offer mortgage modification programs for struggling homeowners designed to lower a monthly mortgage payment to no more than 31 percent of the homeowner's verified monthly gross (pre-tax) income—making monthly mortgage payments much more affordable. If you have a loan that is insured or guaranteed by the FHA, you may be eligible for one of these programs. For information on FHA and participating servicers, call the FHA's National Servicing Center at (877) 622-8525.

5. USDA's Special Loan Servicing: The FHA, the VA, and the USDA also offer programs for rural homeowners to lower their monthly mortgage payment to no more than 31 percent of their verified monthly gross (pre-tax) income. If you have a loan that is guaranteed by the USDA's Section 502 Single Family Housing Guaranteed Loan Program, you may be eligible for a program. Contact your servicer for information.

6. VA-HAMP: If you have a loan that is insured or guaranteed by the VA Department, you may be eligible for a program through the VA.

7. HAFA Program (see Chapter 10): If you can't afford your mortgage payment, and it is time for you to move to more affordable housing, the HAFA program is designed for you. You may be eligible for HAFA if

- You have a documented financial hardship.

- You have not purchased a new house within the last 12 months.

- Your first mortgage is less than $729,750.

- You obtained your mortgage on or before January 1, 2009.

- You have not been convicted within the last 10 years of felony larceny, theft, fraud, forgery, money laundering, or tax evasion in connection with a mortgage or real estate transaction.

HAFA provides two options for transitioning out of your mortgage: a short sale or a deed in lieu of foreclosure. In a short sale, the mortgage company lets you sell your house for an amount that falls "short" of the amount you still owe. In a DIL, the mortgage company lets you give the title back, transferring ownership back to them.

In either case, HAFA offers benefits that make the transition as favorable as possible:

- You can get free advice from HUD-approved housing counselors and licensed real estate professionals.

- Unlike conventional short sales, a HAFA short sale completely releases you from your mortgage debt after selling the property. This means you will no longer be responsible for the amount that falls short of the amount you still owe. The deficiency is guaranteed to be waived by the servicer.

- In a HAFA short sale, your mortgage company works with you to determine an acceptable sale price.

- HAFA has a less negative effect on your credit score than foreclosure or conventional short sales.

- When you close, HAFA provides $3,000 in relocation assistance.

▓ **Tip** Learn more about all these options at www.makinghomeaffordable.gov/pages/default. aspx

---

8. Treasury/FHA Second Lien Program (FHA2LP): If you have a second mortgage and your first mortgage servicer agrees to participate in FHA Short Refinance, you may be eligible to have your second mortgage on the same home reduced or eliminated through the FHA2LP. If your second mortgage servicer agrees to participate, the total amount of your mortgage debt after the refinance cannot exceed 115 percent of your home's current value.

You may be eligible for FHA2LP if you meet the following criteria:

- You are eligible for FHA Short Refinance.

- You obtained your mortgage on or before January 1, 2009.

- You must not have been convicted within the last 10 years of felony larceny, theft, fraud, forgery, money laundering, or tax evasion in connection with a mortgage or real estate transaction.

9. HARP (see Chapter 9): If you're *not* behind on your mortgage payments but cannot get traditional refinancing because the value of your home has declined, you may be eligible to refinance through MHA's HARP. HARP is designed to help you get a new, more affordable, more stable mortgage. HARP refinance loans require a loan application and underwriting process, and refinance fees will apply. This program ends December 31, 2013.

You may be eligible for HARP if you meet all of the following criteria:

- The mortgage must be owned or guaranteed by Freddie Mac or Fannie Mae or have been sold to Fannie Mae or Freddie Mac on or before May 31, 2009.

- The mortgage cannot have been refinanced under HARP previously unless it is a Fannie Mae loan that was refinanced under HARP from March-May, 2009.

- The current LTV ratio must be greater than 80 percent.

- The borrower must be current on the mortgage at the time of the refinance, with a good payment history in the past 12 months.

If you think you may be eligible for HARP, here are three steps you should take:

- First, determine whether your mortgage is owned or guaranteed by Fannie Mae or Freddie Mac by visiting them at www.knowyouroptions.com/loanlookup (Fannie Mae) and www.freddiemac.com/mymortgage (Freddie Mac).

- Second, contact your current mortgage servicer or another that is approved by Fannie Mae or Freddie Mac and ask about HARP.

- Finally, compare rates and costs with other mortgage companies to ensure the best refinance deal.

10. FHA Refinance for Borrowers with Negative Equity (FHA Short Refinance): If you're *not* behind on your mortgage payments but owe more than your home is worth, FHA Short Refinance may be an option that your mortgage servicer will consider. FHA Short Refinance is designed to help you refinance into a more affordable, more stable FHA-insured mortgage. If your current lender agrees to participate in this refinance, they will be required to reduce the amount you owe on your first mortgage to no more than 97.75 percent of your home's current value.

You may be eligible for FHA Short Refinance if you meet the following criteria:

- Your mortgage is not owned or guaranteed by Fannie Mae, Freddie Mac, the FHA, VA, or USDA.

- You owe more than your home is worth.

- You are current on your mortgage payments.

- You occupy the house as your primary residence.

- You are eligible for the new loan under standard FHA underwriting requirements.

- Your total debt does not exceed 55 percent of your monthly gross income.

- You must not have been convicted within the last 10 years of felony larceny, theft, fraud, forgery, money laundering, or tax evasion in connection with a mortgage or real estate transaction.

11. Home Affordable Unemployment Program (UP): If you are unemployed, and depending on your situation, the MHA's Home Affordable UP may reduce your mortgage payments to 31 percent of your income or suspend them altogether for 12 months or more.

You may be eligible for UP if you meet all of the following criteria:

- You are unemployed and eligible for unemployment benefits.

- You occupy the house as your primary residence.

- You have not previously received a HAMP modification.

- You obtained your mortgage on or before January 1, 2009.

- You owe up to $729,750 on your home.

12. Housing Finance Agency Innovation Fund for the Hardest Hit Housing Markets (HHF): Early in 2010, the U.S. Treasury announced that the HHF would provide more than $7.6 billion in aid for homeowners in states hit hardest by the economic crisis. Since then, state housing finance agencies have used the fund to develop programs that stabilize local housing markets and help families avoid foreclosure. HHF programs complement the MHA program but are not limited to homeowners eligible for MHA.

HHF programs vary state to state, but may include the following:

- Mortgage payment assistance for unemployed or underemployed homeowners

- Principal reduction to help homeowners get into more affordable mortgages

- Funding to eliminate homeowners' second lien loans

- Help for homeowners who are transitioning out of their homes and into more affordable places of residence

In total, $7.6 billion have been allocated to 18 states plus the District of Columbia. If you live in one of these states or DC, contact your housing finance agency's program office: Alabama, Arizona, California, Florida, Georgia, Illinois, Indiana, Kentucky, Michigan, Mississippi, Nevada, New Jersey, North Carolina, Ohio, Oregon, Rhode Island, South Carolina, Tennessee, and Washington, DC.

For more information on the HHF, visit www.treasury.gov/initiatives/financial-stability/programs/housing-programs/hhf/Pages/default.aspx or contact your state housing finance agency.

Official Programs vs. Scams

Each of these programs is an official program that is part of HUD's MHA program. There are also hundreds of other programs that are out there to help homeowners who are at risk of going under water. Some of them are legitimate. Others are outright scams intended to defraud homeowners.

Here are three resources that are available to help homeowners avoid real estate scams:

- **FTC:** The FTC has its own YouTube channel that features a video that can help consumers avoid foreclosure rescue scams.

- **Office of the Comptroller of the Currency (OCC):** The U.S. Department of the Treasury's OCC provides tips and materials to help homeowners avoid mortgage modification and foreclosure rescue scams. Go to www.occ. gov to learn more about foreclosure prevention.

- **The Loan Modification Scam Prevention:** This program is a national coalition of governmental and private organizations created by Fannie Mae, Freddie Mac, NeighborWorks America, and the Lawyers' Committee for

Civil Rights Under Law to provide resources to educate homeowners about the dangers of loan modification scams and support federal, state, and local efforts to combat these scams. If you believe you have been the victim of a scam, you can report the scam through the campaign's online complaint form at www.preventloanscams.org.

Beware of Foreclosure Rescue Scams!

Foreclosure rescue and mortgage modification scams are a growing problem in the United States. These scams have the potential to cost you thousands of dollars—or even your home.

Scammers make promises that they can't keep, such as guaranteeing to "save" your home or lower your mortgage, usually for a fee, often pretending that they have direct contact with your mortgage servicer—which they do not.

■ **Tip**   *Get help if you think you have been scammed.* The federal government provides the help you need for free. Just call 888-995-HOPE (4673) for information about the MHA program and to speak with a HUD-approved housing counselor. Assistance is available free, 24-7, in 160 languages.

One Scam Now in Court

One mortgage scam that recently made its way to the New York Supreme Court is the case of *Squassoni et al. v. Blackwell et al.*, in the Supreme Court of New York, Nassau County (No. 3571/12). This case involves a crime called "up-front loan modification fraud." The FTC passed a rule in 2010 that says up-front fees cannot be charged by loan modification companies. The trouble is that lawyers are using this as a loophole to defraud homeowners.[2]

According to the *JD Journal*, "Anthony Blackwell, who is licensed to practice as an attorney in Nevada, set up branches in New York and worked in collusion with mortgage modification company Homesafe America Inc. to extract thousands of dollars in upfront fees from homeowners, purportedly for loan modifications that were never made."

Linda Mullenbach, senior counsel at the Lawyers' Committee for Civil Rights Under Law, told the media that Blackwell's alleged scheme was part of "a

---

[2] www.jdjournal.com/2012/04/05/nevada-attorney-used-loophole-in-new-york-law-to-scam-homeowners/ (Retrieved October 15, 2012).

disturbing trend in which lawyers charge upfront money to homeowners for advice, and then disappear without providing [the] promised service."

According to the *JD Journal*, The Lawyers' Committee for Civil Rights Under Law has filed seven similar lawsuits against different parties over loan modification schemes since 2010, with five of them in Nassau County.

Talking on behalf of the plaintiffs in the Blackwell case, Mullenbach said "Victims who are desperate to try to find a resolution are trusting of the fact that when someone is a lawyer and they need legal advice, they're actually getting legal advice."

Scams like the one alleged in this case are unfortunately not rare. Greed has the power to turn even legitimate professionals into unscrupulous predators. Know that scammers are out there preying on overly trusting underwater homeowners. Keep your eyes open for people who ask for up-front payments without providing promised services.

Watch Out for These Deceptive Acts and Practices

According to a May 2012 preliminary injunction from the Supreme Court of New York, Nassau County, here are some of the deceptive acts and practices or false advertising in violation of New York General Business Law from which Blackwell was forbidden from engaging[3]:

- Falsely promising to offer "legal representation" in connection with consumers' loan modification applications;

- Misrepresenting to consumers the nature and mechanics of Mortgage Loan Modification Services;

- Falsely promising to engage in negotiations with consumers' mortgage lenders or servicers;

- Misrepresenting the progress of loan modification applications;

- Falsely representing that consumers are certain to receive a reduction in mortgage interest rates and/or a reduction in mortgage principal;

---

[3] www.lawyerscommittee.org/admin/fair_housing/documents/files/2012.05.15.Order.Granting.Pl.pdf (Retrieved November 3, 2012).

- Falsely representing that refunds will be issued if the offered Mortgage Loan Modification Services do not lead to a successful result;

- Encouraging consumers to stop paying their monthly mortgage payments and/or to cease communications with their lenders or servicers;

- Charging consumers an up-front fee for Mortgage Loan Modification Services; and

- Forming a business or organizational identity or operating as a "doing business as" organization as a method of evading dissatisfied customers.

If you feel that a lawyer who you have paid to help you straighten out your underwater mortgage has done any of these things, seek help from a reputable organization that can help you clarify whether a state or federal law has been broken or whether a scam has taken place.

Tips to Avoid Scams

Here are some things the FTC says you should keep in mind when talking to people who say they want to help you:

- Beware of anyone who asks you to pay a fee in exchange for counseling services or the modification of a delinquent loan.

- Beware of people who pressure you to sign papers immediately or who try to convince you that they can "save" your home if you sign or transfer over the deed to your house.

- Do not sign over the deed to your property to any organization or individual unless you are working directly with your mortgage company to forgive your debt.

- Never make a mortgage payment to anyone other than your mortgage company without their approval.

What to Do if You Have Been the Victim of a Scam

If you think you have been the victim of a real estate scam, you should file a complaint with the FTC. An online FTC Complaint Assistant is available on the FTC's web site, or consumers can call 877-FTC-HELP (877-382-4357) for assistance in English or Spanish.

Appendices

Glossary of Terms

A credit The best credit rating. If homeowners have A credit, they can get the lowest interest rates and prices that lenders have to offer.

adjustable-rate mortgage (ARM) A mortgage that does not have a fixed interest rate. The rate changes during the life of the loan based on movements in an index rate, such as the rate for Treasury securities or the Cost of Funds Index. ARMs usually offer a lower initial interest rate than fixed-rate loans. The interest rate fluctuates over the life of the loan based on market conditions, but the loan agreement generally sets maximum and minimum rates. When interest rates increase, generally homeowners' loan payments increase; when interest rates decrease, homeowners' monthly payments may decrease. See *convertible ARM.*[1]

amortization The process of paying off a debt by making regular installment payments over a set period of time, at the end of which the loan balance is zero.

annual percentage rate (APR) The value created according to a government formula. The APR is not the note rate on the homeowner's loan. The APR reflects the annual cost of borrowing, expressed as a percentage, and it is always higher than the actual note rate on the homeowner's loan.[2]

appraisal A written estimate of a property's current market value prepared by a professional appraiser.

---

[1] www.federalreserve.gov/consumerinfo/fivetips_protecthome.htm (Retrieved August 12, 2012).

[2] www.realestateabc.com/glossary/glossary1.htm (Retrieved July 10, 2012).

appraiser   A professional with knowledge of real estate markets who is skilled in the practice of generating an appraisal. When a property is appraised in connection with a loan, the appraiser is selected by the lender, but the appraisal fee is usually paid by the homeowner.[3]

assumption   When a qualified buyer is allowed to assume (take over) another homeowners mortgage.

balloon mortgage   A mortgage loan that requires a large payment due on maturity (for example, at the end of 10 years).

Chapter 13 bankruptcy   A type of bankruptcy that sets a payment plan between homeowner and creditors that is monitored by the bankruptcy court. Homeowners can keep their property, but must make payments according to the court's terms within a 3- to 5-year period.

Chapter 7 bankruptcy   A bankruptcy that requires assets be liquidated in exchange for the cancellation of debt.

closing   When selling a house, the process of transferring ownership from the seller to the buyer, the disbursement of funds from the buyer and the lender to the seller, and the signing of all documents associated with the sale and the loan. On a refinance, there is no transfer of ownership, but the closing includes repayment of the old lender.

co-homeowners   One or more individuals who have signed a loan note and are equally responsible for repaying the loan.

collections   The efforts that a lender takes to collect past-due payments.

convertible ARM   An ARM loan that can be converted into a fixed-rate mortgage during a certain time period.

creditor   A person or entity that is owed money by another person or entity.

debt to income   A comparison, or ratio, of gross income to housing and other expenses or debts the homeowner owes.

deed   A document that legally transfers ownership of property from one person to another. The deed is a public record and includes the property description and owner's signature; also known as the *title*.

deed in lieu of foreclosure   A situation when homeowners may be able to "give back" their property to the lender, who then forgives the balance of your loan. There may be income tax consequences, so check with the Internal

---

[3] www.makinghomeaffordable.gov/learning-center/glossary/Pages/default.aspx (Retrieved July 10, 2012).

Revenue Service. This option does not allow homeowners to stay in their home, but it is less damaging to their credit rating than a standard foreclosure. Some lenders impose certain restrictions on taking back property. For example, they may require that the homeowner try to sell the home at a fair market value for at least 90 days.[4]

default When homeowners miss making a mortgage payment when it is due. Usually, this means a payment has still not been made within 30 days of the due date.[5]

deferred payments Loan payments that are authorized to be postponed as part of a "workout" process to avoid foreclosure.

deficiency judgment When a borrower has to make up the difference between the money gained at a foreclosure or short sale and the mortgage loan balance (the deficiency), which includes the lender's costs in bringing the suit.

delinquency The failure to make a payment when it is due. A loan is generally considered delinquent when it is 30 days or more past due.

Dodd-Frank Act A law signed by Congress in 2010 to improve accountability and transparency in the U.S. financial system. Among other things, it was also intended to protect consumers from abusive financial services practices.[6]

eminent domain The government's right to take private property for public use by paying for it at a fair market value. Buildings are often seized under eminent domain before condemnation proceedings.[7]

equity An owner's financial interest in a property, which is calculated by subtracting the amount still owed on the mortgage loan or loans from the current market value of the property.

escrow account A separate account into which a portion of each monthly mortgage payment is placed. This account provides the funds needed for such expenses as property taxes, homeowners' insurance, mortgage insurance, and so forth.

---

[4] www.federalreserve.gov/consumerinfo/fivetips_protecthome.htm (Retrieved August 12, 2012).

[5] www.realestateabc.com/glossary/glossary1.htm (Retrieved July 10, 2012).

[6] www.sec.gov/about/laws/wallstreetreform-cpa.pdf (Retrieved August 10, 2012).

[7] www.realestateabc.com/glossary/glossary1.htm (Retrieved July 10, 2012).

escrow analysis A periodic review of escrow accounts to make sure that there are sufficient funds to pay the taxes and insurance on a home when they are due.

Fannie Mae A government-sponsored enterprise chartered by the U.S. Congress, Fannie Mae's mission is to keep money flowing to mortgage lenders, help strengthen the U.S. housing and mortgage markets, and support home ownership. Like Freddie Mac, it doesn't offer home loans directly.

Federal Housing Administration (FHA) An agency that is part of the U.S. Department of Housing and Urban Development (HUD). The main thing it does is insure residential mortgage loans made by private lenders. The FHA also sets standards for construction and underwriting but does not lend money, or plan or construct housing.

FHA mortgage A mortgage insured by the FHA. FHA loans and Veterans' Administration loans are often referred to as *government loans*.[8]

first mortgage A mortgage that has a first-priority claim against the property in the event the homeowner defaults on the loan.

fixed-rate mortgage A mortgage loan with a fixed interest rate that remains the same for the life of the loan.

forbearance A temporary period of time during which a regular monthly mortgage payment is reduced or suspended.[9]

foreclosure The legal process by which a property may be sold and the proceeds of the sale applied to the mortgage debt. A foreclosure occurs when the loan becomes delinquent because payments have not been made or when the homeowner is in default for a reason other than the failure to make timely mortgage payments.

foreclosure prevention The steps by which the lender or servicer works with the homeowner to find a permanent solution to resolve an existing or impending loan delinquency.

Freddie Mac An organization chartered by the U.S. Congress in 1970 to stabilize the nation's residential mortgage markets and to provide homeowners with reasonable mortgages and affordable rental housing. Freddie Mac does not lend money directly to homeowners.

gold participation certificate (PC) Securities, which are a large part of Freddie Mac's mortgage-backed securities program. Freddie Mac guarantees

---

[8] www.realestateabc.com/glossary/glossary1.htm (Retrieved July 10, 2012).

[9] www.federalreserve.gov/consumerinfo/fivetips_protecthome.htm (Retrieved August12, 2012).

the payment of interest and scheduled principal on all gold PCs, which feature a payment delay of 45 days from the time interest begins to accrue and the time the investor receives a payment.[10]

government-sponsored enterprises (GSEs) Private corporations created by the U.S. government to reduce borrowing costs. The GSEs are chartered by the U.S. government but are not considered to be direct obligations. For example, Fannie Mae and Freddie Mac are GSEs.

HAFA short sale When homeowners sell their property for less than the full amount due on the mortgage. When homeowners qualify for a HAFA short sale, the servicer approves the short sale terms prior to listing the home and then accepts the payoff in full satisfaction of the mortgage. See *HAFA*.

hazard insurance Insurance that must be bought when taking out a mortgage contract. The insurance is used to pay for loss or damage to a person's home or property.

HELOC Or, home equity line of credit, are loans secured by the property. The interest expense is often tax deductible. These kinds of loans were once called *second mortgages*.[11]

Home Affordable Foreclosure Alternatives Program (HAFA) A government program that provides opportunities for homeowners who can no longer afford to stay in their home but want to avoid foreclosure to transition to more affordable housing through a short sale or deed in lieu of foreclosure.

Home Affordable Modification Program (HAMP) A government program that provides eligible homeowners the opportunity to modify their mortgages to make them more affordable.

Home Affordable Refinance Program (HARP) A government program that provides homeowners with loans owned or guaranteed by Fannie Mae or Freddie Mac an opportunity to refinance to more affordable monthly payments.

Home Affordable Unemployment Program (UP) A government program that provides homeowners a temporary forbearance, which is a temporary period of time during which a regular monthly mortgage payment is reduced or suspended.

---

[10] www.freddiemac.com/mbs/html/product/pc.html (Retrieved July 12, 2012).

[11] www.bankrate.com/finance/home-equity/refinance-loan-heloc.aspx (Retrieved August 10, 2012).

home equity line of credit (HELOC)   A bank line of credit that allows homeowners to borrow money against the equity in their home to pay for things such as home repairs, college education, or other personal expenses.

housing expense   The sum of a homeowner's mortgage payment, hazard insurance, property taxes, and homeowner association fees.

interest-only mortgage   A mortgage for which the homeowner pays only the interest and none of the outstanding principal balance on a loan for a specified amount of time.

investment property   A property not considered to be a primary residence that is purchased to generate income, profit from appreciation, or to take advantage of certain tax benefits.

judicial foreclosure   A court proceeding that involves a lender filing a complaint and recording a public notice that announces a claim on the property to potential buyers, creditors, and other interested parties. The complaint describes the debt, the borrower's default, and the amount owed. Twenty-two states use judicial procedures as the primary way to foreclose: Connecticut, Delaware, Florida, Hawaii, Illinois, Indiana, Iowa, Kansas, Kentucky, Louisiana, Maine, New Jersey, New Mexico, New York, North Dakota, Ohio, Oklahoma, Pennsylvania, South Carolina, South Dakota, Vermont, and Wisconsin.[12]

lender-placed insurance   The insurance placed on a home or property by lenders to protect their interest in the collateral that secures the loan.

lien   The lender's right to claim the homeowner's property in the event the homeowner defaults. If there is more than one lien, the claim of the lender holding the first lien is satisfied before the claim of the lender holding the second lien, which in turn is satisfied before the claim of a lender holding a third lien, and so forth.

loan modification   A procedure by which a lender may be willing to rewrite the terms of an original mortgage loan to address a distressed financial situation. A loan modification is designed to make monthly payments more affordable. Changes may include extending the number of years to repay the loan and changing the interest rate, including changing an adjustable rate to a fixed rate.[13]

---

[12] www.mbaa.org/files/ResourceCenter/ForeclosureProcess/JudicialVersusNon-JudicialForeclosure.pdf (Retrieved August 10, 2012).

[13] www.federalreserve.gov/consumerinfo/fivetips_protecthome.htm (Retrieved August 10 2012).

loan-to-value (LTV) ratio This ratio, in real estate lending, is the outstanding principal amount of the loan divided by the appraised value of the property underlying the loan.

MERS Or, Mortgage Electronic Registration Systems Inc.,[14] is a warehouse for loans. According to www.mersinc.org, MERSCORP Holdings Inc. is a privately held corporation that owns and manages the MERS system and all other MERS products. It is a member-based organization made up of about 3,000 lenders, servicers, subservicers, investors, and government institutions. The MERS system is a national electronic database that tracks changes in mortgage servicing rights and beneficial ownership interests in loans secured by residential real estate. According to *The New York Times*, MERS "claims to hold title to roughly half of all the home mortgages in the nation—an astonishing 60 million loans."[15]

monthly gross income The total income of all homeowners who sign a mortgage before any taxes or other deductions are made.

mortgage A legal document that pledges property to a lender as security for the repayment of a loan. The term is also used to refer to the loan itself.

mortgage insurance (MI) Insurance that protects lenders against losses caused by a homeowner's default on a mortgage loan. MI is typically required if the homeowner's down payment is less than 20 percent of the purchase price.

mortgage modification A change in the terms of a loan, usually the interest rate and/or term, in response to the homeowner's inability to make the payments under the existing mortgage

mortgage payment The amount of money paid, on a monthly basis, for principal, interest, property taxes, hazard insurance, and homeowner association fees, if applicable.

mortgage payment guideline The calculation within HAMP that helps determine a homeowner's eligibility. It is calculated as 31 percent of the homeowner's current monthly gross income. If the monthly mortgage payment is above this amount, a homeowner may be eligible for HAMP. See *HAMP*.

negative equity The condition of owing more on the property than the property is worth. See *underwater*.

---

[14] www.mersinc.org/information-for-homeowners/faq-information-for-homeowners (Retrieved August 1, 2012).

[15] www.nytimes.com/2011/03/06/business/06mers.html?pagewanted=all (Retrieved August 1, 2012).

nonjudicial foreclosures A situation in which there is no court intervention in a foreclosure. The ability to do a nonjudicial foreclosure is established by state law. If a homeowner defaults, a Notice of Default is filed. The homeowner may pay off the debt during a prescribed period. If the debt is not paid off, a Notice of Sale is mailed to the homeowner, posted in public places, recorded at the county's recorder's office, and published in area newspapers/legal publications. When the state's legally required notice period expires, a public auction is held and the highest bidder becomes the owner of the property.[16]

partial claim An insurance claim your lender sometimes helps you file if your mortgage is insured by a private mortgage insurance firm. Some insurers provide a one-time, interest-free loan to bring your account up to date. The interest-free loan is due when you refinance, pay off your mortgage, or when you sell the property.[17]

PITI Or, principal, interest, taxes and insurance, which are the components of the housing expense.

preforeclosure A sale when the servicer allows the homeowner to list and sell the mortgaged property with the understanding that the net proceeds from the sale may be less than the total amount due on the first mortgage. Also referred to as a *short sale*. Note: Homeowners may owe income taxes on the deficiency.[18]

primary or principal residence The property in which the homeowner lives most of the time, distinct from a second home or an investor property that is rented.

private-label mortgages Loans that are not owned or guaranteed by Fannie Mae, Freddie Mac, Ginnie Mae, or another federal agency.

refinance The process of replacing an existing mortgage with a new one by paying off the existing debt with a new loan under different terms.

reinstatement When lenders reestablish your loan if you make up the back payments in a lump sum by a specific date. A forbearance may accompany this option.

---

[16] www.mbaa.org/files/ResourceCenter/ForeclosureProcess/JudicialVersusNon-JudicialForeclosure.pdf (Retrieved August 10, 2012).

[17] www.federalreserve.gov/consumerinfo/fivetips_protecthome.htm (Retrieved August 10, 2012).

[18] www.makinghomeaffordable.gov/learning-center/glossary/Pages/default.aspx (Retrieved July 10, 2012).

real estate owned (REO)   When the ownership of a property has reverted back to the mortgage company or bank from the previous owner. Often, this happens after an unsuccessful foreclosure auction. An REO property can be a great bargain for a home buyer, but it is often sold in as-is condition, which means there may be many repairs and unseen costs imbedded in the purchase of the home.

repayment plan   A strategy in which a homeowner promises to pay past-due amounts on a mortgage while continuing to make regular monthly payments on a property.

Second Lien Modification Program (2MP)   A program that provides homeowners a way to modify their second mortgages to make them more affordable when their first mortgage is modified under HAMP.[19]

second mortgage   A loan with a second-priority claim against a property in the event that the homeowner defaults. The lender who holds the second mortgage gets paid only after the lender holding the first mortgage is paid.

servicer   A firm that works on behalf of the lender in support of a mortgage, including collecting mortgage payments, ensuring payment of taxes and insurance, managing escrow accounts, managing communications with the homeowner, and conducting loss mitigation or foreclosure when necessary.

servicing transfer   When one servicer is replaced by another.

short sale   When the servicer allows the homeowner to list and sell the mortgaged property with the understanding that the net proceeds from the sale may be less than the total amount due on the first mortgage. See *preforeclosure*.

straight note   A promissory note that has no payments due until the entire amount is due.

term   The period of time assigned as the life span of any investment.

title   A document that shows that a person or organization has ownership of property.

trial period or **trial period plan**   A stipulated length of time, 3 or 4 months at a minimum, used to determine whether payment of a reduced amount is sustainable. HAMP requires homeowners to enter into a trial

---

[19] www.makinghomeaffordable.gov/learning-center/glossary/Pages/default.aspx (Retrieved July 10, 2012).

period plan before receiving a permanent HAMP modification. During this period, homeowners must submit all required trial period payments.[20]

trust A relationship in which one person or legal entity holds title to property, subject to an obligation to keep or use the property for the benefit of another.

underwater When homeowners owe more on their mortgage than their house is worth. See *negative equity*.

underwriting The process of examining all the data about a homeowner's property and income documentation to determine whether a mortgage modification should be issued. The person who issues the modification is called an *underwriter*.

unpaid principal balance (UPB) The amount of a loan that is due to the lender. The UPB does not include additional charges, such as interest.

weighted average life The average number of years for which each dollar of unpaid principal on a loan or mortgage remains outstanding.

workout A process to resolve or restructure a loan to prevent a homeowner from going into foreclosure through a loan modification, forbearance, or short sale.

---

[20] www.makinghomeaffordable.gov/learning-center/glossary/Pages/default.aspx (Retrieved July 10, 2012).

Additional Resources

The following are just a few of the organizations that can help you if your mortgage is underwater:

Fannie Mae

In 2011, Fannie Mae, the Federal National Mortgage Association, guaranteed or purchased approximately $653 billion in loans, enabling lenders to finance more than 2.6 million single-family conventional loans and loans for 423,000 units in multifamily properties. It also completed more than 328,000 single-family loan workouts to help struggling homeowners avoid foreclosure. And it sold nearly 244,000 Fannie Mae single-family foreclosed properties, helping to stabilize neighborhoods and home values while minimizing taxpayer losses.

Web: www.fanniemae.com

Phone: 1-800-7FANNIE (1-800-732-6643)

Federal Bureau of Investigation (FBI): Mortgage Fraud

From foreclosure frauds to subprime shenanigans, mortgage fraud is a growing crime threat that is hurting homeowners, businesses, and the national economy. The FBI has developed new ways to detect and combat mortgage fraud, including collecting and analyzing data to spot emerging trends and patterns. The FBI is using its full array of investigative techniques to find and stop criminals before the fact, rather than after the damage has been done.

Web: www.fbi.gov/about-us/investigate/white_collar/mortgage-fraud/mortgage_fraud

Federal Trade Commission (FTC)

The FTC works to prevent business practices that are anticompetitive, deceptive, or unfair to consumers; to enhance informed consumer choice and public understanding of the competitive process; and to accomplish this without unduly burdening legitimate business activity. The following URL is a great place to learn about ways to avoid mortgage scams:

Web: www.ftc.gov/bcp/menus/consumer/credit/mortgage.shtm

Freddie Mac

In 1970, Congress created Freddie Mac, the Federal Home Loan Mortgage Corporation, with a few important goals in mind:

- Make sure that financial institutions have mortgage money to lend.

- Make it easier for consumers to afford a decent house or apartment.

- Stabilize residential mortgage markets in times of financial crisis.

To fulfill this mission, Freddie Mac conducts business in the U.S. secondary mortgage market. It does not originate loans. Instead, it works with a national network of mortgage-lending customers. It has three business lines: a single-family credit guarantee business for home loans, a multifamily business for apartment financing, and an investment portfolio.

Web: www.freddiemac.com

Phone: 1-800-424-5401

Hardest Hit Fund

President Obama established the Hardest Hit Fund in February 2010 to provide targeted aid to families in states hit hard by the economic and housing market downturn. States were chosen either because they are struggling with unemployment rates at or above the national average or with steep housing price declines greater than 20 percent since the real estate bubble burst. Hardest Hit Fund programs vary from state to state, but may include the following:

- Mortgage payment assistance for unemployed or under-employed homeowners

- Principal reduction to help homeowners get into a more affordable mortgage

- Funding to eliminate homeowners' second-lien loans

- Help for homeowners who are transitioning out of their homes and into more affordable places of residence.

A directory of state programs is found at the following web site:

Web: www.treasury.gov/initiatives/financial-stability/programs/housing-programs/hhf/Pages/default.aspx

HopeNow

The HopeNow website offers a complete list of mortgage companies (www.hopenow.com/mortgage-directory.php) and a list of state resources that can help homeowners (www.hopenow.com/find-my-state.php).

Web: www.hopenow.com

Phone: 1-888-995-HOPE (4673)

HUD's Housing Counseling Program

Housing and Urban Development (HUD) sponsors housing counseling agencies throughout the country that can provide advice on buying a home or renting, and dealing with defaults, foreclosures, and credit issues. The following web site allows you to select a list of agencies for your state, and you can search for reverse-mortgage counselors or foreclosure avoidance counselors.

Web: www.hud.gov/offices/hsg/sfh/hcc/hcs.cfm

Phone: 1-800-569-4287

Legal Information Institute (LII)

The LII is a not-for-profit organization that believes everyone should be able to read and understand the laws that govern them, without cost. The organization is a small research, engineering, and editorial group housed at the Cornell Law School in Ithaca, New York. Their collaborators include publishers, legal scholars, computer scientists, government agencies, and other groups and individuals that promote open access to law worldwide. *Note:* The LII cannot and does not provide legal advice or interpretations of the law. The LII is prohibited by law from doing so. They will not answer or reply to requests for legal advice, but they do offer a lawyer directory (lawyers.law.cornell.edu).

Web: www.law.cornell.edu

Making Home Affordable (MHA) Program

The MHA program is part of the Obama administration's strategy to help homeowners avoid foreclosure, stabilize the country's housing market, and improve the nation's economy. If you're not behind on your mortgage payments but have been unable to get traditional refinancing because the value of your home has declined, you may be eligible to refinance through the MHA program's Home Affordable Refinance Program (HARP). HARP is designed to help you get a new, more affordable, more stable mortgage. HARP refinance loans require a loan application and underwriting process, and refinance fees do apply.

Web: www.makinghomeaffordable.gov

Phone: 1-888-995-HOPE (4673)

National Foreclosure Mitigation Counseling Program

If you are interested in exploring your options and eligibility for government programs, you can contact a counseling agency for free counseling without being referred by a servicer. If it is determined that you may be eligible for a loan modification or refinance program, a counselor works with you to submit an intake package to the servicer. This service is provided at a low cost or free of charge by nonprofit housing counseling agencies working in partnership with the federal government. These agencies provide you with the services you need to avoid foreclosure under certain circumstances. There is no need to pay a private company for these services.

Web: www.findaforeclosurecounselor.org

NeighborWorks America

NeighborWorks America is the country's preeminent leader in affordable housing and community development. The program works to create opportunities for lower income people to live in affordable homes in safe, sustainable neighborhoods that are healthy places for families to grow. Headquartered in Washington, DC, NeighborWorks America operates through a national office, two regional offices, and seven district offices.

Web: www.nw.org

Phone: 1-888-995-HOPE (4673)

Single-Family Housing Guaranteed Rural Refinance Pilot Program

The U.S. Department of Agriculture launched the Single-Family Housing Guaranteed Rural Refinance pilot program in February 2012 to help rural borrowers refinance their mortgages and reduce their monthly payments. This initiative is part of the Obama administration's ongoing efforts to help middle-class families, to create jobs, and to strengthen the economy. The Single-Family Housing Guaranteed Rural Refinance pilot program operates in 19 states for homeowners who have loans that were made or guaranteed by U.S. Department of Agriculture Rural Development. These states are among those hardest hit by the downturn in the housing market.

Web: www.rurdev.usda.gov/HSF-Refinance_Pilot.html

Phone: 1-800-795-3272

Trulia

Trulia is an all-in-one real estate site that gives users information on homes for sale, rentals, neighborhoods, and real estate markets and trends. You can also find real estate agents, see prices of recently sold homes, and research home values. In addition, you can get advice and opinions from local real estate agents, brokers, and other local experts on "Trulia Voices," Trulia's online real estate community.

Web: www.trulia.com

U.S. Department of Housing and Urban Development

HUD's mission is to create strong, sustainable, inclusive communities and quality affordable homes for all Americans. HUD is working to strengthen the housing market to bolster the economy and protect consumers, to meet the need for quality affordable rental homes, to use housing as a platform for improving quality of life, to build inclusive and sustainable communities free from discrimination, and to transform the way HUD does business.

Web: www.hud.gov

Phone: 1-202-708-1112

USA.gov

USA.gov is the U.S. government's official web portal, where it is easy for the public to get U.S. government information and services on the Web. You can find an index of state and local consumer agencies, including local banking authorities and consumer protection offices, at their web site.

Web: www.usa.gov/directory/stateconsumer/index.shtml

Zillow's Underwater Mortgage Resource Center

Zillow has created an Underwater Mortgage Resource Center that outlines current refinancing options for underwater homeowners. In its resource center, Zillow helps you define what an underwater mortgage is, understand why refinancing is beneficial, and determine whether you can qualify for refinancing.

Web: www.zillow.com/mortgage-rates/underwater/

Index

I

S